Fifty Hikes in the Adirondacks

Scott's Clearing

Fifty Hikes in the Adirondacks

Short Walks, Day Trips, and Backpacks
Throughout the Park

Barbara McMartin

Photographs by the author

Second Edition

Backcountry Publications
Woodstock, Vermont

An Invitation to the Reader

Over time trails can be rerouted and signs and landmarks altered. If you find that changes have occurred on the routes described in this book, please let us know so that corrections may be made in future editions. The author and publisher also welcome other comments and suggestions. Address all correspondence to:

Editor
Fifty Hikes Series
Backcountry Publications
P.O. Box 175
Woodstock, VT 05091

Library of Congress Cataloging-in-Publication Data
McMartin, Barbara.
  Fifty hikes in the Adirondacks : short walks, day trips, and backpacks throughout the park / Barbara McMartin ; photographs by the author. -- Second ed.
    p. cm.
  Bibliography: p.
  Includes index.
  ISBN 0-88150-124-7 (pbk.) : $10.95
  1. Hiking--New York (State)--Adirondack Mountains--Guide-books.
  2. Adirondack Mountains (N.Y.)--Description and travel--Guide-books.
  I. Title.
GV199.42.N652A3445 1988
917.47'53--dc19   88-7456
                                                           CIP

Published by Backcountry Publications
A division of The Countryman Press, Inc.
Woodstock, Vermont 05091

Printed in the United States of America
Typesetting by Sant Bani Press
Series design by Wladislaw Finne
Layout by Ann Aspell
Trail overlays by Richard Widhu

Cover photograpy by Barbara McMartin
Photographs for hikes 6 and 14 by Dennis Conroy; hike 7 by W. Alec Reid; hike 9 by Lawrence King; hikes 16, 17, 18, and 38 by Lee M. Brenning; hike 37 by William J. Burke; hike 41 by Patricia Collier; and hike 42 by James R. Lenney. All other photographs are by the author.

Acknowledgements

In the decade since this guide was first printed, numerous friends rewalked the trails and kept me up to date on changes which were incorporated at each reprinting.

This major revision was aided by the fact that the regional guides of the *Discover* series were nearing completion. My co-authors in that series have been most helpful in this major revision. Lee M. Brenning corrected sections 16–18, which overlaps work he did for the West Central guide. Dennis Conroy went back for a better picture on Peaked Mountain. Edythe Robbins assisted with the revisions of the Eastern guide and this *Fifty Hikes* guide uses pictures she took at Pharaoh Lake.

Pat Collier, James Dawson, and Ed Ketchledge worked on the Northern guide. Their notes were incorporated in this revision, as was Pat's photograph from Pitchoff.

The summer I first researched *Fifty Hikes in the Adirondacks* was notable for its haze. Over the years, I have returned to favorite spots to seek better photographs. My husband, W. Alec Reid, has produced the wonderful new prints used here as well as all the prints used in the *Discover* series.

Margaret Baldwin, DEC cartographer, arranged for us to have a screen of state land showing acquisitions through 1987.

Adirondack Park
(shaded areas are public lands)

Contents

Introduction

The first edition of *Fifty Hikes in the Adirondacks* was written as an introduction to the many different areas of the Adirondack Park. It has been updated four times, but is now completely revised with two new hikes, many new maps based on newly issued USGS topos, and a few new pictures.

When it was first published, it was a companion to three regional guides, each of which covered in depth a portion of the park. In addition to representing almost all the Wild Forest and Wilderness areas of the Park, the *Fifty Hikes* sampled each of the geographical areas that are now described in the *Discover* series. That series of eleven guides is almost complete. So *Fifty Hikes* is a true companion in that it will not only introduce you to the different parts of the Park, it will help you find the *Discover* guide that will allow you to explore your favorite regions in depth. Each of the *Fifty Hikes in the Adirondacks* is typical of the region covered in the *Discover* guides; but the latter contain every hiking trail and path and most of the exciting bushwhacks of each region.

The Adirondack Park is surrounded by a magical Blue Line that sets it apart from the rest of New York State. With nearly 6 million acres, this park is almost as large as the state of Vermont. Calling the area a park is confusing, for the Blue Line in fact delineates a hodge-podge of public and private lands.

The public lands inside the park's boundary have been gradually incorporated into a body known as the Forest Preserve, which was established in 1885 and given the protection of the state constitution in 1894. The Forest Preserve was initially intended to protect forever the state's water resources. At present, the Adirondack Park Agency oversees all of the land within the park, both public and private.

Forest Preserve lands, roughly forty percent of the area inside the Blue Line, are managed by the Department of Environmental Conservation (DEC), which has responsibility for all public trails. The Forest Preserve is managed in a way that permits hunting throughout, but prohibits any cutting of timber. According to the State Land Master Plan that was prepared by the Adirondack Park Agency, the public lands are divided into Wilderness, Wild Forest, Primitive, Canoe, and Intensive Use areas.

The fifty hikes represent as many of the Adirondack's regions, both political and natural, as possible. The guide describes every type of hiking trail, from those well known, to those visited by only a few people. The trails lead you up the tall peaks of the northern mountain ranges as well as up the gentler mountains surrounding the central Adirondack dome. They follow abandoned logging roads and chains of uninhabited lakes. On them you meet wild rivers and distant waterfalls, discover caves and cliffs, and reach a few of the fire towers that still survive. In short, this guide acquaints you with a cross section of trails available to Adirondack hikers.

Of course, I hope this guidebook does more than introduce you to the 360 miles of trails and 60,000 feet of climbing outlined in the fifty hikes. It should make you aware of the geological structures that underlie the trails and their relation to the various types of forest vegetation. It should lead you to observe alpine summits and broad plains, virgin forests and quaking bogs, ferns and wildflowers, birds and wild animals.

Equally important, you should become acquainted with a few of the early settlers who pioneered in the mines and forests, the trappers, lumbermen, and guides whose footsteps echoed on the woodland routes that are today's hiking trails. The Discover series treats each of these themes in greater depth. This guide and all the others contain a list of books that can increase your knowledge and appreciation of the trails' history. These books are chosen not necessarily because they are the most scholarly, but because they have most vividly recreated the past for me. I want this guide to locate where specific historical events occurred.

All the details I have tried to weave into this trail guide are still no more than hints of what you will find. Enrichment is the most important part of this guide and the Discover series. If you let them take you on a true voyage of discovery, you will enjoy much more than the pleasures of hiking. You will come to know the land

and to develop a sense of love and reverence for all that it embraces. That is what I want to share with you.

Before You Start

The majority of these fifty hikes are just that—hikes. This guide is designed to acquaint you with extended walks throughout the Adirondacks. Strenuous hikes are usually associated with the High Peaks Region in the northeastern part of the park, but you can also find them everywhere in the Forest Preserve. To give everyone a chance to discover the wonders of this vast area, however, I have included a few shorter, easy walks. Many more exist, described in the Discover guides.

While all these excursions are dayhikes (although you must pack in and camp overnight to reach the start of one hike), you should be well equipped before starting the longer walks. If you are new to hiking, it will be best to join a hiking group and learn from those with experience. The more experience you have in the woods, the greater will be your enjoyment and your safety. Do not count on this summary of what you need to know to prepare you for every situation you are likely to encounter. This guide was not written primarily for novices, and this introduction is not a primer for beginning hikers. Treat it as a checklist and a set of reminders.

The Weather

Whenever possible, wait for a sunny day. The pleasures are much greater, and the problems more predictable. But even on sunny days you should be prepared for the worst; downpours and cold fronts can occur almost unannounced. The hiking season in the Adirondacks generally extends from May through October, but this does not mean you can't see snow-flakes in July. In May, for instance, the temperature may range from a sweltering 92 degrees Fahrenheit on a trail not yet sheltered by leaf cover, to a frigid 22 degrees Fahrenheit on a mountain path smothered in a foot of new snow. June is no less variable, and by then the black flies, scourge of the north, are out in full force. July and August can be severe on the tops of the higher mountains, and by mid-September you should again be pre-pared for snow. Of course, preparing for the worst does not mean the worst will happen. Remember, the greatest advan-tage in planning day trips is that you can wait until a good day comes before set-ting out.

Preparations

Even with the best of forecasts, your watchword should be to *plan for the un-expected*. Possible changes in tempera-ture mean you should take extra clothing, of which at least one layer should be wool — yes, wool, even in the heat of summer. It is the one material that keeps you warm when wet. In addition to changes of warm clothing, you may also want to carry a change of socks and a shirt, even on a day hike. Experiment with a combination of layers of light wa-terproof gear, warm wool shirts, thermal underwear, and cool, long-sleeved cotton shirts. Your pants should be sturdy and comfortable. If you are modest you might want to carry a bathing suit in your pack. Gloves and a hat usually also find their way into my pack.

Changes in terrain mean you need a sturdy, lightweight, waterproof, over-the-ankle pair of boots. And, you need a pair that fits perfectly and is well broken-in. You need to wear two pairs of socks, an inner lightweight pair and a heavy outer pair that is at least partly wool.

Of course you want a sturdy daypack, large enough to hold your needs. The separate pouch along the side of my pack always contains a whistle, a case with dry matches, a jackknife, a small can-opener, chapstick, and a space blan-ket. I have used them all.

Carry a map and compass (more of that later), a flashlight in case you are de-layed beyond dusk, and a watch so you do not panic if that happens. You also need a small first-aid kit, containing a few bandages, first-aid cream, and moleskin for the unexpected blister.

Buy a small squeeze bottle of insect re-pellent. Carry it all summer long, for the black fly season in spring stretches into the mosquito season of early summer. Deer flies and horse flies follow, and many years see a resurgence of black flies in autumn. If you plan ahead, the bugs are not all that bad. If it is warm and dry enough to walk in early May, you can enjoy a few weeks before the bugs start. They first appear at lower ele-vations and in the south, so try a few higher or more northern hikes until the black flies catch up with you. Most years there is about a week in early June — the timing and length may vary — when you should simply stay home. That week invariably occurs the week the trout fish-ing is best. Although modern science has made great improvements in repellents, nothing really seems to work during this one short period.

I fill a ziplock bag with toilet paper so it stays dry. I also throw in a few "wash and dries" to use before lunch on those dry mountain tops.

All wise hikers are likely to carry these basic items, but my personal list has ad-ditional items you should consider. I al-ways wear unbreakable glasses.

Overhanging twigs and branches have a way of poking eyes. Even if you do not need them for vision, carry dark sunglasses for bright days and a lightly tinted pair for the duller light.

There is always a magnifying glass in my pack for resolving the contour lines on maps and for identifying plant specimens. I would not be without my lightweight pair of binoculars. Distant mountain tops and birds are an important part of what I see. For pure fun I carry an altimeter that works according to barometric pressure. On relatively stable days, it is a good clue to my progress up a mountain, and on an unstable day, it can alert me to sudden changes in the weather.

Managing water has become a problem in the Adirondacks. The appearance of Giardia cysts in once pure mountain streams means that the hiker can no longer drink with impunity. As a general rule, the day hiker ought to carry enough water for his needs. The camper must use other methods, and though there is a variety of opinions about the best methods of water purification, certain filters do work. These can be bulky and expensive and I suggest you consult the latest techniques available in camping equipment stores.

The day hiker may find, as I do, that the lightweight aluminum fuel bottles, used, of course, only for drinking purposes, are the most indestructible and leak-proof water carriers. The introduction of individual cardboard juice cartons has solved the juice and pick-me-up problem for me. They are sturdy, safe, and offer a variety of natural juices, perfect for the hiker.

Remember, hiking should be fun. If you are uncomfortable with the weather or tired, turn back and make the complete hike another day. Do not create a situation where you risk yourself or your companions.

And, *never walk alone*. Be sure someone knows your intended route and expected return time. Always sign in at the DEC trailhead registers where they are available. The unexpected can occur. Weather can change, trail markings can become obscured, and you can fall, and you can get lost. But you will not be in real danger if you have anticipated the unexpected.

Behavior in the Woods

So now you are safe in the woods, but what about the woods? The Adirondack environment that can threaten you can be just as fragile as you are, and you are the only one who can protect it.

Walk dry. Wet soil is more easily compacted, making roots more susceptible to damage, so try to hike when the trails are dry. Stay on trails or rock surfaces, especially on higher summits. Avoid wet places, or walk through them with extreme care. This guide does point out a few bogs; enjoy them without altering them.

Camp at designated areas where they exist or in places where a campsite will leave no trace. Regulations require that you camp 150 feet from water or trailsides and at elevations below 4,000 feet.

Bury your wastes at least 200 feet from water and from a trail or path. If possible, select a leaf- or duff-covered area where a suitable hole can be easily scraped aside. With the appearance of Giardia in some locations, it is imperative that hikers manage human wastes to prevent the spread of this hikers' scourge.

Do not bathe with soap in lakes or streams; when picnicking or camping carry wash water as well as dish water back from the shore. Keep lake or running water pure for drinking and swimming.

If you are camping, carry a stove for cooking, and do not build fires unless they are needed. Then use only dead downed wood, and build your fire on dry stone or on gravelly or sandy soil surfaces, surrounded by a fire ring of stones to protect duff, leaf mold, or organic soils from burning.

Burn organic trash if you can. Otherwise, carry out everything you carry into the woods.

Respect the rights of other—the property rights of private landholders, as well as the privacy of fellow hikers and the wilderness rights of future hikers.

Notes for Using This Guide

Summaries at the beginning of each hike list the hiking distance, vertical rise, time on the trail, and the United States Geological Survey (USGS) topographical map or maps for the area the hike traverses. If the hike is in one of the official Wilderness Areas, that fact is noted. And if the hike climbs a mountain with a fire tower that is still open, that fact is noted along with the days that the observer is not on duty.

Unless otherwise indicated, distances are for the round trip or circuit. Distances have been derived from either state trail

Queen Anne's Lace

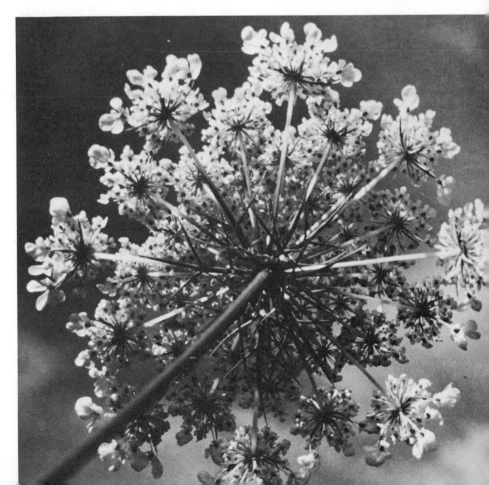

markings or measurements made from the USGS sheets. The latter are correct to within 10 percent. Errors and inconsistencies in the state signing system are described in the text.

Distances are given in miles, feet, and yards. Unless you are an experienced hiker, you probably have little sense of distance. You might want to practice 'guestimating' 100-yard intervals on the level and pacing them out to check. Because the difficulty of a hike can be so affected by elevation changes and the condition of the trail, time is as important as distance in estimating a segment of a trip.

Vertical rise refers to the total rise in elevation for the hike. In cases where the terrain is relatively level a numerical figure has not been used.

Hiking time is given for the total time for a leisurely pace, but it is simply the minimum needed to walk and enjoy the trail as described. The text often tells you to allow more time for sightseeing, and the difference is a good indication of the special things you might encounter on the way.

The maps, the USGS topographical sheets mentioned in each heading, are not absolutely necessary equipment, because the maps in this guide are based on them. (The hike route is shown by a dashed line, and the walking direction of any loop by an arrow.) However, you will have more fun on a mountain top if you can identify some of the surrounding countryside, and the maps enable you to do this.

If you do not know how to read a map you should learn to do so before hiking all but a half-dozen of the simplest trails in this guide. Spend time walking with someone who does know how to read a map. The same instructions are appropriate for the use of a compass. If you are not proficient in the use of a compass,

get help. Or work with a good book on compass reading or orienteering. The skillful use of maps and a compass is only developed with practice.

This book is a guide to fifty great hikes, not a course in using map and compass. Almost all of the routes described are on marked trails, but markings have a way of changing. You cannot always depend on them. Furthermore, bridges wash out, beavers build new ponds, and mountain tops become so clouded in fog that visibility beyond your fingertips is impossible. None of this should bother you if you have developed map and compass skills.

Other Helpful Information

Adirondack Mountain Club
174 Glen Street
Glens Falls, NY 12801

The club (ADK) is active in Adirondack conservation efforts, and its many chapters throughout New York State offer group outings and hikes. ADK publishes regional guides. Membership is currently $30 per year.

Backcountry Publications
Maxham Meadow, P.O. Box 175
Woodstock, Vermont 05091-0175

Publisher of hiking books and *State Parks and Campgrounds in Northern New York* by John Scheib, a great companion for the Adirondack hiker. See page 256 for more Backcountry guides.

City Street Directory, Inc.
35 Sandi Drive
Poughkeepsie, NY 12603

This company publishes "Adirondack Region Atlas," the best road map for locating trailheads in the Adirondacks. The map sells for $4.75.

New York State Department of Environmental Conservation (DEC) is the source of all DEC booklets, trail maps, and campsite information. Some specific titles are: "Nordic Skiing Trails in New York State," "Lake George Islands Map," "Moose River Recreation Area," "Pharaoh Lake Trails Map," "Trails in the Lake George Region," "Trails in the Cranberry Lake Region," "Trails in the Old Forge-Big Moose Region," and "Trails in the Schroon Lake Region."

The DEC operates regional offices throughout New York State. Addresses and telephone numbers for offices in Region 5 are: Lands and Forests Headquarters, Ray Brook, NY 12977, 518-891-1370 (covering Clinton, Essex, and Warren counties); Lands and Forests Headquarters, Northville, NY 12134, 518-863-4545 (covering Hamilton and Fulton counties): and Lands and Forests Headquarters, Hudson Street Extension, Box 220, Warrensburg, NY 12885, 518-623-3671 (covering Saratoga, Warren, and Washington counties).

For Region 6, which also extends into the Adirondack region, offices are: Lands and Forests Headquarters, Route 26A, P.O. Box 3, Lowville, NY 13367, 315-785-2610 (covering Jefferson and Lewis counties); and Lands and Forests Headquarters, 225 North Main Street, Herkimer, NY 13350, 315-866-6330 (covering Herkimer and Oneida counties).

New York State
Department of Commerce
Office of Tourism
99 Washington Avenue
Albany, NY 12245

Among the publications this office issues are the "I Love New York" brochures, camping guides, a tourism map, and the "State Travel Guide."

United States Geological Survey Maps

Maps are available from many local stores. Jimapco of Clifton Park, 518-899-5091 is a good supplier. Phone orders, placed with a credit card number, are quickly filled by Timely Discounts, 1-800-821-7609.

Books About the Adirondacks

Aber, Ted, and Stella King. *The History of Hamilton County.* Lake Pleasant, N.Y.: Great Wilderness Books, 1965.

Beetle, David H. *Up Old Forge Way and West Canada Creek.* Lakemont, N.Y. and Old Forge, N.Y.: North Country Books, 1972. (One-volume reprint of two books composed of articles published by the *Utica Observer-Dispatch,* Utica, N.Y., 1946 and 1948.)

Carson, Russell M.L. *Peaks and People of the Adirondacks.* Glens Falls, N.Y.: Adirondack Mountain Club, 1973. (Reprint of 1927 edition.)

Donaldson, Alfred L. *The History of the Adirondacks.* Vols. I and II. Harrison, N.Y.: Harbor Hill Books, 1977. (Reprint of 1921 edition.)

Dunham, Harvey L. *French Louie: Early Life in the North Woods.* Saranac Lake, N.Y.: North Country Books, 1970.

Fox, William F. *History of the Lumber Industry in the State of New York.* Harrison, N.Y.: Harbor Hill Books, 1976.

Gallos, Phil. *By Foot in the Adirondacks.* Saranac Lake, N.Y.: Adirondack Publishing Company, Inc., 1972.

Grady, Joseph F. *The Adirondacks, Fulton Chain–Big Moose Region: The Story of a Wilderness.* Old Forge, N.Y.: North Country Books, 1966. (Reprint of 1933 edition.)

Graham, Frank, Jr. *The Adirondack Park: A Political History.* New York: Alfred A. Knopf, 1978.

Hyde, Floy S. *Adirondack Forests, Fields and Mines.* Lakemont, N.Y.: North Country Books, 1974.

Jamieson, Paul F. "Adirondack Eskers." *Adirondack Life,* November/ December 1978, p. 20.

_____. *Adirondack Canoe Waters: North Flow.* Glens Falls, N.Y.: Adirondack Mountain Club, 1975.

_____. *Adirondack Reader.* Second Edition, Glens Falls, N.Y.: Adirondack Mountain Club, 1982.

Ketchledge, E.H. *Trees of the Adirondack High Peak Region.* Glens Falls, N.Y.: Adirondack Mountain Club, 1967.

Masten, Arthur H. *The Story of Adirondac.* Syracuse, N.Y.: Adirondack Museum and Syracuse University Press, 1968. (Reprint of 1923 edition.)

McMartin, Barbara. *Caroga: The Town Recalls its Past.* Caroga, N.Y.: Town of Caroga, 1976.

_____. *Discover the Adirondacks.* Series of regional guides. Backcountry Press, Woodstock, Vermont. See pages 254–255 for map and description of the individual guides.

Murray, William H.H. *Adventures in the Wilderness.* Syracuse, N.Y.: Adirondack Museum and Syracuse University Press, 1970. (Reprint of 1869 edition.)

Newland, D.H., and Henry Vaughn. *Guide to the Geology of the Lake George Region.* Albany, N.Y.: University of the State of New York, 1942.

O'Kane, Walter Collins. *Trails and Summits of the Adirondacks.* Boston and New York: Houghton Mifflin Company, 1928.

Pilcher, Edith. "Nehasane." *Adirondack Life,* September/October 1979, p. 14.

Rickett, Harold William. *Wild Flowers of the United States, Volume I: The Northeastern States.* New York: The New York Botanical Garden and McGraw-Hill Book Company, 1966.

Simms, Jeptha R. *Trappers of New York, or a Biography of Nicholas Stoner and Nathaniel Foster.* Harrison, N.Y.: Harbor Hill Books, 1982. (Reprint of 1857 edition.)

Street, Alfred B. *The Indian Pass.* Harrison, N.Y.: Harbor Hill Books, 1975. (Reprint of 1960 edition.)

Van De Water, Frederic F. *Lake Champlain and Lake George.* The American Lakes Series. Indianapolis and New York: Bobbs Merrill, Co., 1946.

Van Diver, Bradford C. *Rocks and Routes of the North Country, New York.* Geneva, N.Y.: W.F. Humphrey Press, 1976.

Wherry, Edgar T. *The Fern Guide: Northeast and Midland United States and Adjacent Canada.* Philadelphia: The Morris Arboretum of the University of Pennsylvania, 1972.

1

Buck Mountain

Distance (round trip): 6.6 miles
Vertical rise: 2,000 feet
Hiking time: 4½ hours
Map: USGS 7½' Bolton Landing; USGS 7½' Shelving Rock

Buck Mountain lies on the southeast shore of Lake George, and it is a perfect introduction to the Adirondacks. Pick a bright day in May, and start your Adirondack hiking with a great climb.

The views from Buck Mountain's summit encompass thousands of square miles of the Adirondacks to the north and west, parts of Vermont's Green Mountains to the east, and two large bodies of water that have figured significantly in the settlement and military histories of this region and indeed the United States. Lake Champlain and Lake George were major water highways connecting the Hudson and its river settlements to the south with the St. Lawrence and its settlements in French Canada to the north. Both lakes were important military routes, as the number of old forts and battlefields along their shores attest.

Lake George was christened Lac du St. Sacrement by its European discoverer, Father Jogues, in 1609. From that date until the end of the War of 1812, the lake was the scene of many bloody battles among the Indians, French, English, and American patriots. During that entire period, no peaceful settlement graced its shores, although there was a military

presence after 1755, when Fort William Henry was erected on its southern shore. Much of the lake is still bordered with stands of solemn evergreens, so that in places it looks very much as it did to the first white men who visited it.

Buck Mountain is only one of Lake George's mountains. Those planning additional hikes in this long-favorite resort region should investigate some of the area's state campgrounds. The Lake George Beach State Campground has picnic facilities only. Both the Hearthstone Point State Campground, 2 miles north of Lake George Village, and Rogers Rock State Campground near the north end of the lake have good camping facilities. Perhaps the most beautiful campsites are those scattered among the many state-owned islands in the lake. All of these campsites are accessible only by water. The required permits may be obtained from island caretakers on Glen, Long, and Narrow Islands, or through Ticketron. You will also want the campsite recreation circular, available from the DEC (see introduction).

Like Buck Mountain, many of Lake George's mountains are within the public lands of the New York State Forest Preserve, and several have excellent trails, the majority of which were constructed as horse trails in the 1930s by the CCC. The trail on Buck Mountain is one of the best designed in the Adirondacks. Spring comes early here, so any of these mountains is ideal for that first spring hike. Fires have swept most of the summits, leaving bare rock promontories with great views. Because of the sparseness of the cover near the summits the trails are hot and dry in summer, so you will probably find spring or fall preferable for hiking here. You must be sure to carry water. Finally, rattlesnakes inhabit the rock crevices on many of the mountains. Their infrequent presence on trails should not deter you, but do wear sturdy, high boots, and watch where you place your hands.

To reach the start of the trail up Buck Mountain take Adirondack Northway (I-87) to either Exit 21 or Exit 22, head into Lake George village, and pass Fort William Henry and the Minnehaha Boat Landing. Continue east around the south end of the lake .4 mile to NY 9L. Turn left on that highway, which follows the eastern shore of Lake George north for 6.8 miles and forks. The way left is marked "Pilot Knob, 4 miles." The state parking turnout for the Buck Mountain trailhead is 3.3 miles along this dead-end road on your right and is well marked.

You begin walking along an abandoned roadway at the east end of the parking lot. The trail is marked with yellow DEC hiking trail signs and light blue horse trail signs. The trail is raised and dry as it immediately plunges into a hemlock bog with many osmunda ferns, their huge root clump masses rising from the soggy ground. As the forest changes to tall hardwoods, the heavy vines of fox grapes are reminiscent of typical Hudson Highland cover.

At this lower elevation, the trail intersects several logging roads: at the first fork turn right, and at the second, at .3 mile, turn left. You cross Butternut Brook, then begin to climb the deep, hemlock-covered slopes that shelter the brook. You pass another old woods road forking left, you cross the stream, Butternut Brook, and continue beside it, climbing a slope beneath a deep hemlock-covered ledge. The trail zigzags as it climbs seriously, and if you look down on your right you should see a picnic table beneath the hemlock and beside the stream.

Another indistinct woods road coming from the left will remind you that this area was once farmed and logged. You are now climbing moderately and are already high enough to see the blue water of Lake George through the trees. Rock ledges rise on your left where the trail has been carved into the hillside. After walking for about a half-hour you pass an old stone fence. It leads to a promontory with a small opening and a view of mountains to the south. Beyond that you walk through an open field and cross a small stream on a slippery log. The stream cascades in a pretty series of small waterfalls down to Butternut Brook. Follow the stream for 100 yards to an intersection, where a sign says it is 1.5 miles back to Pilot Knob trailhead. (Pilot Knob itself is privately owned and inaccessible.) You probably walked that distance in forty minutes.

At the intersection the blue trail bears right to Inman Pond, 3.1 miles away. Take the left fork, which heads north to the summit of Buck Mountain, 1.8 miles distant. Here the trail is deeply cut into the hillside, with high banks on either side, and the route is somewhat boulder strewn. You begin a gradual but steady climb with gentle switchbacks into a scrubby deciduous forest. Refreshing level stretches curve between the steepest segments. About twenty minutes from the intersection, a logging road joins from the left, and you turn sharply right, uphill. At this point there are so few trail markers that you may be misled.

A couple hundred yards past the logging road, water pours from a spring-fed pipe to the right and spills across the trail to join the small stream on the left. About twenty minutes beyond the logging road you cross the stream again. The forest cover of small maple, beech, and birch is home to a multitude of birds, and you may even spot a nesting pair of scarlet tanagers. About ten minutes from the second stream crossing, in a level between climbs, the trail has been widened to avoid a wet seep. This is the only place where the route might be confusing. Look for the yellow markers on your left to show you where to begin the climb again, with the steepest grades so far encountered. Even the stretches between switchbacks seem steeper now. The forest is more open, with scrubby oak indicating the summit is near.

You soon reach the first real overlook,

with views southeast to Crosset Pond. Beyond it the trail climbs and then flattens out, heading north across a shoulder of the mountain. Pine, hemlock, and tall birch fill the level ground below the last rise. The path, narrow here, crosses a boggy area lush with wild iris, clintonia, spring anemones, bunchberry, golden thread, putty root orchid, *corallorhiza trifida,* and huge clumps of polygala, or gay wings. As open rock and the summit appear ahead, you realize you still have a way to walk. Yellow arrows painted on the bare rock direct you between scrubby patches of cherry, maple, birch, popple, and blueberry. The view begins to unfold, and after two and a half hours of walking, you reach the summit. In a cleft filled with garnet sand near the summit, a sign indicates that the trail continues northeast toward Shelving Rock Road, 2.5 miles away.

Buck Mountain rises steeply from the deepest part of Lake George. From the 2,330-foot summit you will not only enjoy views of the lake, which lies in a deep

View south from Buck Mountain toward Lake George village

fault valley whose ends are blocked by glacial debris, but you will meet some of the other peaks described in this guide. Crane Mountain (Hike 29) lies almost due west, and Gore Mountain with its tower and ski slopes is to the north. Just north of Gore on the horizon is the distinctive flat-topped hump of Blue Mountain (Hike 36). In the distance between Crane and Blue lies Snowy Mountain (Hike 33). It is 43 miles away and distinguished by the jagged knob whose cliff face reflects white, prompting the name.

On the north-northeast beyond Little Buck Mountain lies Sleeping Beauty, with Erebus to its left and Black Mountain (Hike 2) just peeping up behind. If it is a clear day in summer, when there is little definition between rocks and trees, the cliffs on Sleeping Beauty may not show up in such a way that they reveal the form of a reclining female stretched like a romantic billboard across that mountain's southwestern slopes. Pharaoh Mountain (Hike 26) rises almost 21 miles away in the direction of magnetic north. Beyond it and more than 40 miles distant, range the Adirondack's High Peaks, with Giant (Hike 48) to the right of Pharaoh, and the cluster that includes Nippletop and Marcy to the left.

Northwest of Buck, lying against the western shore of Lake George, is Green Island, with the rebuilt Hotel Sagamore. Look beyond it to the hills on the horizon. South of a line to Green are the cliffs on Moxon Mountain, which mark the route toward Vanderwhacker (Hike 43). Sight above the middle of the island to Hoffman Mountain, whose western notch makes a great day's trek (Hike 46). From the eastern promontories you can enjoy the sweep of the Champlain Valley with the Green Mountains behind.

When you start your return, retrace your footsteps, being careful to follow the designated route on the open summit. That way you will not disturb the fragile plants that have managed to find niches in cracks along the open rock.

The long sweep of the shoulder you traverse points to Pilot Knob Mountain on the south. Your zigzag descent to the shoulder and the trek across it should take no more than twenty minutes; you then begin the series of switchbacks that will bring you within forty-five minutes to the piped spring. When you reach the trail intersection, less than a half-hour beyond, most of the steep descent is finished. Native columbine and sweetfern shrub edge the route. The rest of the walk is so easy that a half hour will suffice for the last 1.5 miles, unless you pause to look at wildflowers.

Black Mountain

Distance (around loop): 8.5 miles
Vertical rise: 1,100 feet
Hiking time: 6 hours
Map: NY Department of Transportation 7½' Shelving Rock and
  NY DOT 7½' Whitehall or USGS 15' Bolton Landing
Fire Tower; closed Thursday, Friday

Black Mountain, at 2,646 feet, is the highest peak in the two ranges of mountains that shelter Lake George, and the views from the summit are more than proportional to its height. One of the trails to its summit rises steeply from the shore of Lake George, but it is accessible only by water. Your route on Black Mountain is a loop that requires a bit less climbing, but it still traverses part of the reputedly more handsome trail from the lake. This loop also allows you to visit a series of charming ponds that lie south and east of the summit.

There is a fire tower on Black Mountain, and although you might appreciate the fire observer's help in identifying distant mountains, Black's summit is mostly open rock so overlooks in every direction can be found at ground level.

Black Mountain is about halfway along the eastern shore of Lake George. You reach the trailhead from NY 22. From the north and west, take Exit 28 off the Adirondack Northway (I-87) to NY 74, and follow that route east to NY 22 at Ticonderoga. Head south on NY 22 to Clemons. From the south, pick up NY 22 at Fort Ann and continue north to Clemons. This latter route takes you on a

beautiful drive through the Champlain Valley and across the South Bay of Lake Champlain above Whitehall.

At Clemons drive 2.6 miles west toward Huletts Landing on County Route 6, and then bear south (left) on Pike Road for .8 mile to the trailhead. Signs at the trailhead indicate that the Black Mountain tower is 2.8 miles away, and that the Lapland Pond Lean-to, which you pass on your return leg, is 2.5 miles distant.

On the drive from Clemons west, you will have views of Black Mountain as well as of Knob Hill and Sugarloaf, two unusual small mountains whose distinctive shapes you will be able to identify again clearly from Black's summit.

The trail begins along a gravel road that leads to a private residence. Red trail disks on telephone poles, which you will follow all the way to the summit, mark the route. A splash of the wildflowers that make every walk in the Lake George region special brighten this otherwise dull roadway. Trillium, blue cohosh, crinkleroot, twisted stalk, Solomon's seal, and clintonia are only a few of the flowers you may see.

You reach an intersection in .9 mile.

Across the field of the nearby farmhouse the tower still looks a long way away. The trail follows the right side of the field and continues gently uphill through a more mature and taller woods, making pleasanter walking. You should spot the rattlesnake fern, which will remind you to be watchful of rattlesnakes on this mountain, as on all of Lake George's mountains.

After a half-hour or so, in just over 1.2 miles, the trail to the Lapland Pond Leanto and the ponds to the south forks left, marked with blue disks. You take the right-hand trail, still marked with red disks. The sign indicates it is 1.6 miles to the tower. The trail continues to follow an old roadway, which has stretches of corduroy. Look to the edges for trailing arbutus and foamflower. A snowmobile trail forks right at a second intersection. It winds toward the summit by a more circuitous route, with a lower grade than the hiking trail. You will meet it again just below the last pitch on the summit.

For the hiking trail, go left, on the less obvious route. Fortunately a plethora of red disks marks the intersection. The trail quickly takes you across a little stream where water falls over a series of small horizontal ledges.

The trail turns sharply left uphill and really begins to climb, following the little watercourse to a rock ledge. The trail heads straight up the ledge, so steeply that you will probably have to pause and catch your breath. Beyond, the trail, wide enough that vehicles once used it, is worn to bedrock. The forest is fairly open, and within an hour you can look back toward Knob Hill. You pass through an area of heavy blowdowns where winter has taken its toll of many treetops, leaving a scene of destruction. Then you continue climbing through spruce forests with some hemlock, low balsam, and striped maple. The underbrush becomes thick before finally opening by moss-covered ledges near the summit.

It will probably take you a little over an

hour and a half to reach the open, wind-swept summit, which picnic tables, two cabins, and the tower share. A sign points south where the red-marked trail continues to Black Mountain Point on Lake George, some 2.7 miles away.

From the tower you can't help noticing first the Tongue Mountain Range (Hike 3) on the opposite shore of Lake George. The Range Trail and Fivemile Mountain, Fifth Peak, and French Point Mountain are easily identified. You will appreciate from this vantage the lumps and valleys on the Range Trail that make it so chal-lenging and difficult: the deep valley to the south of Fifth Peak, the height of the two unnamed knobs to its south, and the deep valley between French Point Moun-tain and First Peak reveal how much climbing there is.

Elephant Mountain lies northeast of Black on the east shore of Lake George. Sabbath Day Point, Silver Bay, and The Hague stretch north on the lake's western shore, with the slopes of Rogers Rock sil-houetted beyond. Slightly south of Rogers Rock, on the west shore, An-thony's Nose raises its unmistakable pro-file. In the distance to the northeast Lake Champlain is visible, with the Green Mountains beyond.

If it is a really clear day, you can iden-tify the mountains on the horizon that lie between the northern end of the Tongue Mountain Range and Catamount, the long mountain northwest of Sabbath Day Point. Sight beyond Catamount to Giant Mountain. Dix rises directly over Fivemile Mountain, and continuing to the left, you see McComb, Nippletop, Basin, Hay-stack, Marcy, Skylight, and Redfield. Pha-raoh Mountain, just to the left of Nippletop, is much nearer. Still in the closer range, Hoffman Mountain is farther left, with Santanoni to its left on the hori-zon. Vanderwhacker is next left, its steep cone standing isolated. This panorama

occupies the skyline defined by Fivemile Mountain and the valley between it and Fifth Peak. Over that valley is the flat top of Blue Mountain.

Once you have climbed back down the tower, the views south are best as you begin your descent, continuing along the red trail. At the end of the promon-tory, ledges to the right overlook Erebus Mountain and the islands that fill the nar-rows of Lake George. This is the best place from which to appreciate the deep trench of the down drop fault, or graben, that forms the lake. Here the bent forms of wind-shaped trees frame the views, and clusters of misshapen cherries, ma-ples, and elderberries provide little shel-ter from the sun. The trail, built up with rock, hugs the steep slopes and begins its twisting, turning descent, dropping rapidly and without views below many cliffs and ledges. The switchbacks (I lost track of the count after twenty) allow you to descend quickly to a magnificent look-out southeast to the chain of ponds you are about to visit, as well as southwest to Lake George.

Below the overlook, the trail becomes less steep and the woods become deeper, changing to a high, open forest of huge birch. You have passed the imaginary line that separates the sharp knob of Black Mountain's summit and the valley below. On the upper slopes, which rise 800 feet in .5 mile, rock work was necessary to build the trail against the mountain, but here it is beautiful, soft, and wide. After walking only a few min-utes on the wider trail, a total descent of forty minutes (if you did not pause too long for views) you reach an intersection. The well-used, red-marked trail turns right toward Black Mountain Point, but you turn left on the yellow-marked trail. This intersection 200 yards below the lookout is not obvious. If you are still on the red trail heading downhill when it crosses the

Lapland Pond

outlet of Black Mountain Pond, you have followed it about 200 yards too far. Retrace your steps and look for the intersection with the yellow trail. It is easier to spot when walking in this direction. This little-used route will take you .3 mile to Black Mountain Pond, .7 mile to Round Pond, and a bit over 1 mile to Lapland Pond.

You begin beside a boggy swale with handsome birch. Next, climb to a hemlock knoll above Black Mountain Pond, which is hardly visible at first below the ledge on which you are walking. Descend to the muddy shore of the marshy little body of water, complete with beaver house and bog plants. Continue up another knoll topped with huge paper birch, and walk on high ground to Round Pond. The trail dips to its shore beside a hemlock-covered hillside that makes a great place to camp.

Just east of Round Pond you intersect a snowmobile trail. Your yellow-marked route continues east, winding alongside a hemlock marsh, and reaches a three-way junction fifteen minutes from Round Pond. (The sign indicates it is .77 mile from Black Mountain Pond. You will notice that distances vary in the Adirondacks sign to sign; the sum of the mileages rarely adds up to the totals given at the trailheads.) The entire walk between intersections takes no more than thirty minutes, unless, of course, you could not resist stopping at one of the ponds. The yellow-marked route heads right (south) toward Millman and Fishbrook ponds. You take the blue-blazed trail left, which the sign indicates heads toward Pike Brook Road. Walk along it for no more than five minutes, about .2 mile, to another intersection, where a spur trail heads back southeast along Lapland Pond's eastern shore to a lovely lean-to high on a rock slide.

Lapland is the largest and deepest of the three ponds and has beautiful shores. You will surely stop here for a rest or swim before continuing north. The trail north is marked both with blue hiking trail disks and orange snowmobile trail disks. It follows a long level valley on an old road, and although the woods are handsome, the walking is not good. The level roadway may be flooded, even in dry times. Within ten minutes you begin a long descent, first following a stream and then continuing through the saddle high and dry above the stream, which you ultimately cross. Thirty minutes probably suffices for the walk from Lapland Pond to the last trail intersection and the end of the blue-marked trail. You fork right on the red trail to retrace your steps for the final 1.2 miles to your car.

Tongue Mountain Range

Distance (around loop): 12.4 miles
Vertical rise: 3,000 feet
Hiking time: 8 hours
Map: USGS 15′ Bolton Landing

The Tongue Mountain Range is a great block fault thrust up in the midst of the fault valley that Lake George has filled. On this loop hike you first climb its ridge, then follow the backbone of the Tongue that thrusts south into the lake, and conclude with a walk back north along the shore of Northwest Bay. From countless vantage points along the ridge, views of Lake George and The Narrows are superb. French Point Mountain, halfway along the portion of the Range Trail you hike here, lies just far enough out of line with the rest of the Tongue Range to have long, uninterrupted views both north and south. Because the lack of tree cover on the ridge permits a completely different range of flowers from those found in the deep woods that fill the slopes along Northwest Bay, this hike also introduces you to an amazing variety of Adirondack flora.

The Tongue Mountain Range is a good choice for spring hiking. The trail is among the first to dry out enough to walk, and in May the cover of wildflowers is magnificent. The long stretches of open ridge that are a plus in spring discourage hiking in summer months, when a canopy of shade trees is more desir-

able. The abundance of hardwoods makes it a spectacular fall hike.

This is a most strenuous trip, however, so if you plan to go in early spring be sure you are up to it. The hike is long, and the vertical rise is equivalent to that on Giant or Algonquin mountains, the two highest peaks described in this guide. You rise 1,560 feet directly from lake level to Fifth Peak, and then snake across the peaks to the south as if you were following the Great Wall of China, soaring to each summit from a deep intervening valley.

For the easiest route to the trailhead from the Adirondack Northway (I-87), exit at Interchange 24 and follow County Route 11 east, toward Bolton Landing and NY 9N. After descending the long hill toward the lake, head north on NY 9N. From the intersection you will see the Tip of the Tongue and a portion of the ridge you will walk.

Drive north on NY 9N for .4 mile, past signs for a boat launching site and the Tongue Mountain–Clay Meadows trailhead, to a parking area beside an old quarry on the east side of the road. If you have allowed enough time for a full day of hiking, take a few minutes now to

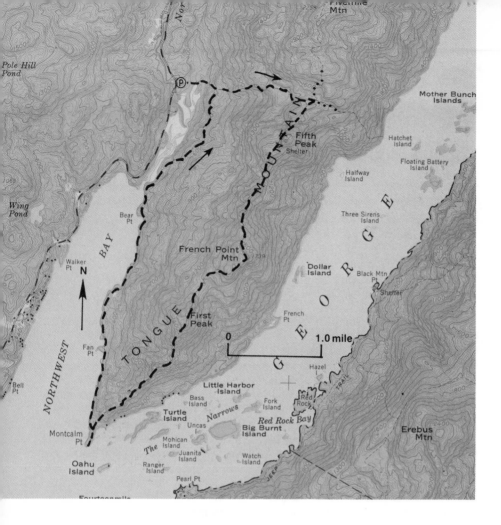

cross the road just south of the parking area and walk about 100 yards along the evergreen-covered promontory above Northwest Bay Brook to a handsome little falls in the deep hemlock-shrouded gorge.

Signs at the trailhead direct you east toward the Tongue Mountain Range. You begin at the blue markers by walking through a tall red pine reforestation stand—the site of the old farm that gave the area the name Clay Meadows—and then crossing the marsh beside a small inlet of Northwest Bay. The marsh sports many ferns and in spring brilliant yellow clumps of marsh marigolds.

Within ten minutes and .3 mile, you reach a junction. You will return later in the day by way of the trail to the right. For now, go straight ahead on the red-marked trail (there are few visible markers). The trail follows a small stream that flows from Fifth Peak on your right. Although you hardly ever see it, you can almost always hear it. Five minutes from the intersection you may want to leave the trail to walk right toward the stream at the top of its plunge down a deep, shaded gorge.

The well-worn trail climbs steeply, crossing three bridges, two over intermittent streams. Watch as ledges appear along the trail on your left; one of these is manmade and is the clue to turn sharply left for a switchback that covers the last steep pitch before a plateau. This is the only place where the relative absence of trail markers might cause confusion. You then round the hemlock marsh that fills the plateau and cross the stream that feeds it, here without benefit of a bridge. You climb steeply again, a pitch covering about 160 vertical feet, before reaching a second plateau and the major intersection with the Range Trail. It is 1.9 miles from Clay Meadows to this spot, and the climb should take nearly an hour and fifteen minutes.

Here the red route continues straight ahead and down to the shore of Lake George. The left, or north, branch of the blue trail leads to Fivemile Mountain and Deer Leap. (A trailhead farther north on NY 9N offers easier access to these peaks in the Tongue Mountain Range and is described in *Discover the Eastern Adirondacks*.) Your route is right on the blue trail, south to the Tip of the Tongue.

The roller-coaster trip along the ridge begins mildly enough with a .5-mile climb of under 300 feet toward Fifth Peak. You leave the blue trail on a yellow-marked, .2-mile-long spur to reach the actual peak and its nearby lean-to. Note that there is no water at all on the peak. Hikers who detour to the peak often bushwhack southwest from there, descending a few tricky ledges to intersect the blue trail farther along, rather than retrace steps along the spur.

Beyond Fifth Peak, the trail shows much less use, and the trail markers are more numerous and definitely necessary. In places under the leaf cover the footpath is hardly visible, although the trail shows signs of its superior CCC construction.

There is a second lookout on Fifth Peak from a shoulder .2 mile south of the summit. In 1985, in the area of the second lookout on Fifth Peak, a forest fire burned many acres on the east flank of the mountain, a reminder that this area is very prone to fire damage. Only a small portion of the trail was affected by the fire, however. Just beyond the trail crosses the ridge to afford a view straight down Northwest Bay. Then it starts to drop into the valley south of the peak. "Drop" is scarcely the word for the long rock slide with several extremely steep pitches. You will lose almost 350 feet in elevation in .2 mile. As you descend, look back to the cliffs behind you. And while you are grappling for handholds on the descent, you might be amused to think that Robert Moses, the master roadbuilder, had plans to build a highway that would encircle Lake George's shores. The prospect always conjures images of a huge flying span across the gulf between Fifth Peak and the unnamed knob to its immediate south.

You no sooner hit bottom than you immediately start climbing again, heading up that knob. It is just short of 1 mile from Fifth Peak to the top of the first knob. There is a view back to the cliffs on Fifth Peak, but the trail leads you immediately on, plunging down the next southern slope. Here you turn sharply, below the cliff, and head away from the lake. Another steep drop takes you to a hemlock swale where you must look carefully for the turn left to head up a second knob.

Again, you will make a short, sharp descent before continuing on the ridge without the aid of many trail markers. Your route gradually heads southeast to French Point Mountain. It takes a good hour to walk from the south shoulder of Fifth Peak to the summit of French Point Mountain, because of the scramble over and around the unnamed knobs.

Your hike has lasted about three hours so far, and you have covered 4.6 miles. That makes French Point Mountain (elevation 1,739 feet) the perfect place to stop for lunch. You will find a perch suspended almost 1,400 feet above the lake, with fantastic views northeast up the lake and south toward The Narrows, which are choked with tiny islands, just a few of the 200 that grace Lake George. The DEC map for the island campsites of Lake George (see introduction), which shows the campsites and day-use areas on the islands below you, is the best guide to their names. Opposite your perch lies Paradise Bay, whose deep green, gem-clear waters are visited by the steamer Mohican on its regular trips on the lake. During your lunch stop you will certainly see one of the steamers, successors to those that plied the lake as long ago as 1817. Black Mountain is a little north of east across the lake, and Erebus, Sleeping Beauty, and the Buck Range are to the south.

If you have been keeping count, you should tally the wildflowers you have seen on the way. A list that exceeds thirty-two is not unusual and in season probably will include: pale corydalis, four kinds of violets, twisted stalk, red trillium, dwarf ginseng, wild oat, foamflower and myterwort, toad flax and Canada mayflower, lady's slippers, clintonia, Dutchman's-breeches, bluets, saxifrage, early buttercup, cucumber root, pipsissiwa, three-toothed cinquefoil, wood betony or lousewort, and the amazing fields of trailing arbutus for which the Tongue Mountain Range is famous.

After leaving French Point Mountain, cross over the ridge, guided by blue daubs on the bare rock, for another view of Northwest Bay. You can now almost see the Tip of the Tongue, or Montcalm Point. Imagine the scene during the French and Indian War when Montcalm's army of attacking French rounded the tip toward Northwest Bay. You head down toward the bay in as steep a descent as that which followed Fifth Peak. Walk along the vertical side of the mountain with cliffs below, and then turn away from the bay, still descending, in a switchback heading toward Lake George. The scrub cover of beech, butternut, shadblow, white pine, ash, oak, and hop hornbeam is not thick enough to block the views. The drier, sparser cover contrasts with the deep rich woods of the western slopes. Most of the time now you are walking right at the exposed edge of the cliffs overlooking Lake George.

After climbing another small promontory you will see that First Peak, your next destination, is maddeningly far away on the opposite side of another deep valley. Here, the talus slopes make rugged walking.

When you reach First Peak, a forty-five minute walk after lunch, you are rewarded with a view back to French Point Mountain. You can appreciate the magnificence of the cliff that falls away from it, dropping to water level. The reason for your difficult walk is clear, for looking back north is like viewing the ridges of a dragon's back. Someone said the trail was laid out along the teeth of a giant saw.

The sawblade continues southwest to the very Tip of the Tongue. Green Island is opposite the tip, and Dome Island lies farther south in the middle of the lake. From First Peak the trail drops steeply at first and then levels out, as it twists and turns along the top of the ridge on a fairly well-marked route. From an outcrop a spectacular cliff drops away to Turtle Bay, and you overlook Turtle Island and Shelving Rock across The Narrows. The trail continues into a narrow slot between ledges where the talus makes for very difficult footing.

You have been walking for almost two hours since lunch, and you haven't reached the Tip yet. After still more rock outcrops with views and one last knoll to climb, you descend nearly to lake level and reach a junction. Continue straight ahead on a .2-mile spur to the Tip and a well-earned rest soaking your feet in the cooling waters of the lake. The sign says you have traveled 2.5 miles from French Point Mountain, descending 1,426 feet. It doesn't say how much you climbed in that "descent." After returning from your detour to the Tip, you will have walked 7.6 miles, but you still have 4.8 miles left to reach Clay Meadows again.

The blue trail along the shores of Northwest Bay is level at first, but before you have time to enjoy the flatness, you have to climb around a small piece of private land. Beyond it, the trail continues at lake level, sometimes wet underfoot, and usually close to the water, but shortly the steepness of the shoreline forces you to climb again.

You cross a small creek and then turn sharply left, to edge a small bay. About forty minutes from the intersection, you cross a stream with a waterfall; ledges beside it drip with mosses and maidenhair spleenwort. For those who count ferns, this could be the twentieth species of ferns you have seen along the hike.

Rock work edges the trail, which was originally constructed as a bridle path. The walking is easier as you cross two bridges in a beautiful deep hemlock stand, but only briefly. You climb again, now around the marshes that edge Northwest Bay Brook. When you reach a final bridge, you are just 200 feet short of

View from French Point Mountain across Lake George

the trail intersection you passed at the outset. Here you head left to the highway and your car.

By the end of your trip you will certainly have walked for eight hours, but if you have paused to enjoy the spectacular scenery you will probably have been on the trail for at least ten hours.

Look up at the Tongue Mountain Range when you leave to drive south along the highway. You will have a great respect for the sinuous route that the trail takes along the bumps and ridges of the Tongue Mountain Range.

Hadley Mountain

Distance (round trip): 4 miles
Vertical rise: 1,550 feet
Hiking time: 2½ - 3 hours
Map: USGS 15' Lake Luzerne
Fire Tower; closed Thursday, Friday

With a summit of only 2,700 feet, half the height of Mount Marcy, Hadley might not sound like much of a mountain. This just proves how little elevation can figure in the true pleasures of mountain climbing. Views from the fire tower on Hadley or from its open summit are among the most spectacular in the Adirondacks. In the north you can see many of the eastern High Peaks; in the south, the major summits of the Catskills; and in the east, an open panorama of the hills beyond Lakes George and Champlain ranging to Vermont's Green Mountains and the edges of the Berkshires in Massachusetts. The view southwest is across Great Sacandaga Lake and northwest to a multitude of southern Adirondack mountains. Once I climbed Hadley on a perfectly clear day, and I remember the trip as one of the most beautiful I have ever had in the mountains.

Hadley is near the southern end of a chain of summits that together comprise West Mountain, a ridge in the southeast corner of the Adirondacks. There are many open spots along the ridge's north-northeast to south-southwest ranging axis, and you should plan to extend your visit to Hadley by walking along it, watch-

ing the perspectives change. The lichens growing in niches between open rock make a multicolored carpet and easy crunchy walking through the scrub. Here, moving from open rock ledges to scrubby promontories can hardly be called bushwhacking.

The only difficult part about climbing Hadley is locating the trailhead; no markers point the way, and there are few road names to assist in the search. If you are driving from the west, along the shores of the Great Sacandaga Lake, the signs are pretty clear. The north shore road is County Route 4. Just before the Paul River Hardware Store turn north onto Hadley Hill Road. The intersection is in Day Center, almost a thirty-minute drive east of Northville. Follow Hadley Hill Road for 5.2 miles to Tower Road, on the left. The parking turnout for the tower is 1.4 miles north on Tower Road.

From the south, east, or north, take NY 9N, which passes through Lake Luzerne. Turn left in Lake Luzerne to Hadley, then go north on Stony Creek Road. Hadley Hill Road is a left turn at a marked intersection just over 3 miles north of Hadley. Drive west on Hadley Hill Road for nearly 3 miles and turn right on an unnamed road. Follow the road for .8 mile to a Y where the macadam road bears right. Go straight ahead on the dirt road. After 1.7 miles, a small sign on the right indicates the parking lot for the Hadley tower. This will probably be the first sign you see for the tower.

At the trailhead a sign states: "Successive fires in 1903, 1908, 1911, and 1915 severely burned 12,000 acres of the surrounding forest land." In response to fires in the late nineteenth and early twentieth centuries, the state erected a series of fire towers across the Adirondacks. From early spring to snowfall, these towers were manned by dedicated observers who often trudged long distances with heavy packs to supply their week-long stays on the mountaintop. The men were dependent on fragile telephone lines for communication and usually had to maintain both the lines and the trails to their towers. From the earliest days, each tower was assigned the days its ranger could take off; since the territories of adjacent towers overlapped, the pattern established meant the area was continually under the watchful eye of one or another

fire observer during the dangerous months.

Most of the southern Adirondack mountaintops are heavily wooded, so the towers provide the only opportunities for views from their summits. The fire towers have long been favorite hiking destinations, and the recent closing of a substantial number is mourned by many. The daily plane flights that took their place may provide adequate fire surveillance, but they deprive hikers of many fine views. Fortunately, Hadley's tower remains open, although there are great views from the summit, even without the tower.

Fires alone did not create the bare peaks. As recently as ten thousand years ago, retreating glaciers scraped the mountaintops and left huge boulders and glacial erratics perched precariously on even the highest summits. What little organic soil had accumulated in the geologically short interval since the last glacier was quickly consumed by the raging fires.

What caused these great fires? When settlers first advanced into the Adiron-

View from Hadley Mountain

dacks, cutting the towering pine and hemlock for building lumber and later harvesting hardwoods for pulp, little thought was given to the methods of harvesting timber. Tops and slashes were left in huge, loose piles across the once-forested hills and valleys. The early years of the twentieth century were unusually dry, and the tinder piles were easily ignited by lightning and careless sparks. Nearly a million acres of New York's forest land were burned. Charred stumps and bare soil can still be found on many mountains, and the soil's ability to retain water has been completely disrupted. Only the vigilance of fire observers prevented further burning, and although many dry, bare summits persist, the forests have begun to recover.

Enough of background, history, and directions to the trailhead—the directions along the trail are quite simple, and the trail needs almost no description, even though it is sparsely marked by red disks. It is simple and direct and wide and open. Much of the route is over exposed bedrock. The high cover of beech and birch soon gives way to smaller trees. The route is fairly consistently steep.

Three-fourths of the way to the summit, the road turns sharply left. Telephone lines angle right through a cliff-lined draw. Those with youngsters may prefer to scramble to the summit under the telephone lines, the little ledges and cliffs providing a bit of sport. Going down, though, it is safer along the road.

On the 2,700-foot summit you can spend hours playing "name that peak." Among the features you should spot is the edge of the Helderberg escarpment over the Great Sacandaga Lake. North beyond Roundtop, which is a part of West Mountain, you can see Baldhead, Moose, and Crane mountains. To their left lie Bearpen and Mount Blue. Further left, the knob of Snowy's summit rises above the line of mountains on the horizon. Nippletop and Dix are easily identified in the High Peaks 50 miles away. Pharaoh Mountain can be spotted in the north-northeast, and the peaks surrounding Lake George in the northeast.

You will have no trouble at all filling a day with things to do on this lovely mountaintop.

Murphy, Middle, and Bennett Lakes

Distance (one way): 7.2 miles
Vertical rise: 500 feet
Hiking time: 4 hours
Maps: USGS 15' Lake Pleasant; USGS 15' Harrisburg

During the early nineteenth century, settlers traced a network of roads into the valleys of the southern Adirondacks. These routes were used after the Revolutionary War to reach the rich stands of timber in the northern wilderness and to establish new settlements in the Adirondack interior.

Today some of these old roads are the routes of modern highways. Others remain concealed in the wilderness, completely forgotten. And a few are the trails we now follow. The hamlets of Hope, Hope Falls, and Pumpkin Hollow, on the Sacandaga River and East Stony Creek, were established by settlers who built roads north from Northville immediately after 1800.

One road started near Hope Falls and headed north past several homesteads, a paint mine, and a string of small lakes. Today that road is a fine trail, short enough for a one-day, one-way trek if you spot a car at each end, and interesting enough for an extended camping expedition. There are several good camping sites and a lean-to near the lakes.

The northern end of the trail is the easiest to find; I suggest you arrange to leave a car there. Distances are given from the NY 30 bridge over the Sacandaga River, about 3.5 miles north of the fork to Northville. From the bridge, drive north on NY 30 for 7.2 miles to Pumpkin Hollow Road, which is on the right, or east. A snowmobile trail signboard also marks the turn. The northern end of the trail is 1.6 miles along Pumpkin Hollow Road and is marked. There is parking off the road near the trailhead.

There are two ways to reach the southern end of the trail by Hope Falls. Just over 3 miles north of the Sacandaga Bridge turn right, or east, from NY 30 onto Creek Road, and drive east for 2.5 miles to the trailhead, which is on the north side of the road and marked. A prettier approach is from Northville on the Hope Falls Road, which approximates the route used by early settlers. Follow Hope Falls Road north to Creek Road and then bear left for .5 mile to the trailhead. The Hope Falls Road and its extension north make a nice drive along East Stony Creek.

The trail has been marked with both yellow hiking and orange snowmobile disks, although the colors are worn. The old road is so easy to follow, you should not be bothered by the indistinct markings. The first mile north skirts private land along a road that has been recently used for logging, with hemlock, sugar maple, and beech remaining. The route is uphill, and the road has eroded and washed out. As you approach a height-of-land, white pine and yellow and gray birch appear. After about twenty-five minutes, you will notice that the forest cover changes to a small, dense population of pine, birch, and beech. You can see the old stone wall of one of the nineteenth-century farmsites on your left. Just beyond, a cable marks the boundary of state land.

No more than five minutes beyond the cable you arrive at the old paint mine, now hardly more than a depression in the ground. The red-stained rocks and soil indicate a low-grade hematite, the color that made barns and homes deep red. Imagine using this road to walk to school, as children did in the late 1800s, and coming home by lantern light after dark every evening.

The trail continues through a mature mixed forest around the side of the hill. Less than 1.5 miles and forty minutes from your start, you will glimpse Bennett Lake down through the trees on your right. Within 200 yards an unmarked path forks right toward the lake. Follow it down a relatively steep grade for 150 yards to a flat place along the shore, where there are several good camping spots, an outhouse, a fireplace, and a sandy beach.

Returning to the main trail, continue west, climbing a small hill. You will pass an unmarked loop that quickly rejoins the main route and reach a small brook at the top of the rise.

Approximately ten minutes after you pass the creek, you will have your first glimpse of Middle Lake. The distance between Middle and Bennett lakes is 1.6 miles, and the walk between them should take about forty minutes. The trail continues on the hillside, about 50 feet above the lake. The lake is .6 mile long and very narrow, with steep, evergreen-covered shores and several small islands. One side path leads 100 feet to a camping spot, and shortly beyond that fork the main trail approaches the lakeshore and follows it past many campsites. The remains of an old foundation are visible on

Middle Lake from the cliffs on the unnamed hill

the lakeshore. There are impressive views of the cliffs on the mountain to the north.

At the northern end of Middle Lake the trail turns left and enters a small, thick, wet forest. Only fifteen minutes is required for the .5-mile walk between Middle and Murphy lakes. The approach to the latter is signaled by a mature hemlock stand. As you come to the lake there are spectacular views of cliffs on the small knob to the north as well as those on the mountain to the east. Adventurous bushwhackers will want to find a route to these cliffs for a view of the lake (see *Discover the Southeastern Adirondacks* for a description).

A lean-to and several campsites border the trail at its southern approach to the lake. Continue along the trail, north to a huge boulder on the shore. You can enjoy both a great view of the lake and a swim from the boulder.

The footpath around the lake is not always easy to follow, but for .6 mile you stay close to the shore until you reach the northern inlet, crossing that small brook on a log bridge. Continue along the shore, heading southwest, for .2 mile to the outlet. From here it is 2.8 miles northwest to the trailhead via the snowmobile trail. The first part of the route beside Murphy Lake outlet is the prettiest. Then you cross the creek, pass a beaver flow with views east to the cliff-faced knob, recross the creek, cross Doig Creek, and end with a rather ordinary and level stretch on the old logging road.

Stone Dam Lake and Chub Pond

Distance (round trip): 13.4 miles
Vertical rise: 280 feet
Hiking time: 7 hours
Maps: USGS 7.5' North Wilmurt; 15' McKeever

The low foothills of the southwestern Adirondacks rise gradually to the central mountain dome. It is a region of sandy plains—the borders of ancient glacial lakes. Flat logging roads crisscross the lower slopes. Today, most of these are trails for hikers and snowmobilers; they are generally broad routes, with firm surfaces that make for very easy hiking. All of these trails are described in greater detail in *Discover the Southwestern Adirondacks.* One such long level route does not follow old roadbeds; for most of its distance it is a narrow, wilderness track. It will lead you past two ponds and the aftermath of a tornado, a scene of destruction that resulted from a cataclysm of nature in one of its most violent forms.

While you are discovering this route, you can explore one of the major highways into the southwestern Adirondacks. The trailhead is on North Lake Road. North Lake was dammed to assure water for the Black River Canal and its feeders. The dam was finished in 1856, creating North Lake Reservoir from tiny, 60-acre Sophie Pond. Reservoirs were also constructed on the South Branch of the Black River (South Lake) and Twin Lakes where a marsh was flooded. Modern

trails explore both of these areas, though much of North Lake is now in private hands and the surrounding lands are part of the very private Adirondack League Club.

The dam on North Lake was responsible for the worst flooding ever in the Black River basin. Snows were particularly heavy in the winter of 1869 and by April of that year the run-off was enormous. The gatekeeper, who lived in State House, which stood not far from the dam, slept through the night of quickly rising water. The water behind the dam should have been lowered in anticipation of the floods, but it was not. The earth and timber dam gave way, flooding the valley below, just minutes after the residents of Forestport were warned of impending disaster.

Sawmills, gristmills, tanneries, wagon factories, bridges, flumes, and downstream dams were all swept away. The devastation was felt as far downstream as Watertown. The *Utica Weekly Herald* described "logs thirty feet long, catching in the drift [and] thrown end over end and snapped like pipe stems. The crashing and pounding together of the fallen monarchs of the forest drowned for a time the roar of the waters. An eye witness said: 'The logs seemed to be fighting with each other, and when caught in the drift, would be almost instantly stripped of their bark, twisted, split and broken like straws.' This immense weight of driftwood and water was thrown against the dam at Forestport. Those who were at work upon the dam had barely time to make their retreat in safety, when the North wing gave way. Through this gap nearly all the lumber above the dam was carried. The current tore out a channel nearly 40 feet deep."

The dam was rebuilt, and you can drive to the end of North Lake Road to see the lake the new dam created. The damage from the flood 120 years ago has disappeared, but this hike along the trail that begins on North Lake Road will take you to a scene of destruction no less awesome than that flood.

Turn off NY 28 at Forestport, immediately north of the bridge over Black River, and head east. At 1.2 miles you cross the tracks of the abandoned Adirondack Railroad and just beyond is the Buffalo Head Restaurant—a very old establishment that offers such sizable meals you have to walk at least the 13.4 miles of this round trip to justify eating there. You won't be out of place in hiker's clothes, but you may need a reservation on busy weekends.

The trailhead is 6.5 miles from NY 28 along this road. The trail heads north into the woods, following at first a wide old woods road. Side paths branch off leading to Little Woodhull Creek. You are walking through a tall forest with ferns and witchhobble below. After a five-minute walk, you cross a tiny stream, and shortly (at .3 mile) begin to hear Little Woodhull Creek. The route turns northeast to follow the creek on a ridge high above it. After a bit more than a ten-minute walk, at .5 mile, you cross an-

Hurricane devastation along the trail near Chub Pond

other small stream on a slippery log bridge. You continue close to the creek, but far enough away that you cannot see it.

At 1 mile, a twenty-minute walk, you head down the bank to cross the creek on a wonderful two-log bridge. A waterfall tumbles below the bridge, upstream there is a stillwater, below are rapids. The route, now generally north following the valley of Stone Dam Lake Outlet, crosses several small ridges. Farther north you are close enough to the creek to hear it, but never close enough to see it. The forest is broken by an occasional erratic. The trail does a lot of winding about, up and down or around little ridges. There are tiny wet areas and openings but basically this is a very deep, dark forest. Fifty minutes from the trailhead, about 1.8 miles, you climb a very small hill and pass a very large erratic. Here low ledges border the trail.

The trail shows little sign of use; there are a number of markers, and you need them to keep on the route. The route is uphill over a ridge, downhill, contouring northwest, and across an intermittent stream flowing to your right. Lots of big, old, moss-covered fallen trees testify to a long-ago blowdown. At 3.3 miles, almost an hour and a half into the trip, you can see a meadow and open water of Stone Dam through the trees to your right. The trail is now along a spruce-covered ridge. There is a jet black pool in a hollow to the left of the trail, which has gradually turned northwest, briefly almost west, to follow the marshes along Stone Dam's inlet.

At 3.6 miles you turn north to cross the inlet stream and climb a low ridge. The climb is gentle through maple and beech stands. A little draw leads to another ridge from which you can see a meadow, and a marsh appears on your right. There is also a small marsh on the left. The trail begins to wind about again, and be cautioned that if you stray from it here, you would be hard pressed to find it again. The foot tread is so faint you can cross the route and not even be aware of it. This is a relatively newly cut trail—a real wilderness route.

The trail is now in a densely ferny valley—woodferns and hay-scented fern predominantly. After two and a half hours of walking you pass another marshy opening, and at 4.9 miles you cross Big Brook, which *is* a fairly big brook at this point. It flows to your left, the west. Past it, the trail climbs a small hill, reaching a height-of-land at 5.3 miles, beyond which the trail descends through a small draw. Beech drops border the trail here. You cross an intermittent drainage, and angle right across a ridge where, suddenly, a scene of destruction spreads out in front of you. The massive blowdown was caused by the tornado of August 30, 1984. You can follow its route in a line through the valley. Trees snapped like toothpicks, jumbles of fallen limbs, and leaning trunks border the trail.

The trail stays along the edge of the blowdown, then crosses the path the tornado took, forcing you to climb over upturned stumps and root masses. In this area look for *dryopteris clintonia,* a fern of the deep wet woods, which is having a hard time surviving on the dried and exposed forest floor. The tornado's path is a couple hundred yards wide here.

At 5.9 miles, a two-hour-and-forty-minute walk, the trail descends to a T where the yellow trail you have been following ends. The way left has snowmobile markers that lead to the Gull Lake Lean-to and Bear Creek Road. A blue-marked trail and the snowmobile trail head right to the Plumley Lean-to and on around to the shore of Gull Lake. Actually a blue-marked side loop takes you across a small bridge to the lean-to that sits undisturbed in the middle of the blowdown. Continuing on the snowmobile trail, you reach the marshy shore of a bay that is filled with bottled gentian, cranberries, blue flag, and yellow bladderwort. Across the lake on a sand bank sits the other lean-to.

Blowdown is so dense you cannot leave the trail to reach the shore at any other point near the trail. If you follow the trail back west, returning to the T at 6.5 miles, you can head west to circle around Chub Pond. You are still following the swath cut by the tornado, and the trail (an old road) is very wet. An occasional tree broken by the tornado arches over the trail. At 7 miles, fifteen minutes from the T, you reach a bridge over Woodhull Creek. You can see the scene of devastation where it follows the creek for a bit. You can continue nearly a mile to the second lean-to; but if you are making a day outing of this trek, it is time to turn around and head back.

From the T at 7.5 miles, you turn south. Assume thirty minutes to Big Brook crossing from the T, another forty minutes to cross the inlet of Stone Dam where the trail angles southeast. Ten minutes beyond, when you can see Stone Dam through the trees, leave the trail and bushwhack north along a promontory to the marshes that border Stone Dam. After a brief respite here, you have an hour and a half walk south to your car, but you may be tired enough that it will take a good two hours.

7

Cathead

Distance (round trip): 2.8 miles
Vertical rise: 1,100 feet
Hiking time: 1½ hours
Map: USGS 15' Lake Pleasant
Fire Tower; closed Thursday, Friday

Cathead, at the southern edge of the Forest Preserve, may be a small mountain (it is only 2423 feet high), but it is the threshold to a great green wilderness that stretches north almost unbroken for twenty miles. No other area is as dense and trailless as the Silver Lake Wilderness to the north and west of Cathead. To the north and east are the gentle mountains that rise beyond Great Sacandaga Lake. And to the south lies the civilization hikers are anxious to escape. From the summit of Cathead you can spot the Helderberg escarpment that rises beyond the Mohawk Valley, edging the plateau that becomes the Catskill Mountains farther south. On a really clear day and with strong binoculars you can even define buildings in the state capital of Albany.

To reach the trailhead, drive north on NY 30 from the southern border of the Adirondack Park. At the intersection 3.2 miles past the bridge to Northville, turn left, or west, toward Benson. The intersection is marked with a sign designating the road as the Northville-Placid Trail. The narrow macadam road immediately climbs away from the Sacandaga Valley through an old farming community where many homes have been converted to seasonal dwellings. Two miles from NY 30 you pass a bridge and Chartier Road, and .7 mile farther you reach dirt North Road, on the right. Turn here. A sign at the intersection points to the Cathead Mountain Fire Tower. Just before you reach this intersection you will see the mountain itself with its tower ahead and to your right. The dirt road can be rough after a bad winter, but it is usually smoothed in early spring by the Town of Benson.

Land on both sides of the 1.2-mile-long road is posted and private, as is the land the trail traverses. However, a new parking lot has been constructed at the end of the road, alleviating previous conflicts with nearby landowners. No vehicles are permitted beyond the parking lot and dogs must be on a leash.

This is a good place to emphasize that the Adirondack Park is in reality a confusing mosaic of private and public lands. It is important to respect private property here and elsewhere. Many landowners who have granted public access across their land have seen it abused by a few careless hikers and other outdoor people. There is a great need to preserve the good will that permits this and other important accesses to public trails.

The road on which the trail begins leads through a logging operation. One hundred yards past the barrier, a sign points left away from the roadway. The Cathead fire tower is just over 1.4 miles from here along a blue-marked trail that follows telephone lines to the summit. The trail winds in a narrow footpath through the wide swath that is cleared below the lines.

Using a series of log bridges, the trail at first traverses a wet area grown over with royal fern. The third bridge, just before the trail begins its upward course, crosses a running brook. The fourth, 100 yards farther along, at .5 mile, marks the edge of the recently logged area. Beyond, the tree cover becomes taller, cov-

ering patches of strawberries, bluets, violets, trillium, foamflower, wild oat, twisted stalk, cucumber root, and dwarf ginseng. A few tall hemlock mingle with the hardwoods of the dense forest. You are now climbing steadily. Only a few battered trail markers denote the route, which is so obvious the shortage is not even noticeable.

The lower slope of the hill contains a few particularly tall and straight maples. The tall, arched cover makes a cathedral ceiling over the trail, which begins to mount the first of the series of small, open rock ledges. These giant stepping stones continue all the way to the summit. The tread becomes all rock, with a stream flowing along it in spring.

The trail is particularly straight, heading north-northwest, right up the hill, with the

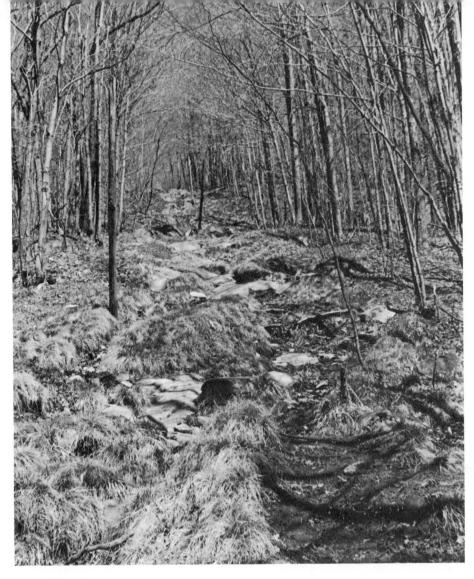

Cathead Mountain Trail

emphasis on up. You climb most of the 1,100 feet in under .7 mile. You will probably pause often for breath, and if you are hiking in late spring, your pause will have to be brief. The plague of the Adirondacks, hordes of black flies and mosquitoes, will descend on you in swarms and make you wonder what they would find to attack if you were not there.

Within an hour the forest cover becomes shorter, ledges begin to edge the trail, and you emerge in a tiny opening by the ranger's cabin and a sign reminding you to carry out what you carry in. The tower is 200 yards ahead up the rock slope. A hint of roadway leads to the left through a depression below rock ledges on the same level as the cabin.

To the right of the rocky summit is a new helicopter pad. It was needed when an addition was put on the tower, nearly doubling its height to provide a tele-phone relay. A huge windmill roars be-side the tower, providing power for the relay. It is not exactly a pristine sight for this border of the wilderness.

The tower is currently manned and the rocky summit is filling with blueberries and small cherry trees, but there are some views even if you do not climb to the tower. Below the mountain to the west is Grant Lake, which is nearly filled with a marsh. Beyond it rise Wallace, Three Ponds, and Silver Lake mountains. To the north you should be able to figure out which of the foreground hills are Finch, Hamilton, and Speculator. You will have no trouble detecting Snowy's white face shining on the horizon, but you need a really clear day to discern the mountains to its north.

Part of Great Sacandaga Lake stretches to the southeast, and beyond it the skyline is almost flat, rising only with the edge of the Helderberg escarpment. Part of the Capital District is visible on an exceptionally clear day, but for that field glasses are essential.

Almost none of the mountains you see have trails to their summits, and almost all the summits are heavily wooded. You see a few cliffs and steep hillsides, but most of your view is filled with the soft, gentle mountains of the southern Adiron-dacks. The skyline varies little, for the foothills are not spectacular. But the view is deceptively benign, for the soft green hides one of the Adirondacks' most im-penetrable wildernesses, where you could pick almost any heading north and not meet a sign of civilization for nearly twenty miles.

After you return to NY 3 by the same route, you may want to head north along the Sacandaga River. The Sacandaga Campground, south of Wells, is only a short drive north, and it is a lovely place to camp before heading on toward other adventures. Along this part of NY 30 there are several parking turnouts where you can stop for a picnic close to the river.

Falls on the West Branch of the Sacandaga

Distance (round trip): 6 miles
Vertical rise: minimal
Hiking time: 6 hours
Map: USGS 15' Lake Pleasant
Silver Lake Wilderness Area

The falls on the West Branch of the Sacandaga will leave you amazed that such a place can exist so close to the fringes of civilization. The access route is incredibly challenging, the falls themselves are little known, and much around them remains to be explored and discovered. The remote stretch of river by the falls has been known for years to a few hunters and fishermen, but only in recent years have hikers begun to appreciate its beauties.

The West Branch of the Sacandaga uncoils about the Silver Lake Wilderness. The river is formed at the confluence of three south-flowing outlets from three separate ponds; their union flows west, then north, then east, and finally south again, enclosing one of the Adirondacks' most secret realms. The gem of that interior is certainly the series of falls on the West River, as natives have called this branch of the Sacandaga since the day when lumbermen and trappers first penetrated its wild recesses.

The trail, path, and bushwhack route described here will take you to the first pair of falls. They are almost 3 miles upstream from Whitehouse, the site of a lovely old lodge whose chimneys today

stand forlornly guarding the spot where the Northville-Placid Trail crosses the river. If you are really adventurous and want a great challenge, you should extend the bushwhack through the deepest part of the West River's gorge to a second pair of falls, past a quiet flow, and to a final falls that are just below the flow formed where the outlet of Piseco Lake joins the West Branch. (See my *Discover the Southern Adirondacks* for a description of that route.)

Your adventures on the West Branch begin when you leave NY 30 at the southern end of the hamlet of Wells and head west on Algonquin Drive. West River Road forks left .7 mile from NY 30 and continues 1.7 miles to Blackbridge. Over the next 1.7 miles west to Jimmy Creek, the road is close to the river and its wild rapids. Then the road pulls away from the river, continuing west for a total distance of 8.6 miles from Wells to Whitehouse, where a parking area now occupies the site of the lodge.

The trailhead for the Northville-Placid Trail is west of the parking area. Head northwest on that trail for .8 mile to a fork. The marked trail continues north, but you turn left to continue west. Al-

Falls along the West Branch of the Sacandaga

50   *Falls on the West Branch of the Sacandaga*

though the route is unmarked, it follows an abandoned roadway. After .6 mile you reach Hamilton Lake Stream in an area used for camping. Cross the stream by hopping rocks in low water, or wading if it is high. The washed-out bridge has not been replaced. Across the stream a faint path heads southwest toward the river. Because hikers have taken many different routes, you may have trouble finding an obvious path, the best of which roughly follows the hypotenuse of a triangle, the two legs of which are the stream and the river, so you cannot get lost. You will approach the West Branch just below the flow called Big Eddy, which will make you wish the entire route had been along the river. There is a camping spot here.

The footpath continues west along the north shore of the river, and you should follow it as far as you can. The majority of visitors here are fishermen whose des-

tination is the pools in Big Eddy, so the foot tread rapidly disappears. A path of sorts exists beside Big Eddy as far as the crossing of Cold Brook, which empties into the West River with a small waterfall. Look out for poison ivy on the bank beside the confluence of Cold Brook and the river. West of Cold Brook the path really disappears, and you must follow the shore, or, in low water, hop along the rocky stream bed. You pass one more deep pool with an overhanging ledge before reaching the boulder-strewn waterway that leads into the deep gorge.

So far the hike has been relatively mild. You will probably need only a bit more than twenty minutes to hike the section on the Northville-Placid Trail, an almost equal amount to reach Hamilton Lake Stream, and about forty minutes to cover the .8-mile distance to Cold Brook. However, you will need more than forty minutes to trek the next rugged .6 mile distance through the deepening gorge to the first falls.

By the time you reach the falls the cliffs of the gorge walls are nearly 400 feet high. The growing mound of boulders and blocks leading up to the falls makes an increasingly difficult walking route.

The level of the water has a great impact on the difficulty of the walk and on the beauties of the gorge. In high water, walking becomes difficult, and you may have to approach the falls by scaling the hill behind the cliffs. In low water you can find a route over the boulders within the narrowing gorge, but then the falls are less dramatic.

The second falls are scarcely 200 yards beyond the first, but since the ravine curves, you can't see them until you are nearly upon them. Even more peculiar than the visual separation of the falls is the length of time it takes to walk between them. In high water you definitely must climb the hill behind the cliffs from the east. Even then you will have to be content with a view from above, for de-scending to the second falls is all but impossible. In low water I have spent at least forty minutes clambering over boulders the size of buses, through openings in the pile of blocks, and leaping across crevices to reach the second falls. If you attempt this section, be careful.

As you climb along the ledge you will notice that the high-water mark is more than 20 feet above summer low point. Swirls of natural foam frost pools of tea-colored water. In dry times the sprays that cascade from the narrow clefts are almost lost in the complex of boulders. In spring, or after periods of heavy rain, the water falling 240 feet through the mile-long gorge creates a roar that barely hints at the brutal force capable of tearing boulders from ravine walls and hurling them into the huge piles that are the West River's falls.

In any season, a trip to the falls is a rough experience. You will remember your day's trip to this dramatic spot as a truly great adventure.

Good Luck Cliffs

Distance (round trip): 4.4 miles
Vertical rise: 700 feet
Hiking time: 3 hours
Maps: USGS 15' Piseco Lake; USGS 7½' Canada Lake

The trek to Good Luck Cliffs is one of the best short hikes in the southern Adirondacks. The route combines a walk along a snowmobile trail with a climb through a small gorge on a footpath. A jumble of easily explored boulders and crevices line the gorge. The footpath circles behind the nearly 500-foot-high cliffs to emerge on a small overlook with a dramatic view across the foothills of the Adirondacks to the skyline of hills south of the Mohawk Valley.

The footpath is fairly well defined, but there are three points at which you may have difficulty, so take a map and compass and pay close attention to the landmarks along the route. The trek through the gorge is not marked by trail disks. The footpath was flagged in an experiment by the state to discover if hikers would create a defined path along marked routes where no trail cutting and grooming was to be done. Here the results are clear, for a footpath has developed and it is a delight to follow.

The trail starts opposite a parking turnout on NY 10, 100 yards north of a bridge over the Sacandaga and 6 miles north of the intersection of NY 10 and NY 29A.

The trail is marked with a signboard designating the distances to Good Luck Lake, Dexter Lake, and Potters Homestead. Follow it west for just under .5 mile to an intersection. The route to Dexter Lake is straight ahead, but you should turn left on the trail to Good Luck Lake and Spectacle Lake. Here the trail follows an old logging road down a gentle incline for .7 mile, and as it approaches the first low point you can see Good Luck Lake through the trees on the left. This is the easiest approach to the lake via this trail. With a short bushwhack (200 yards) you can quickly find informal footpaths connecting the good campsites on the lake's handsome and dry northern shore. If you do this, you really should stay above the marsh that edges the western shoreline.

If you want to visit the lake as part of your visit to the cliffs, the easiest approach is a short, informal, and unmarked footpath that leaves the highway opposite the parking area and 50 yards southeast of the marked trailhead. It leads to Good Luck's northern shore in .5 mile.

Good Luck was named not for its good fishing, although fishermen visit it regularly, but because of an incident on its shores that ended well. As Jeptha R. Simms relates in *Trappers of New York,* the party surveying and laying out the roadway, now called the Nick Stoner Trail, through the Sacandaga Valley, was working at Good Luck Lake to hollow out a canoe from the trunk of a tree. The son-in-law of the chief surveyor, Lawrence Vrooman, spotted a loon on the lake and "discharged his gun at the loon, off on the water. The piece burst and scattered its fragments harmlessly in every direction. The accident terminated so fortunately, that the name the lake now bears was entered in the surveyor's field book."

To find the cliffs, continue on the snowmobile trail until it crosses a small stream within sight of the lake, about a twelve-minute walk from the four-way intersection. There are currently some planks at this crossing. Continue 150 yards up a rise and down to a second stream. This one has a snowmobile bridge and just beyond it the trail, which has been on a southwesterly course, takes a curve to the south. You will leave the trail at this stream to follow a faint footpath on its eastern side. After 200 yards, you go straight where the stream swings west.

The footpath and the stream meet again in about 300 yards and this time you cross the stream and continue to the northwest close to the stream.

Hikers have here taken several routes. After 50 yards, you will see a path, or paths, angling left away from the stream. They all seem to zigzag uphill as the route gets steeper. The first pitch is fairly steep; you attain 300 vertical feet in just 250 yards. The cliffs become visible through the trees on your right, as do the boulders and slabs that have fallen from them to litter the floor of the draw. Do not follow any route that takes you more than 50 yards from the base of the cliffs, although the chasm below the cliffs is such an impenetrable mass of blocks and crevices, it is often difficult to get much closer. Where the path levels off somewhat, a smaller footpath heads 30 feet down a slide to the base of a huge mass of boulders. Stop and explore the area: peer into the 12-foot-deep cave created by overhanging ledges, climb the boulders to observe the cliffs above and the valley below. The perch is overhung by a thin slab 40 feet tall.

The footpath continues northeast for 50 yards, crosses the stream, and climbs steeply again below the cliffs in a more

End of the cliff on Good Luck

northerly direction. You walk beyond the cliffs to climb the summit from the west. The last 50-foot pitch to the summit ridge is quite steep and currently ends in a tangle of small spruce and blowdowns of larger spruce. Push through and walk to the right, down a small depression on the summit and up to the overlook on the opposite side.

You emerge on a small rock crest exposed to the south and west, overlooking Spectacle Lake and the foothills of the Adirondacks as they fade into the Mohawk Valley.

You should follow the same route for the return. Remember, this is not a marked trail and you should be prepared to search for the route as well as for the features created by the fallen boulders.

Pine Orchard

Distance (round trip): 4.8 miles
Vertical rise: minimal
Hiking time: 2½ hours
Map: USGS 15' Harrisburg

Pine Orchard is a gem of a walk wrapped in the deep woods of the southern Adirondacks. Inside Pine Orchard you will discover a treasure that is rare anywhere in the park, yet here very easy to find.

Virgin pine once covered large sections of the Adirondacks. As lumbermen and settlers moved into the mountains after the Revolutionary War these magnificent trees were the first to be felled. They not only made the tall masts for sailing vessels, but their building quality was unsurpassed. The giant pine, some fifteen feet in circumference, are the eastern equivalent of the Olympic rain forests' redwood; a walk among them is equally awe-inspiring.

A few virgin stands remain, and one of them covers a small hill northeast of Wells. You will find larger stands on the Oswegatchie, but none so close to a trailhead. I have been impressed with Pine Orchard for years, but it was not until I had seen many of the other notable Adirondack pine forests that I could truly appreciate its significance.

Fire played an unusual role in the development of the Adirondack forests. Stands of giant hemlock only occur in areas where there have been no fires, but groves of pine only spring up after a fire or blowdown. Most people are unaware that a pine forest is not a climax forest. Pine seedlings do not sprout beneath their elders. Spruce, balsam, and birch can pioneer below a tall pine stand, and here at Pine Orchard, the pines are so old that maturing yellow birch and maples are filling the niches beneath the remaining giants.

Pine of 5 and 6 feet in diameter were common in the early eighteenth century. Adirondack logs were traditionally cut in 13½-foot lengths, and sometimes the butts, or first cuts, were too large to be moved by man or horse. Charges of black powder in a special splitting tool were used to break the huge ends in two so they could be carried off to mills.

Core samples indicate that Pine Orchard's trees date back to 1815. It is likely that a hurricane about that year felled all the existing trees on the knoll. White pines quickly pioneered on the knoll and they might have been too small to cut when the region was first logged. Whether this explains the origins of Pine Orchard or not, you will find the trek to Pine Orchard among the most delightful

of nature walks, and it is certainly the
easiest of hikes, following the relatively
level stretch of an abandoned roadway
once used by loggers.

To reach Pine Orchard, drive north on
NY 30 through Wells, and turn right on
Griffin Road at the north end of the
hamlet, just south of the bridge where
NY 30 crosses the Sacandaga River.
Follow Griffin Road north along the east
side of the Sacandaga for .8 mile and
turn right on Windfall Road, which parallels Mill Creek for a short distance. Follow Windfall Road for 1 mile, and turn
right at the first road on the right. Drive
along that road for 1.9 miles, past
stretches of Forest Preserve, to a private
inholding. The owner has posted a "Visi-
tor Parking" sign on a small turnout on
the right. He permits hikers on their way
to Pine Orchard to park here, on his
land. The trail begins along the continuing road, past his house, and heads into
the woods, very quickly reaching state
land again. At that point a cable blocks
the roadway. Please respect the private
property, touching nothing as you walk

through, so this much-appreciated permission to park and cross the private
land will continue.

Walk east past the cable on the continuing roadway that is now marked as
a snowmobile trail. It connects with the
trail from Willis Lake, which comes in on
the right, or south, just beyond the cable. See *Discover the Southeastern Adirondacks* for a description of this route,
which passes the Fury Ponds. The direction you walk, now northeast, is labeled with a sign showing a destination
of NY 8 at Georgia Brook, 8.2 miles to
the north.

You start gently downhill, viewing the
flow created by a new beaver dam on
the right. In twenty minutes and 1 mile
from the parking area, you cross a
stream. A new snowmobile bridge carries
you over the tributary of Mill Creek. A
gravel area just beyond has been used
as a campsite. So far the trees are not
very large, and the mixture of spruce,
hemlock, and birch is occasionally quite
small and very dense. Ten minutes past
the bridge you will see the first big pine.

By the giant white pine

Five minutes later, about .6 mile from the bridge, a washed-out bridge helps you across a small stream that feeds the flow. The trail continues with another little stream on the right and then heads north up a slight rise. More giants greet you as you climb the hill, and a few significant spruce appear among the pine. The trail makes a sharp right turn and then circles toward the crest of the hill. Most of the giant pines are near the top, with the highest to the right of the trail. The trail continues north, and as soon as it leaves the crest it enters a grove of enormous hemlock. You reach the hemlock, marking the end of Pine Orchard, after a leisurely, hour-long walk of 2.4 miles.

You may want to try and find the largest tree in the pine stand. It appears that most of the pine of 15 feet in circumference are doubles, a phenomenon that occurs when blight strikes. The largest single trunk I found was just over 13 feet in circumference or over 4 feet in diameter. Try some elementary trigonometry to estimate the height of the larger trees. Unfortunately, the giants in the orchard crowd so densely together that it is difficult to see the tops of most of the pines, and measuring the base of a right triangle to an established sighting angle is equally difficult. I calculated a few that approach 150 feet in height. Even without trying to measure the trees, you will enjoy strolling in the parklike open understory beneath these Adirondack giants.

11

Echo Cliffs on Panther Mountain

Distance (round trip): 1.4 miles
Vertical rise: 600 feet
Hiking time: 1⅓ hours
Map: USGS 15' Piseco Lake

Echo Cliffs curve around the western slopes of a shoulder of Panther Mountain overlooking Piseco Lake, and the view from the cliff tops is more than ample reward for this short and easy climb. The mountain is a good destination for a first hike into the southern Adirondacks region.

Piseco lies in the middle of a region of hills and mountains where every valley seems to contain a small and often remote and uninhabited lake. Nearly one hundred hiking destinations in the country of the West Branch of the Sacandaga River, the area just south of Piseco, are described in another of my guides, *Discover the Southern Adirondacks*. A day hike to Echo Cliffs, which offers a sweeping overview of that area, is an excellent introduction to some of those adventures.

The trail begins near the Little Sand Point State Campground on the western shore of Piseco Lake, the middle of three handsome state campsites offering good camping, boating, fishing, and access to hiking trails.

From the intersection of NY 8 and NY 10 by the southeast shore of Piseco, head west on NY 8 for 2.8 miles to West Shore Road. Follow that road north for 3.6 miles to an unmarked trailhead, and park along the road's shoulder. The spot is .5 mile south of the entrance to Little Sand Point Campground.

There are no signs and few trail markers to indicate where the trail enters woods on the west side of the road. The footpath is well used, as the initials carved on the smooth bark of every beech tree along the way indicate. You could almost conclude that the beech die-back was a protest at such desecrations, but the real reason so many beech are dying is that there is a preponderance of mature beech. Those trees were not harvested when local forests were either stripped of their softwoods or culled for their valuable hardwoods. The die-back, which you will observe on this climb, is nature's way of restoring balance, while erasing the tempting slates on which those hikers with no reverence for the woods have left their feeble marks.

The rocky and washed-out stretches also indicate that the trail is fairly popular. Many flowers of the deep woods bloom here in their seasons: violets, trillium, jack-in-the-pulpit, dwarf ginseng, and the dogtooth violets. As you start to climb, magnificent maple line the trail. Then, continuing generally west, you pass through a hemlock glen.

As the trail makes a distinct curve to the right, in the vicinity of one of the few trail markers, look right, northwest through the trees, and you may catch a glimpse of the cliffs. In early spring or late fall their 200-foot vertical rise is easy to spot; in summer you may miss them entirely.

The climb steepens, and boulders line the route where you approach a ledge and turn right below it. You pass a small intermittent stream with hardly enough flow for a drink in wet weather and then begin a short, steep climb below tall spruce whose roots provide stairs on the sharp incline. Your route is now behind the cliffs. Shortly you have a glimpse of the lake through the trees. Cross the spruce- and hemlock-covered promontory to emerge on the narrow ledge. This ledge, at 2,420 feet in elevation, is well below Panther's 2,716-foot summmit.

The evergreens open to a panorama of the Silver Lake Wilderness across Piseco and Spy lakes. Few tall mountains are visible in the distance, and the dense forest cover is broken only by streams and ponds. Hawks soar in the updrafts above the cliffs. The water of Piseco Lake mirrors cloud patterns.

Summer homes dot the shores of Higgins Bay opposite Echo Cliffs. The narrow strip of land between the bay and Spy Lake was the site of the area's first settlement, which began in the 1820s and was called Rudeston after one Eli Rudes. Several sawmills were built in the vicinity.

In 1838 a village was designed for the north shore of Piseco by Andrew K. Morehouse, who envisioned a thriving community with a "gristmill, sawmill, machine shop, a large hotel and boarding house and some half-dozen dwellings." Strong inducements were offered to settlers, but fewer than 200 of them stayed more than a week.

This saga of disappointment in the wilderness is typical of most early nineteenth century settlers' adventures. Details of many such failures are chronicled in the Hamilton County History by Aber and King. Read the chapter on the

Town of Arietta to gain insight into the land you survey from Echo Cliffs. Its abandonment explains why so much of the southern Adirondacks was incorporated into the Forest Preserve, creating the largest chunk of state land in the Adirondack Park.

View across Piseco and Spy lakes from Echo Cliffs

T Lake Falls

Distance (round trip): 11.5 miles
Vertical rise: 1,200 feet
Hiking time: 8 hours
Map: USGS 15' Piseco Lake
West Canada Lakes Wilderness Area

Caution: In the last decade three people have died in falls from the top of T Lake Falls. It can be a dangerous place. This hike is not for pets or small children. Follow the route described, and observe all the cautions.

It is unfortunate to have to preface this hike to such a great place with a caution. Do not let it deter you, for many careful hikers have found the trip to T Lake Falls one of the truly great wilderness treks in the Adirondacks.

The outlet of T Lake drops 350 feet into a tiny pool from the rounded crest of an escarpment. If the falls were a sheer drop of this distance, statisticians would consider the claim that it is one of the highest in New York State. It is the highest in the Adirondacks and tall enough so that Adirondack writers have exaggerated its height to 640 feet, or "twice the height of Niagara." The danger comes when hikers venture out on the smooth rock seeking better views and fail to notice the gradual curve of the rounded, slippery lip until it is too late to turn back safely.

Below the falls, the outlet turns southwest and joins outlets of several small ponds to form the South Branch of the

West Canada Creek. A continuing track through that valley was once used by Indian hunters and early settlers. One of the first descriptions of a visit to the falls was written by Ephraim Phillips in the 1860s. He was Hamilton County's sheriff from 1843 to 1847 and the proprietor of hotels at Lake Pleasant and Piseco Lake.

The trail you follow to T Lake Falls makes a fairly strenuous one-day trip. There is a lean-to at T Lake 1.8 miles from the falls that makes a good spot to stop if you prefer an overnight expedition.

The trail begins from the northernmost of the three state campgrounds on the western shore of Piseco Lake. To reach the start, drive 2.8 miles west from the intersection of NY 8 and NY 10 at the southeast side of the lake, and head north on West Shore Road for 4.9 miles to the Poplar Point State Campground. If you are coming from the west, the shore road is clearly marked with a sign indicating the three campsites. If you are approaching from the north via NY 8, bear right, or west, toward Piseco and continue around the lake's northern shore.

There is a day-use fee at Poplar Point. The marked trailhead is 100 yards south

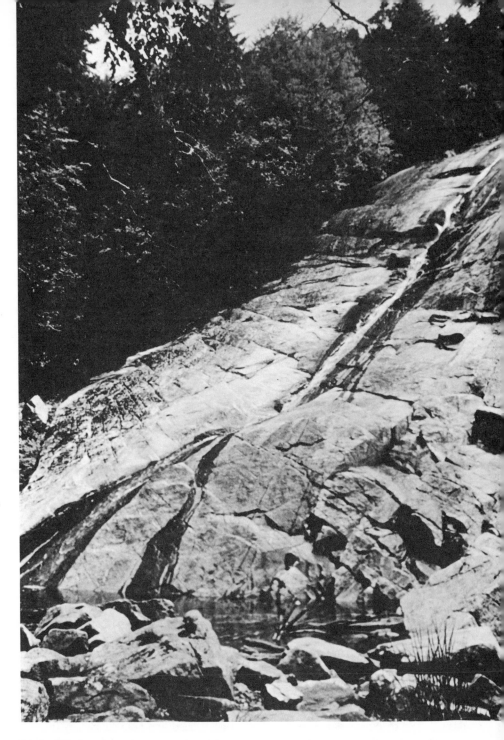

T Lake Falls in summer

of the campground entrance, where a sign indicates the distance to T Lake as 3.65 miles.

The first stretch of trail is fairly new. It heads up a southern shoulder of Piseco Mountain after crossing a cement dam for an unused reservoir. The climb into a forest of giant yellow birch with good-sized beech and maple is fairly steep for twenty minutes. Then, in just over .5 mile, you climb into a small boulder-strewn col. Here the trail takes you along a fairly level stretch through the rather rugged valley. In five minutes or so you will see a stream in a draw on your left. After the short rise that follows you will cross a small wet, boggy saddle between a knob on the south and high cliffs that face the mountain proper.

Nearly forty minutes and just over 1 mile into your walk, you cross a ridge and descend a small draw crowded with thick growth that is filling in areas left by dead beech. Walls and ledges continue above on your right, and there is a drop to a deep valley on your left. A small draw at 1 mile marks the valley between Piseco and Stacey mountains. Within another five minutes you reach a height-of-land on Stacey and begin the long, gentle descent into the valley that separates it from T Lake Mountain. Shortly the trail picks up the stream that drains that valley, follows it north for 200 yards before crossing it, and then, within 100 feet, crosses a larger stream that flows from the southern flanks of T Lake Mountain. Their confluence is on your right, and the pink feldspar rock lining the streams makes the spot quite handsome.

Just beyond the stream crossing you should spot old corduroy and other signs that indicate the trail is now following a very old road. This road entered the valley by way of Warner Lake (to the southeast). A field of touch-me-nots, or jewelweed, partially conceals a stand of horse nettles. Watch out! Huge spruce edge the trail, which now begins to climb the eastern edge of T Lake Mountain. Soon the slopes of that mountain drop off to your right, and a rock wall appears on your left. The trail makes a ninety-degree turn left and heads west up to a rock outcrop. You are now about 2.5 miles from the start, and you have walked about one hour and fifteen minutes.

If you are clever at spotting old trails, you may see the intersection, about five minutes beyond the sharp turn, where the trail from Mill Stream used to come in from the east. But at this point the trail bends to the left, so most likely you will not spot the old trail until your return, when you should take care not to continue straight on it. Just beyond the intersection a valley opens out on your right; it is the valley of the fault that contains T Lake. The trail begins an up-and-down course, and again, a real woods detective could see where the old trail headed southwest to T Lake Mountain where there was a fire tower. An abandoned coil of telephone wire may be the only real clue; it is amazing how quickly these southern Adirondack forests can conceal old roads and trails.

You can look across the fault valley to unnamed mountains to the north, and you may even notice water from the small arm of T Lake down the slopes on your right. Here walking is easy, for the trail is wide, open, and relatively level. After a gradual descent to lake level, you reach the lean-to alongside the small eastern tip of the lake. Rocks east of the lean-to make it easy to get into the water without churning the muddy bottom of the shallow lake.

The best part of the trip starts here, but because T Lake Falls have proven so dangerous, the trail west of T Lake is officially closed and not maintained. This makes for a more rugged walk along the surviving footpath, which has not been cleared of blowdown. Continuing west, the path is gorgeous. You first edge the shore of T Lake in a rich evergreen forest with a deep understory, then pass the end of the bay with its natural rock dam, and walk close to the outlet in a small rock gorge that leads to a beaver meadow. Twenty minutes past the lean-to you will pass a deep water channel created by a beaver dam that tops a second rock ledge. Preceding the dam site the path has been flooded, and you will have to detour around a small swamp or trust your footing on a fallen log.

Bunchberry and sorrel carpet the woods floor, filling crevices between spruce roots, which makes walking difficult on the narrow trail. You pass a twelve-foot waterfall that drops from a small ledge edging a second beaver meadow. This one stretches west for .5

mile. Where the trail skirts the flow you will want to pause to look for birds.

The valley narrows, and the sound of water falling over the rocks at the west end of the flow will make you think you are almost at the falls, but you still have some way to go. Steep ledges rim the hillside above on the south as you drop into a narrow gorge. Cliffs of recently bared slides rim the north.

An hour's walk past the lean-to, or 1.8 miles, the view west opens to reveal the outline of the West Canada Creek valley. Now is the time for caution. A cable that used to make crossing the stream safe is now missing, and without it the ford is tricky. Slippery mosses may make you lose your footing, and most of the smooth rock is just as slippery. Note that you cannot see the waterfall from the end of the path. Do not walk down along the smooth rock, looking for it. There is no place on the escarpment from which to see the pool at the bottom of the falls. If you wish to descend to the base of the falls, do so through the woods south of the falls. Crossing the outlet near the top of the falls is dangerous as is the bare rock north of the falls.

It will take you at least half an hour to climb down beside the falls. From the pool you can look up at the creased and lined rounded slopes over which T Lake Falls tumbles. In wet weather a real torrent splashes into the pool. In dry times you will know how the side of an elephant looks to an ant.

The pool is not quite all the way to the bottom of the valley. If you follow the stream 100 yards farther west, you pass another camping spot, where a sign says it is 6 miles along the old Indian path to Mountain Home, a trailhead in the southwest.

You will need at least twenty minutes to scramble back up the slopes beside the falls. Again, resist the temptation to walk toward the edge of the escarpment. You will have enjoyed just as good views across to the valley from the safety of the trees beside the slope.

The walk back beside the flows is even prettier than the trip out, for the trail east offers better views of the wide expanses of meadowsweet and grasses.

Peaked Mountain

Distance (round trip): 8.2 miles, 6.4 miles if you approach the
  trailhead by canoe
Vertical rise: 1,245 feet
Hiking time: 5 hours
Map: USGS 15' Thirteenth Lake
Siamese Ponds Wilderness Area

Peaked Mountain and its eponymous pond lie in the northeastern corner of the Siamese Ponds Wilderness Area, just west of the shores of Thirteenth Lake. Thirteenth Lake, over two miles long and very thin (less than a third of a mile wide), occupies a fault valley that extends south beyond the lake, along the headwaters of the East Branch of the Sacandaga River to NY 8. Gore, Harvey, Balm of Gilead, and Durant mountains—the garnet hills—rise to the east of the fault. Ruby Mountain and a cluster of little cones rise to the west of the fault. The cluster includes Big and Little Thirteenth, Hour Pond, Slide, and Peaked mountains. The sharpest of the cones are Slide and Peaked; both have rock outcrops, cliffs, ledges, and narrow views. Peaked Mountain has a newly flagged trail.

The garnet history of the region is told in *Discover the South Central Adirondacks,* where trips to many of the garnet hills are described. The trail on Peaked Mountain has a different story, a modern one, that illustrates the way the Adirondacks is being managed and will be managed in the future.

In the 1960s, there were many threats to the Adirondacks. Modern vacationers

with their leisure time and mobility flocked to the mountains in record numbers. (Think about how recently the automobile affected accessibility to the mountain recesses—automobiles were not widely used until after World War II, until the 1950s.) There were suddenly proposals for huge developments of second homes in an area where there was almost no land-use planning. Snowmobiles and motorized vehicles began to penetrate every corner of the wild public lands. The concerns of those interested in preserving the Adirondacks in their natural state became focused after a brief and abortive attempt to make a part of the Adirondacks into a federal park. As a result, then Governor Rockefeller, appointed a Temporary Study Commission, which was chaired by Harold K. Hochsild. With the work of a professional staff, the commission produced a report in 1970, *The Future of the Adirondack Park,* with 181 recommendations and documents describing the natural resources of the park that substantiated the recommendations.

One of the recommendations was that the Adirondack Park Agency (APA) be created. The Adirondack Park Agency

Act, passed by the state legislature in 1972, detailed how the agency was to regulate development on private lands. It also stated that the agency should prepare a State Land Master Plan (SLMP) outlining how the public lands, the Forest Preserve, were to be managed by the Department of Environmental Conservation (DEC). The SLMP divides public lands into categories: Intensive Use Areas, which are the campgrounds managed by DEC; Canoe and Wilderness Areas, in which no motorized access is permitted; and Wild Forest Areas, the principal recreation areas of the park. The SLMP defines Wilderness in a manner that is similar to the federal definition.

Fifteen Wilderness Areas were delineated and their characteristics described in the SLMP. Guidelines for Wilderness management were detailed. But, the SLMP left the DEC the responsibility for creating detailed management plans for each Wilderness Area that would interpret the SLMP. For a decade, efforts to establish Unit Management Plans floundered. Finally, the process began. The Siamese Ponds Wilderness Area was the first for which a Unit Management Plan was begun and completed.

Writing the plan was a difficult and prolonged process. Many individuals—local residents, preservationists, sportsmen,

and hikers—met regularly to hammer out the details. Their recommendations were further modified by the APA and finally, in 1987, the plan, with some of the advisory group's recommendations, was approved by the Governor. In a way, the plan they produced is a prototype of those that have followed. It exemplifies the way Adirondack Wilderness is to be protected—and used.

The Siamese Ponds Wilderness Area Unit Management Plan sets aside areas that will remain trailless, identifies areas and accesses that the state should purchase, closes certain roads that penetrated the Wilderness, and recommends the marking of a new trail. Peaked Mountain is the locus of that trail. The justifications for it are many—there are few trails to mountains with views in the region; there existed a marked DEC trail to Peaked Mountain Pond at the foot of the mountain; and the climb up the mountain had long been a favorite bushwhack route, along which many hikers have managed to get lost. It is a short, steep, but confusing little cone, so the new trail is most welcome. However, in the manner suited to Wilderness Trails, this route will be marked sparingly, preserving the region's wilderness character. Even the route to the pond will remain difficult, since the trail builders are losing the ongoing competiton with the beavers who manage to discombobulate the trail regularly.

From North Creek, head west on NY 28 along the Hudson River to North River and turn south on Thirteenth Lake Road. That road climbs steeply away from the Hudson. At 3.5 miles, bear right. The way left leads to Garnet Hill Lodge (a good place to stay for hiking and cross-country skiing in the region) and to the major trailhead for interior trails in the Siamese Ponds Wilderness Area. The way right leads less than .5 mile to a parking area for Thirteenth Lake where you will find fireplaces, a swimming beach, and a place to launch canoes. You can canoe or walk to the trailhead, which is .9 mile south along the west shore of the lake.

By canoe, head to the first cleft in the steep mountains on the west side. Here a slanted rock provides a landing and a footpath leads south for 100 yards to the trail. The spot is just south of the last rock ledge in a low area not far from Peaked Mountain Brook.

If you are walking, the trail from the parking area stays close to the shoreline, generally a few feet above it. There are outcrops and views and few markers as you walk south. Note that the trail turns west just to the north of Peaked Mountain Brook, the first real stream you meet, so if you reach it, look about for the beginning of the trail.

The trail, sparsely marked with red disks, begins by following the stream uphill. (Mileages begin at lakeshore.) There are few markers, but many lovely little waterfalls. The trail is moderately steep beside the brook's boulders and cascades for .6 mile, a fifteen-minute walk that climbs 325 feet. Then it is more gentle, until at .8 mile you cross the brook by hopping rocks. You stay in the valley all the way to Peaked Mountain Pond,

but wind from side to side across the flooded brook because of the beaver. A little more climbing brings you at 1 mile, in thirty minutes, to views of the first flow along the brook and of the mountain beyond it. You stay south along this first flow.

About 100 yards past the first flow, red DEC markers and new flags—a multitude of markings at present—direct you across the stream and slightly uphill to the north of the second flow. This route has minimal foot tread, so the marks are temporarily needed. It takes you over a little ridge and through deep forest and out again to a beaver meadow, this one currently flooded and very full of water. There is even a sign and arrow indicating the direction of this rerouting, so you can easily follow this new route. You can see Hour Pond Mountain to the south across this flow.

The trail crosses the stream again, heading to the south side of the next flow. Note that the entire time you are making these S curves, you are near the bottom of the very narrow valley. The third meadow at 1.6 miles is a wonderful little place with views of Peaked across it. Flooding in this meadow has forced hikers to veer more and more to the south away from the prescribed route. You wind around several large boulders, then just short of 2 miles (a good hour's walk) you continue briefly west through the woods. As you cross a little stream, watch closely for the red marker that directs you up over a ridge to a rock ledge on the south side of the outlet of the pond at 2.2 miles, an hour-and-ten-minute climb of 425 feet from Thirteenth Lake.

Peaked Mountain looms above you. There are paths along the south shore, but to find the trail up the mountain, you head along the north shore. First you must cross the outlet brook—just one good jump if you do it right at the outlet of the pond—and you will find a narrow footpath along the north shore. New red trail markers now mark the route all the way to Peaked's summit. The trail goes up and over a knoll and down to a campsite at water level. It continues along the north shore of the pond, around a bay, and, with more than adequate red disks, leaves the shore at 2.6 miles. The 660-foot climb from here to the summit is under .6 mile long and takes about half an hour.

The new route leaves water level of the pond by making two very steep zigzags before attaining the narrow ridge and settling down into a steep climb to the north. The trail is back from the edge of the cliffs and away from danger; but it is so steep in places it is already becoming eroded. The route up the cone is well flagged, but you should pay careful attention to it. At one point you climb up below a rock ledge and really have to scramble to round it. Above the scramble, you go through a narrow passage walled by spruce and balsam and emerge on a flat rock with your first view.

At this point, the trail heads left, away from the cliffs, and zigzags back toward them for the final approach to the tiny 2,919-foot summit area. From it there are views down into the pond, west all the way to the mountains west of Indian Lake, and directly over to Slide from a tiny vantage at the top of the cliffs on

Peaked Mountain

Peaked's northeastern face. From this point you can trace your route along the brook past the flows.

There are still problems to surmount on the return. The first is near the summit—watch closely for the flags. You must make a sharp zigzag to the left and then right onto open rock to stay on the marked route. Do not be tempted to head off west onto open rock there. Your route is only temporarily a steeper way. The red disks should keep you from making the mistakes bushwhackers have made in the past. As you descend along the ridge, remember the last zigzag that will take you to water level. Here you turn left from the ridge, again following a steeper course for 100 feet or so.

There are sufficient new markers to take you around the pond, but stay close to its shore until you are across the outlet. Then plunge into the woods and pick up the old route again. It is even possible to stray on the return, especially where a number of footpaths have been worn to circumvent the beaver flooding. Remember to stay low in the valley, so even if you do wander from the trail, you will quickly return to it. The places the trail changes direction to cross the brook are and should remain well marked. If you do not stray from the route, it should take less than two hours for the return from the peak to the shore of Thirteenth Lake.

14

Moose River Plains

Distance (four walks): 5.4 miles
Vertical rise: minimal
Hiking time: 3½ hours
Maps: USGS 15' West Canada Lakes; USGS 15' Old Forge

The Moose River Recreational Area has long been a sportsmen's paradise. In 1963 the state acquired 50,000 acres from the Gould Paper Company, the heart of the region surrounding the South Branch of the Moose River in western Hamilton County. The area is now open to sportsmen, campers, and hikers. You will find that there are many exciting destinations in the recreational area besides those outlined in this hike and in Hike 15, Beaver Lake; and all of them are described in *Discover the West Central Adirondacks.*

A good dirt road runs almost 24 miles through the recreational area, starting on the east at the Headquarters Gate by the Cedar River Flow and ending on the west by Lake Limekiln Gate, south of Inlet. Over 150 campsites have been designated in several districts along the roadway, so if you prefer camping from your car to carrying a backpack, the Moose River Plains area is for you. The campsites are dispersed along various access roads, well separated from each other. Signs indicate safe springs beside the road. A few campsites are near lovely streams, some are near accesses to ponds, and a few are in deep woods.

Tent camping is allowed on any of the sites or at any undeveloped site in the interior. If you are spending the night or just driving through you must register at the booths at either end of the access road. You will need a camping permit if you stay longer than three nights. The area opens to the public about Memorial Day, or after the dirt road has dried out. Consult the DEC Moose River brochure for complete details (see introduction). You will most probably want to visit here later in summer, when the black flies have diminished. But you should go before hunting season begins, when access is limited to cars with chains or four-wheel-drive. And you certainly will want to bring along a fishing pole and canoe. The Moose River's ponds are quite accessible.

One 3-mile long stretch along the Moose River is natural meadow and open field. These plains are as intriguing to Adirondackers used to unbroken forests as a water hole is to visitors to the desert. The scrub growth infrequently dotted with trees is a natural phenomenon explained by the poor sandy soil remaining from a glacial lake that once covered the area. The vast expanse is so

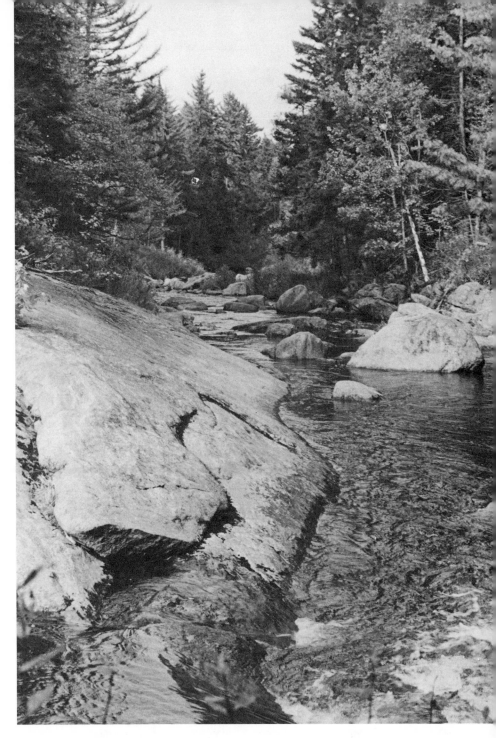

Behind the campsite near Beaver Lake trailhead

unusual in the Adirondacks that early visitors were convinced the plains were man-made, specifically the work of Indians. They were reputed to have regularly burned the plains to provide a habitat for deer and game. The berries and low browse are natural and attract deer especially. In winter The Plains becomes a huge deer yard.

Because it has been less than twenty years since the last logs were taken from parts of the area, scrub forests, thick with small new growth, cover much of the remainder of the recreational area. However, there are significant stands of large pine and black spruce and magnificent tamarack edge the road. A network of logging roads covered the area, and those not open to vehicles are now the area's foot trails. All are easy for walking. This "hike" actually takes you on four separate short trails, to give you a general introduction to the Moose River Recreational Area.

Start at the eastern end of the road through the recreational area. To reach that entrance drive west from Indian Lake on NY 28-NY 30 for 2 miles and turn south on Cedar River Road. It is almost 12 miles to the Headquarters Gate near the Cedar River Flow. You pass the trailhead to Wakely Tower (Hike 34) just before you reach the gate.

The Northville-Placid Trail forks left 1.2 miles from the gate, leading to lean-tos by the Cedar River Flow and in the interior of the West Canada Lake Wilderness. At 1.7 miles you reach a section of land recently sold to the state by International Paper Company. Currently, the marked campsites begin at 3.3 miles.

South of the road you begin to see Little Moose and Manbury mountains, which rise more than 1,200 feet above The Plains. You will cross several small streams, including Cedar and Bradley brooks, all flowing into the South Branch of the Moose River, which is south of the road. Just beyond, where you cross Silver Run, interesting cliffs overhang a lovely flow north of the road.

At 9.3 miles turn left for a quick look at the Moose River. Several of the nearby camping spots are nicer than most. As you start west again you begin to see in the distance Mitchell Pond Mountain with its interesting cliffs guarding the west end of The Plains.

The preponderance of low cherry, elderberry, birch, and mountain ash explain the area's wildlife, but now a few of the truly giant pine appear. At 10.8 miles you reach a side road that leads north toward Lost Ponds, the first of your destinations on foot. Drive .4 mile from the main dirt road and park. You'll want to pick a few blueberries before you start walking north on the dirt roadway, following the yellow trail markers. The trail is so smooth and easy that fishermen use wheeled carrying devices to transport canoes to Lost Ponds. At an unmarked intersection by a campsite, just before the roadway bridges the outlet of the eastern pond, turn right, or east, onto a very narrow footpath. It leads 100 yards to the eastern Lost Pond. Its shores are fairly swampy, and the lake is more suitable for exploration by boat than by foot.

Continue on the yellow-marked roadway beyond the bridge and then fork left. (The sign says only "trail" to differentiate this route from the myriad interconnected logging roads.) This path leads to the south side of the western pond, where there are signs that deer have heavily browsed the banks. A rock ledge topped with enormous pine faces the north shore of this very handsome pond. This is brook trout water—no bait is allowed. I am not sure about the fish, but the plants are varied and interesting, with trillium and trailing arbutus, lots of woody bog plants, and, of course, blueberries. If you are just exploring, the 1.2 mile round-trip walk to visit both ponds should take under an hour.

Returning to the main dirt road, continue west for another 1.5 miles to a turnout on the left, or south, for Helldiver Pond. You can drive this side road for .2 mile, leaving but .3 mile to walk to the pond. It is named for the hell divers, or grebes, that have nested here. From the parking area beneath notably tall pines, you plunge into a dense, dark spruce thicket on a yellow-marked trail. The path veers right and emerges in a wet field on a corduroy walkway across the sphagnum mats that ring this boggy pond. You will want a camera. This is one of the great quaking bogs, with bog rosemary, pale rhododendrum, leatherleaf, Labrador tea, mats thick with cranberries and sheep laurel, and painted trillium, creeping white winterberry, and golden thread along the borders. The pond delights naturalists as well as fishermen.

To find your third destination, return to the main road and continue west another .8 mile through the most open part of The Plains to a major intersection. Bear south for .5 mile to a sign for the trail to Icehouse Pond. Park at the roadside, below one of the region's giant pines, which serves as the best signpost for the trail. Head east through fields typical of The Plains: small cherry, popple, shadblow, willows, and birch are dotted with clumps of larger spruce, balsam, or tamarack. A fence keeps deer out of a small area

where trees really thrive, demonstrating how the forest can grow when not browsed by deer. Another feast of blueberries awaits summer hikers. This short trail quickly leads to beautiful deep woods surrounding the pond. Clumps of over-sized painted trillium fill the banks beneath tall spruce.

Returning again to your car, head back north toward the intersection, crossing the outlet of the last two ponds you visited .2 mile from the trailhead. Stop and look at the impressive 4-foot-tall, mud-packed beaver dam that stretches for 100 feet across the swamps beside the outlet.

At the intersection head north and then west, following the road past many lovely vistas of bogs, brooks, and ledges for 3.5 miles to an intersection beside the Red River. For your last destination on this day in The Plains, turn left, or south, on a road that takes you to the western boundary of the recreation area, to the edge of the private lands of the Adirondack League Club.

The road follows the meandering Red River for 3.9 miles to a trailhead on the left, or east, side of the road. Here a sign indicates where a very narrow yellow-marked trail heads downhill into the woods, descending to the level of a sphagnum bog. A footbridge carries you dryly across. Notice how much larger the stumps of harvested trees are than anything else growing here.

You reach an intersection with an old logging road and turn right. More bogs and wet places fill the level route. You do need the trail markers, for the foot tread of other hikers is barely visible. There is one exceptional patch where the bright, light greens of sorrel are massed beneath a deep, dark spruce stand. You begin to hear water after only a half-hour, so the trail seems shorter than the 1.8 miles stated on the trailhead sign.

You have reached the confluence of the Red and Moose rivers. Both are blocked by a smooth natural rock dam, with quiet flows above and rapids below. This is a spot for summer swimming after a day of exploring and hiking. There is a campsite on a spruce knoll beside the dam. You have had a good woods walk to a special place, a suitable finish to a day of discovering the Moose River Plains.

If you wish to follow the main road out to the western gate, return to the major intersection by the Red River and bear left, or north, toward Limekiln Lake and NY 28 at Inlet.

Beaver Lake

Distance (round trip): 4.6 miles
Vertical rise: minimal
Hiking time: 2 hours
Map: USGS 15' West Canada Lakes

Beaver Lake is the largest lake in the Moose River Plains. Along the trail to the lake you will find a few giant trees, including pine, like those that once covered parts of the Moose River Valley. The trail is short and easy, so you can extend your day here by exploring two other nearby ponds or walking other short trails in the Moose River Recreational Area described in Hike 14. Read that hike description as an introduction to the area and the regulations governing it, and for general driving directions.

If you enter from the west, registering at the Limekiln Gate, drive southeast on the main dirt road for 10.6 miles to a major intersection. This intersection is 13 miles west of Headquarters Gate at the eastern end of the road. The distances do not sound great, but even when the dirt road is in good condition, travel is slow.

Bear south at the intersection; within 1.5 miles you cross the South Branch of the Moose River. Beyond the bridge turn right, west, onto a dirt road. After .2 mile, at the confluence of Otter Brook and the South Branch, this road is barred to vehicular traffic. The trail begins here, fol-

lowing the abandoned roadway.

The trail traverses fields of butterflies and meadows that border the Moose, and then begins a very gentle uphill trek into deep woods. A stand of large yellow birch hints at the mature forests that once covered this part of The Plains. The tall, open forest gives way to a dense spruce grove. Within twenty minutes, or about .8 mile from the trail's start, you attain a slight height-of-land in a beautiful forest of spruce, maple, and birch. A soft, spongy layer of needles on top of sand cushions the broad roadway, making walking easy. Ground pine, golden thread, bunchberry, sorrel, foamflower, and sarsaparilla make a marvelous carpet beside the road.

In another ten minutes you see the first of the huge white pine, and beyond, the hollow trunk of one whose diameter exceeded 6 feet. Near it, stretching 120 feet along the south side of the road, lies one of the fallen giants.

The hollow trunk is more than halfway to the lake; only a fifteen-minute-walk beyond it you see water through the trees, and shortly after that you come into a meadow. Cross the meadow heading south, down toward the lake. It is hard to believe that an elegant summer home was built on this spot in 1904.

Beaver Lake is fairly shallow, but it has a sandy bottom. Even the good-sized spruce and hemlock around the shores are dwarfed by the scattering of pine that have survived the logging. There is a lovely campsite here, and another lies along the shore to the east, beyond a spruce thicket, guarded by a few enormous pine stumps.

The lake seems to have a resident loon family, but no beaver. Anyway, it appears that the lake's name did not derive from previous residents, but from its shape. It is a very short-tailed beaver (on the USGS map, his tail extends west into the Old Forge quadrangle).

On the north side of the Moose, near its confluence with the Otter, is the site of Wellington Alexander Kenwell's hunting lodge. He ran the lodge for ten years after 1891 during the time the road from Headquarters on the Cedar River was 19 miles of wagon ruts. His son later had a hunting lodge at the end of what is now an abandoned and unmarked trail near the Plains bridge over the Otter.

It is difficult to imagine the isolation of these settlers in the wilderness, but Beetle's account of Kenwell in his book *Up Old Forge Way* provides a good illustration. Kenwell was asked to name the worst noise he had ever heard in the woods. Not wolves, not panther, not owls, but a "dreadful scraping sound, Mrs. Kenwell scraping the bottom of the flour barrel, and he knew he had to go 11 miles in a spring thaw to get more."

When you return to your car, you might want to head south along the access road to discover other lakes. Immediately south of the Beaver Lake trailhead, there are several very handsome campsites between the road and Otter Brook. Beyond the Otter Brook bridge, the Plains road angles west for 1 mile to a major trailhead for the West Canada Lakes Wilderness Area. A sign 2.4 miles beyond that trailhead marks the start of the .45-mile-long trail to Squaw Lake.

The road continues southwest for al-

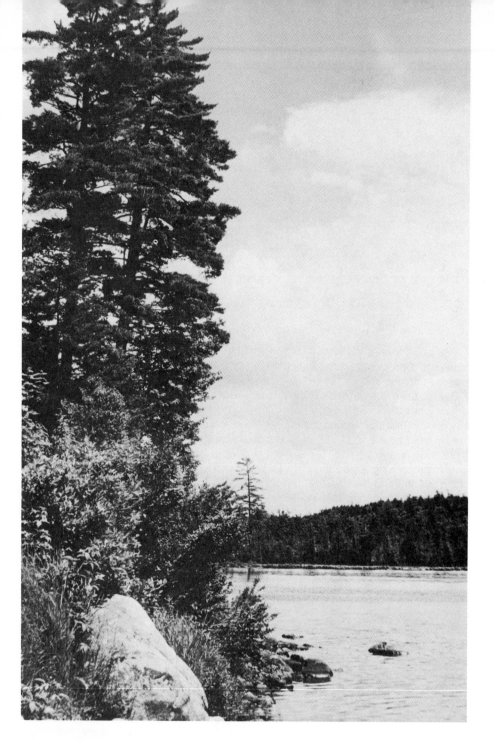

Near Beaver Lake

most 2 more miles, passing the flow near Muskrat Lake. The swampy trail that leads .2 mile to Indian Lake is being re-routed to higher ground, and the road will be barred to vehicular access beyond the new trailhead.

In most of the Adirondacks, you have to walk a good distance to find an isolated and secluded lake bursting with wildlife and bordered with a colorful array of blooming plants and shrubs. The Moose River Plains is a major exception. Both Indian and Squaw lakes have loons and sometimes mergansers. Rarely do you meet other hikers visiting them in summer. You can count on one hand the number of other uninhabited Adirondack lakes that are this lovely and this close to a road. The Moose River Recreational Area is an enormous expanse of recovering wilderness with a system of trails well designed around its access road so that you need to hike only short distances to reach any of its diverse lakes and ponds.

John Brown's Tract

Distance (full circuit): 9.6 miles
Vertical rise: minimal
Hiking time: 8 hours
Map: USGS 15' McKeever
Ha-de-ron-dah Wilderness Area

A hike in John Brown's Tract takes you farther west than any other route in this guide, beyond the mountain region that generally distinguishes the Adirondack Park. You will visit the rolling country that tempted early settlers. Their story is as fascinating as the walk through the deep quiet woods that now conceal almost all evidence of their presence.

The story of John Brown's Tract is a tragedy of greater proportion than any of the other failures that marked early attempts at Adirondack settlement, and it is one of the oldest tales in the mountains. It began in Rhode Island with the family and fortunes of John Brown, a businessman whose generosity to Rhode Island College caused that institution to be renamed Brown University. In 1796, one of his sons-in-law misspent a $210,000 fortune on the disputed title to 210,000 acres in Herkimer County. John Brown spent another $250,000 straightening out his son-in-law's folly and clearing title to the parcel, which was a part of the McComb purchase. Brown then divided the purchase into townships with the names of virtues he espoused: Industry, Enterprise, Perseverance, Unanimity, Frugality, Sobriety, Economy, and Regularity.

John Brown only visited the area once, but he had a 25-mile-long road built from Remsen, north of Utica, for the settlers he enticed to his community of Middle Settlement in Township #1, Industry. No sign remains of Industry's log houses, barns, and clearings, but the hike outlined visits Middle Settlement Lake, and follows in part a trail along John Brown's Road.

The tragedies that befell a second son-in-law, Charles Frederick Herreshoff, were even more devastating. But, from the failures of Herreshoff's attempts to bring settlers to Township #7 sprang some of the Adirondacks' most notable events. The community he founded later grew into the lovely resort of Old Forge. Otis Arnold acquired Herreshoff's mansion and turned it into the Adirondacks' first hotel. And that hotel was visited in 1856 by the first woman to make a camping trip across the Adirondacks. The isolation of that Adirondack wilderness is graphically illustrated by the story that that first female traveler, Lady Amelia M. Murray, lady-in-waiting to Queen Victoria, was said to have been the only woman other than their mother that six of Arnold's twelve daughters had ever seen.

You will want to read more of the history of the ill-fated settlements; the story of the failure of Herreshoff's iron mine, one of the first in the Adirondacks; and the adventures of the wild days when trapper Nat Foster occupied Herreshoff's mansion and murdered an Indian. Either Donaldson's *The History of the Adirondacks* or Grady's *The Adirondacks, Fulton Chain–Big Moose Region,* would be a good introduction.

Your hiking introduction to John Brown's Tract is a long, level loop generally following the valleys between long ridge hills. The hike takes you past several lakes in the Ha-de-ron-dah Wilderness, each desirable as a camping or fishing destination. The route is designed to give you a feel for the wilderness that greeted those first settlers.

Trailhead parking for the Scusa access is at a large turnout on the south side of NY 28, 3 miles south of the railroad overpass near Thendara. The trail begins opposite the turnout, and it is in better shape than any road the settlers ever saw.

The surrounding forests were burned in one of the worst of the 1903 forest fires, ignited by a spark from a wood-fired locomotive on the rail line near Thendara. In spite of that fire, the forest through which you will walk has almost regained wilderness stature.

The trail, marked in red, heads up a ridge through state land. You can walk

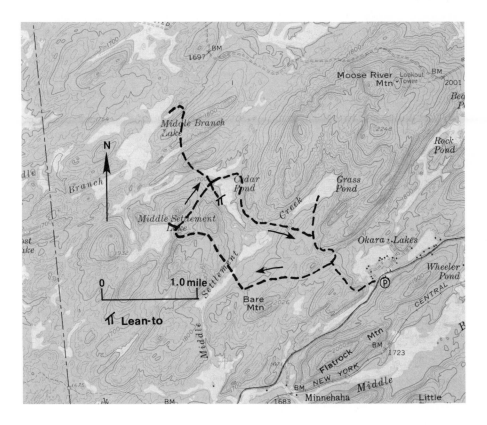

the .6-mile distance to Brown's Tract Road in fifteen minutes. You will return to this junction on the right-hand fork from Grass and Cedar ponds. For now, turn left on the yellow-marked Brown's Tract Road. It is a lovely, smooth path, leading south-southwest around Bare Mountain. Only a few glacial erratics lie beneath the forest of enormous beech, birch, and maple. In twenty minutes, .9 mile from the junction, you should reach a second intersection. Here you will fork right on the blue trail, heading 1.7 miles to Middle Settlement Lake.

Narrower and showing much less use, this trail is a good stretch-your-legs, wilderness route. As you wind along a ridge only slightly elevated from the surroundings, you can see swamps opening beside Middle Branch Creek. There is a particularly beautiful vista across a ferny meadow on your right as you cross a double-log bridge. I was most impressed with the openness of this forest's understory, and I stopped at least a half-dozen times to watch for black-throated blue warblers, vireos, and thrushes. You know you are nearing Middle Settlement Lake when suddenly, in the midst of the unbroken forest, one of the Adirondacks' great big boulders appears. It is a part of the facing cliff that has split away. At the trail junction below the cliff you turn left on the yellow-marked route to walk the short distance to Middle Settlement Lake.

The trail winds across a wet inlet area between boulders and starts along the northern shore of this swampy little lake, whose shores are made muddier by the flooding of recent beaver work. No matter, for it makes a better home for the nesting loons you are sure to find. Within 260 yards of the inlet a red-marked trail forks right for a short detour up a steep pitch and around to the top of the cliff. The view is crowded by maples, but you do look out across the pond. Return to

water level. The yellow trail continues west. To continue the loop, however, head back to the intersection below the cliff to take the yellow trail east. One overhanging section of cliff forms a small cave that appears to have shelterd hikers. You wonder if early settlers also found shelter here.

The yellow trail starts out along the left side of the draw, behind the huge split boulder and beneath the cliff. By this route it is just over .9 mile to Cedar Pond. After a twenty-minute-walk the trail crosses the end of the ridge and heads down and crosses Cedar Pond Outlet. Where you can see a marsh through the trees is about the closest you will get to Cedar Pond on a trail. Cedar Pond is a small pond surrounded by a beautiful long meadow full of big, twisted stumps.

Ten more minutes should suffice to get you to the next intersection, where a right fork leads south to a new lean-to. You could shortcut your circuit of John Brown's Tract at this point and head back south on the red trail, but if you are still game for adventure, head north for 1.3 miles to Middle Branch Lake. The trail starts up a series of short ledges, goes over a height-of-land and down into a swale, and then cuts down more steeply and crosses a stream on the predictable split-log bridge. Only a thin layer of sand covers the valley bottom, revealing the glacial wash that is typical of the tract's long valleys. Beyond the stream you head up beside big ledges and round a cliff on your left. Across the second height-of-land you start to descend, and before long you reach still another intersection where you can see Middle Branch Lake through the trees. The right fork, still marked with yellow, heads to a DEC truck trail that circles back to Thendara. The left fork leads along a red-marked trail to a lean-to where you should stop for lunch. This is certainly the

Middle Settlement Lake lean-to

prettiest of the lakes you visit; its loons may swim by quite close and its shores are lined with Labrador tea.

The return from Middle Branch Lake to the junction near the Cedar Pond lean-to takes about forty-five minutes. Beyond the lean-to the trail shows much heavier use. The first stretch is very handsome, through a dense spruce bog with a beautiful ground cover of sorrel, bunchberry, creeping white winterberry,

and beech fern. You keep to the long winding ridge of an esker with deep bogs on both sides.

The next unbroken chain of wilderness is measured by a series of minor events: two stream crossings; a stand of tall straight trees towering over a parklike setting where a variety of ferns carpets the forest floor a mottled rich green; a ledge covered with huge black cherry trees; more impressive fern-crested ledges; another small stream crossing; and finally, after nearly an hour of walking, the crossing of Middle Branch Creek, which is the outlet of Grass Pond. Beyond, the trail makes a ninety-degree turn left, and the tree cover becomes smaller. The long level walk begins to lose its excitement just about the time you reach the Grass Pond trail junction, an hour and ten minutes from Cedar Pond lean-to. This section is 1.7 miles long.

To visit Grass Pond, turn left and walk for .5 mile (fifteen minutes). A very old beaver dam holds almost no water. However, the pond is not merely grassy, for you can find sundew, lady's slippers, and the hoof prints of many deer along the shore.

When you return from the side trip to Grass Pond, you have .5 mile to walk to Brown's Tract Road. Head south along the red-marked trail to a newly marked intersection. The way left leads to O'Kara Lakes. You go straight, across new planking built by DEC and ADK's Iroquois Chapter in 1987. The trail makes a sharp right turn to avoid private land, then reaches Brown's Tract Road. You are now heading briefly west but shortly make a left turn to head south for the final .6 mile to the highway and your car. It takes about thirty minutes to walk from the new planking to the trailhead.

Vista Trail and Bald Mountain

Distance (total trip): 8.1 miles
Vertical rise: 1,300 feet
Hiking time: 7 hours
Maps: USGS 15′ Old Forge; USGS 15′ Big Moose
Fire Tower; closed Tuesday, Wednesday

The western foothills of the Adirondacks diminish to a series of long ridges whose major axes point slightly north of east. Few rise more than five or six hundred feet above the surrounding countryside, but glacial scraping has left many with steep cliffs flanking their long sides. The most visible and dramatic ridge is the row of hills along the north shore of the Fulton Chain, stretching from First through Fourth lakes.

Two trails on that escarpment connect a row of extraordinary vantages that stud the ridgeline like gems on a necklace. For the best walk in the Old Forge area, you should combine both trails into one long day's outing. The combination is possible because the Vista Trail ends at the trailhead for the Bald Mountain route.

If you have only a little time, you should just climb Bald Mountain on the western end of the chain. O'Kane's description of this trail in his 1928 classic *Trails and Summits of the Adirondacks* as ranking "first or nearly so in the amount of reward that it offers for a minimum of climbing" is still accurate. But if you want a full day's adventure and a long hike, you will want to combine the Vista Trail with the hike up Bald Mountain. For this

trail, and for the combined outing, it is best to have two cars, one at each trailhead.

The Vista Trail winds along the eastern slopes of the chain north of Fourth Lake. The mountain range is sometimes known as Onondaga Mountain, while a peak above Mountain Pond is called Scenic Mountain.

The Fulton Chain, best known for its canoeing opportunities, dominates most of the views on this hike. Old Forge, at the west end of the Fulton Chain, was the major settlement in John Brown's Tract (see Hike 16), but unlike most of the tract, it failed to fade into the wilderness. In fact, it grew into a thriving resort community and now has many vacation possibilities. See Beetle's *Up Old Forge Way* for a delightful series of stories about this community. Several state and private campgrounds are nearby, and a visit to the Northeastern Forest Industries Exhibit Hall, .6 mile east of town, is most informative. In addition, you should not miss a lake cruise on the Clearwater, which makes a 28-mile tour of the Fulton Chain starting at Old Forge.

The new official Bald Mountain trailhead, which is also the trailhead for the

western end of the Vista Trail, is on Rondaxe Road just north of its intersection
with NY 28, 4.6 miles east of Old Forge.
If you are hiking the complete route,
leave one car here and continue east another 3.1 miles to the County Lake Gift
Store. That store is 1.5 miles west of Big
Moose Road at Eagle Bay. The eastern
trailhead is on the north side of the road
100 yards east of the store.

The yellow-marked trail immediately
heads northwest up the ridge. As you
near the height-of-land, you will see a
narrow footpath angling up the ridge to
the west, left. The more obvious trail,
which you take, continues straight. It
leads to Bubb and Sis lakes, two pretty,
shallow ponds. Bubb is a mere fifteen-
minute walk from the highway. One of
the area's typical long ridges frames its
northern shore. The trail skirts its south
shore and forks. The way right heads
north around Bubb Lake to Moss Lake;
the left fork leads 100 yards through a
spruce thicket to Sis Lake. It takes no
more than fifty minutes to visit both and
return to the junction near the height-of-
land.

Now bear right, west, onto the Vista
Trail on Scenic Mountain. Blue markers
denote the trail. The eastern end of the
trail was closed for a couple of years
during the Indian occupation of Moss
Lake in the late 1970s. When the route
was reopened to the public, it was
cleared, new markers were added, and
sign posts gave it a new name—Vista
Trail.

You now begin climbing directly up
ledges. Within five minutes you reach the
beginning of the ridge and in another
five come to the first opening, Becker's
Outlook, with very limited views. Now
heading south of west along the razorback ridge, you continue climbing, but at
a more gradual rate. The water of Fourth
Lake is visible through the trees. Fall,

with its brilliant colors and sparser cover,
might be the most desirable time for a
trek along this ridge. All the vistas are
growing in, and all but two are now very
limited.

After walking forty minutes on the razorback ridge, you reach a rock overlooking Fourth Lake and the rolling hills
stretching away to its south. Within ten
minutes a second overlook with small
views follows, just before the trail starts a
short descent. Head down into the col
between the ridge and the higher hill on
the right. Angle right, crossing the valley
floor then up the higher ridge that follows. Another opening follows, this one
with a fireplace. You will then find the
trail confusing as it goes from one open
patch to another, but it always stays
close to the ridgeline.

After an hour and twenty minutes on
the ridge you reach open rock edged
with deep moss and spruce trees. If you
have made the trip to Bubb and Sis
lakes, this is two hours and twenty minutes from the start. You may want to stop
here or at the next overlook for lunch.
The through-the-trees view is east along
Fourth Lake, past Gull Rock Point and
several islands, to the right of which you
can spot a broad mountain with a fire
tower. That is Wakely (Hike 34), 18 miles
away.

Two excellent overlooks follow, separated by a minor dip. From the first there
is a broad view east, with Black Bear
Mountain and Estelle Mountain, which is
southeast of Raquette Lake, now visible.
Best of all, is the shot straight down,
south, to Fourth Lake, which almost
seems tucked below the intervening cliffs.

From the second overlook, you seem
to hang directly over the lake. You are
on the the narrowest part of the razorback ridge at the top of a nearly vertical
cliff. The crescendo of improving vistas
continues, for not only is this perch

placed dramatically and precariously on top of a nearly 400-foot vertical drop, but it permits points to the west to come into view. This spot marks the end of the long stretch of unbroken ridge line. If you pause often, as the changing perspective encourages you to do, your walk on just this section of ridge should take more than an hour.

The trail now ducks back into the woods and descends into a small valley. As you climb the next knob, stay left, on the Fulton Chain side of the ridge, going around and below ledges that form a 12-foot-high cliff near the top. This is a very difficult spot to navigate since you go around and below the knob and then up to it.

As you continue descending the ridge line, the forest suddenly becomes much taller and more handsome, but openings allow you some glimpses of Second and Third lakes. At the bottom of the next steep descent, you turn away from the Fulton Chain Lakes and intersect a freshly marked blue trail which is the present official route of the Vista Trail. The left, or south, branch goes down to

an abandoned railroad right-of-way. For more views, take the right branch. Mountain Pond greets you almost as soon as you turn north. Beaver have recently raised the level of the water in that pond, so dead spruce trees edge it and the walking can be muddy and terrible.

Beyond the south end of the pond the trail heads up a ridge, climbing 100 feet into the saddle between two knolls. An extraordinarily tall and handsome spruce and hemlock grove greets you as you mount the ridge. Just as you cross the ridgeline a red-marked trail forks right up the knoll by a sign pointing to "scenic overlook." Of course you cannot resist another detour, so head up, staying right as footpaths branch off near the summit. You soon come to an overlook of Mountain Pond. From here, its deep emerald water looks infinitely more inviting than from the shore. You also see Lake Rondaxe and the meadows that stretch east from it, with the cliffs of Slide Off Mountain facing the ridge behind. You will recognize that mountain as a carbon copy of the ridges you have been following. Beyond, a series of long hills stretches

Vista Trail looking north

toward Big Moose Lake. You will be glad you took the side trip to this beautiful hilltop.

Returning to the main blue-marked trail, you drop precipitously along slippery needle-covered slopes in a hemlock grove, then zigzag right along a contour before dropping again, this time swinging left around the northern marshes of Carry Pond. High water here almost floods the trail just before it emerges on the roadway, where you turn right, back north, crossing the marsh on a causeway. On the far side of the causeway a state historical marker tells you that you are walking along the route of a standard gauge railroad that was constructed in 1899. Until 1933 the line carried passengers between Raquette Lake and Carter Station. The railroad had the first oil-burning

locomotive in the Adirondacks, thus preventing the forest fires that were regularly ignited by the wood-burning monsters.

That sign at the end of the causeway is the only indication that here the blue trail turns left. It is .7 mile to the trailhead. The railroad continues north to Lake Rondaxe, but you walk south along the shore of Carry Lake. (The USGS map spells it Cary, but local signs and logic favor Carry.) This is a lovely stretch of trail with a needle-covered tread and views back to the mountain you just descended.

You cross an inlet on a log bridge and then climb another small rise, beyond which you can see Fly Pond. The trail heads south and up another ridge for .3 mile before reaching Rondaxe Road opposite the trailhead. The sign indicates it is 1.7 miles back to Mountain Pond, and with the additional detour to the overlook, you probably need one hour and fifteen minutes for that segment of the hike.

For the second part of this trek, where the view is equal to the sum of those along the Vista Trail, you simply climb Bald Mountain. From the parking area the ascent is only 400 feet in less than 1 mile. If the climb were not too short to call a hike, or if you were not apt to meet hordes of other hikers, it could be one of the most satisfying treks in the Adirondacks. But, since you have certainly enjoyed a measure of solitude on the Vista Trail, you should complete the day with this trip.

You do not really need directions for the trail. After a short level stretch, it begins to climb along the razorback ridge, angling up and over it, and reaching the first outcrop with a view in ten minutes. Gentle switchbacks bring you to the north side of the ridge, where you make a sharp left turn to cross a boggy swale on a bridge. Just beyond, the grade levels out. This is where the old trail from NY 28 up the south flanks of the ridge used to join the new route. The intersection is all but invisible now. Turn right to follow the ridge. The vista opens to include First and Second lakes and Moose Mountain. Stop and enjoy the amazingly narrow spine, the magnificent view of Fourth Lake, and the incredible drop of the cliffs below to the south. Hollow footsteps on the exfoliated sheaves tell of ice-loosened slabs that may one day fall away like the ones you see against the forest below. The serpentine ridge continues west to the fire tower, to which the state has assigned the name Rondaxe Mountain Tower. It is open to the public, but you scarcely need to climb it for the view. The only significant improvement the short tower affords is a clearer look at two peaks in the distant northeastern horizon. The one on the right is Marcy, 56 miles away, and the one on the left is Colden. You can be certain of their identity if you are looking to the left of Blue Mountain, which, only 25 miles distant, has an identifiable stubby profile. The best part of the view from the 2,350-foot summit is unquestionably the panorama of the Fulton Chain spread out parallel to the knife edge of cliffs that constitutes Bald Mountain.

Cascade and Queer Lakes

Distance (one way): 9.7 miles
Vertical rise: some
Hiking time: 6½ hours
Map: USGS 15′ Big Moose
Pigeon Lake Wilderness area

Unusual names are not uncommon in the Adirondacks, but why would anyone name a place Queer Lake? No deep mystery surrounds this strange name; it probably only reflects the lake's eccentric shoreline. But, to appreciate just how queer the lake's shape is, you have to walk there, and the best way is on a route that also touches Cascade Lake and Chain and Windfall ponds.

These lakes lie north of Fourth Lake in the Fulton Chain and south of Big Moose Lake. Natives in the nearby hamlets of Eagle Bay and Inlet will tell you just how the latter lake, Big Moose, and the surrounding country figured in the murder that Theodore Dreiser immortalized in his *An American Tragedy*. To reach the trailhead, drive to Eagle Bay on NY 28, 9.1 miles east of the information center in Old Forge and turn north onto Big Moose Road.

You will want to make this walk with friends so you can leave a car at each end of the loop. Start at the Cascade Lake trailhead, which is .9 mile north of Eagle Bay. There is a parking turnout on the east side of the road around a bend past the trailhead. This trailhead will shortly be located .2 mile farther north.

Arrange to leave a second car at an unmarked turnout 2.5 miles farther north, where a yellow-marked trail comes out from Queer Lake. The sign at the Cascade Lake trailhead clearly indicates that the dirt road heading east is the beginning of the 5.5-mile-long Cascade Lake Cross-Country Ski Loop, which is also designated as a hiking and horse trail. Your trip follows that roadway to the lake and then north along it a short distance, before continuing on to the other lakes.

The dirt road used to be the principal access to an old estate that later became a girls' camp. It is wide and improved with gravel, so you certainly do not need what few red trail markers there are to guide you. Trees along the roadside have been cut back for such a distance that the forest cover of tall, mature trees hardly forms a closed canopy. The road is so wide and straight you can see quite a distance ahead, sometimes as much as .2 mile, a most unusual phenomenon on Adirondack trails. The route takes you up a short hill and then down a long, gradual incline. An old road forks right as you cross a corduroyed section. Continue straight, through a spruce glen with marvelous bunchberry beneath, to a large field. Your trail is along its left border, which is edged in pine with a carpet of sarsaparilla and Canada mayflowers. Several good campsites can be found not far from the trail.

After crossing the outlet of Cascade Lake on a small bridge, the trail turns east for 100 yards to a junction that is 1.1 miles from Big Moose Road. A sign points north, left, to a narrow footpath with red markers. Routes connected to it lead in 1.6 miles to Chain Ponds, in 3.2 miles to Queer Lake Lean-to, and in 2.3 miles to Windfall Pond.

Unless you made a late start, continue straight for a trip along the north shore of Cascade Lake, a mile-long, thin body of water that is ideal for camping and canoeing. The only drawback is its proximity to the trailhead; the lake is so popular it is sometimes crowded. The roadway is

smooth enough for transporting a canoe the easy way, on a bicycle-wheeled contraption.

Many campsites are secreted along the several evergreen-covered promontories that edge the lake's shore. From the lake or its east shore, you can see the 200-foot-high cliffs that face the mountain to its north, but if you are going to finish the loop you will not have time for more than a .5-mile trek down the lake and return.

Back at the trail intersection, the narrow footpath climbs almost 200 feet to a spruce bog filled with lady's slippers, blueberries, and clintonia. Red trail markers define the route, which crosses the wet area and then rises gently to a mature forest with many yellow birch. Within twenty minutes you reach a height-of-land in a sort of natural rock garden where ferns seem to have found

Cascade and Queer Lakes **95**

perfect niches among the boulders and tall straight trees.

Huge yellow birch, the first of the giants you see on the hike, appear beside the trail. The trail winds through the mature hardwood forests and then angles left in a sphagnum bog covered with tall spruce. Beyond the bog, you climb a small rise and then reach a trail junction, 1 mile from Cascade Lake. Both continuing trails are marked with blue disks; the left leads 1.3 miles to Windfall Pond and then out to Big Moose Road, and the right, the one you follow, continues .6 mile to Chain Ponds and 1.4 miles to your first approach to Queer Lake. As you turn right you enter a small valley with an unusual ledge off to your left and an enormous birch growing from a boulder on your right.

The short walk to Chain Ponds is through a beautiful and majestic forest of hemlock and spruce, one of those deep evergreen pockets all too rarely encountered. A bog appears through an opening on your right just before you reach the outlet of Chain Ponds. Cross the outlet on a natural bridge of well-placed stones and stop for a moment to look up the lake and examine the old beaver dam that raised the water level, creating a typical Adirondack stump forest around the shores.

The trail climbs a ridge on a carpet of sorrel and interrupted fern. Ledges 20 to 30 feet tall face the hillside on your right. Look for a balancing boulder on one cliff top. The walk along the shore is one of the day's high points. You pass a spruce-covered peninsula formed by the continuation of a rock shoulder that edges the left side of the draw that the trail now enters. The deep, dark valley formed by the beautiful cleft in the rocks is overhung on the right by moss-covered ledges. Caves and crevices are sources of cool air. Mystery and a feeling of suspense ac-

company you. As the draw narrows, the trail is squeezed between boulders and huge slabs that have fallen from the cliffs.

The draw is all too short, and within fifteen minutes the trail emerges and starts to drop sharply. Here the trail is narrow and rooted, and again you will be awed by the size of some yellow birch. In ten more minutes you reach a trail junction within sight of Queer Lake. An informal path angles back right along its shore. A yellow-marked trail heads west, left, 2.6 miles to Big Moose Road. This is the route you will follow after you have explored Queer Lake. For now, bear right, where a sign points to the Queer Lake Lean-to, Mays Pond, and the West Mountain Trail.

You glimpse a small portion of Queer Lake as you cross the marsh at its western end on a slippery log bridge. You might notice an informal path that continues along the northern shore, but the trail, with its yellow markers, makes a sharp left turn uphill behind the lake. After a five-minute climb, you turn east and walk along the ridge, reaching another three-way junction within fifteen minutes at 3.8 miles. Here all the trails have yellow markers. The way left goes to Mays Pond and the route straight ahead leads to the lean-to in .5 mile. Continue right on the narrow trail that winds along the flat-topped ridge high above the lake, and then turns to descend, meeting on the way down still another trail. The yellow-marked route turns north, left, in 2.3 miles to Chub Lake, and the red-marked trail drops down to Queer Lake.

Your first approach to Queer Lake is at the beginning of a boggy isthmus linking the shore with the long narrow peninsula that almost divides the lake in two. Using a split-log bridge to cross the bog, you will walk along the north side of the peninsula under big spruce for 200 yards and then cross to a wind-swept promon-

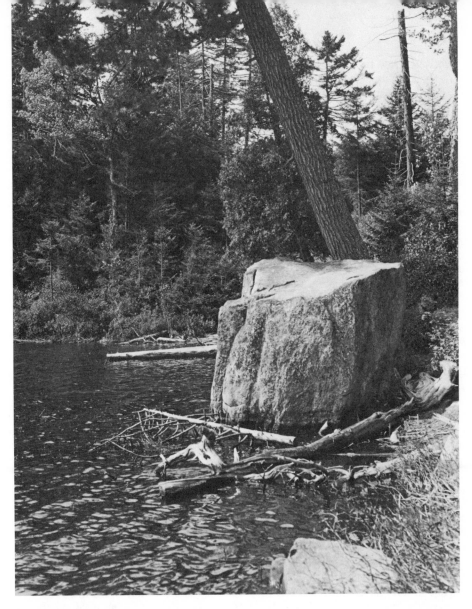

Queer Lake near the lean-to

tory overlooking the larger portion of the
lake. Here a lean-to has been placed to
enjoy the best of both views and
breezes.

An informal path continues from the
lean-to to the end of the peninsula, leading to ledges from which there is good
swimming in deep, clear water. This peninsula almost reaches the western shore
of Queer Lake. When you are in one portion of the lake, the separation is so complete you have no hint of a lake on the
opposite side. The shape is certainly peculiar!

When you start back, walk slowly along the boggy spit that takes you to the "mainland." Tall spruce protect an eerie shoreline edged with the naked spires of dead spruce, swamp laurel, and Labrador tea.

Return to the principal trail junction at the lake's western end and head right, west. Now is the time to enjoy the huge yellow birch. In the next hour of walking, you should spot dozens of these magnificent giants, some with diameters approaching four feet.

The trail begins through a valley, with low ground on the right and a steep hill on the left. Wet places make walking less than perfect, and roots poke out occasionally. A series of split-log bridges takes you across a wet meadow filled with lush ferns, clumps of oak fern, or *gymnocarpium*. An arrow directs you left. The turn is poorly marked, but if you miss it, you will quickly see the buildings of a private inholding. The trail heads up the hill and across its face before continuing in the valley in order to avoid this private land.

Past the detour, you reach another intersection where a sign indicates you have traveled .7 mile from Queer Lake. There is no indication of the distance to Big Moose Road, but it is just about 2 miles; the walk out takes just over an hour.

Stay straight ahead on the yellow trail to Windfall Pond, walking generally up the side of a hill for a half-hour on a ledge below long thin ridges. The footpath is narrow and appears infrequently used.

A spruce-covered plateau for camping lies between Windfall Pond and the trail. The lake is deep, its dark green waters reflecting the high hills that rim it. Its rock-edged shoreline invites swimming. The trail skirts the lake on the north as far as the outlet, staying most of the time 100 feet back from the water.

From the outlet it is 1 mile to Big Moose Road. The trail follows the stream, dropping through a rocky gorge in a narrow valley with ledges above and a tumble of boulders below. When you reach a meadow of ferns and Canada mayflowers, turn left. The sign says "Beaver Meadow," which is obvious, but it is curious. Do you suppose it was placed there when beaver had flooded the meadow, making people think that this was Windfall Pond? Yellow paint blazes and trail markers mark the trail as it circles the meadow. You cross a small stream on a split-log bridge, and beyond it, stop on a real bridge to watch the stream below flowing over smooth bedrock into a miniature chasm, complete with diminutive cliffs and a dark evergreen canopy. The trail pulls away from the stream up the valley's right side, following the stream for a short distance on a ledge and then dropping down to recross it on a log bridge.

Instantly the trail is wider. You have reached the point where "inbound" hikers stop, five minutes from the road. You turn away from the stream and a campsite that seems attractive to many (but think of all the beauty of the more remote spots you reached on this walk). In no time at all you are back at the unmarked trailhead and waiting car.

Stillwater Mountain

Distance (round trip): 2.4 miles
Vertical rise: 560 feet
Hiking time: 1¼ hours
Map: USGS 15' Number Four
Fire Tower; closed Thursday, Friday

The western Adirondacks have relatively few mountains to cimb. This fire tower peak is almost too small to be called a mountain, and its short trail hardly offers a hike, but it is among the few mountains in this part of the Adirondack Park with a view. Finding the trailhead takes you on a journey of discovery to an area with which you ought to become acquainted.

The mountain is south of Stillwater Reservoir, an enormous impoundment for hydroelectric power. From a state boat launching site on the reservoir you can gain boat access to 117 miles of shoreline and forty-two islands. Canoe or motorboat destinations include many wilderness campsites and lean-tos. North of the reservoir lies a region of four dozen lakes, with the Pepperbox Wilderness on the west and the Five Ponds Wilderness on the east flanking a section of private land along part of the reservoir's northern shore. There are few trails in the region, so its forests and lakes are among New York's most inaccessible.

Even driving to the trailhead is a trek into the wilderness. Turn north from NY 28 onto Big Moose Road at the hamlet of Eagle Bay on the north shore of Fourth

Lake in the Fulton Chain. In 6 miles bear left near Big Moose Lake toward Stillwater. You cross the Adirondack division of the New York Central Railroad 1.8 miles from the fork. Just beyond, in the hamlet of Big Moose, the road turns left and then right and adds Stillwater to its name. Most of the continuing road is hard-packed dirt. The surrounding land is owned by International Paper Company, which permits day use but no camping.

Traveling toward Stillwater is an adventure in itself. On an early summer day I counted a half-dozen deer, including one doe with a fawn, placidly grazing right beside the road. You pass a designated picnic area and a bay with views of the reservoir in the 9.7 mile drive from the fork at Big Moose to the trailhead, which is nothing more than a small parking turnout on the shoulder of the dirt road.

The trail heads uphill at a fairly gentle rate, generally below the telephone line leading to the tower. It follows a roadway and crosses an old logging road about halfway up. It is amazing how thin the Adirondack soil is even on these moderate slopes. You walk on bedrock a short distance before passing a cabin. The tower is not much farther, and the whole walk hardly takes thirty minutes, even at a slow pace.

Trees on the 2,264-foot summit crowd the view, hiding much of the reservoir, but you can look beyond it north to a series of low rolling hills. Farming country rolls away on the distant southwestern horizon. West Mountain lies due east, almost directly in line with Blue Mountain so only a portion of Blue is visible to the left of West. At 120 degrees magnetic you can spot Wakely Tower, over 27 miles away, with Snowy to its right.

North of east stretch the High Peaks, reduced at this distance to a range of small and not easily identified summits. Even on a clear day and with good binoculars it is hard to distinguish Santanoni, 48 miles away, from the MacIntyre Range, almost 8 miles beyond and

slightly to Santanoni's left, the two appearing as one connected ridge. Clouds often top the High Peaks, and their cluster from this angle is maddeningly dense.

The trip down takes no more than twenty minutes. A summer walk through the rich hardwood forest on Stillwater's slopes makes it hard to imagine that the deepest snows and lowest temperatures in the state are often recorded nearby.

To extend your adventure here you can walk from the parking turnout to a stump-filled spit of the reservoir, or you can continue driving west toward the Stillwater settlement. Immediately beyond the trailhead you pass the fire observer's cabin. There is a spring at the roadside nearby.

In just over 2 miles a sign directs you to a turn right toward the boat launching facility and the ranger's headquarters, where you must register if you use the lake. You will even find a hotel and store in this outpost, whose location at the western edge of the Adirondacks places it almost as far from civilization as you can get in the park.

Bay on Stillwater Reservoir, near the trailhead

High Falls on the Oswegatchie

Distance (round trip): 11 miles
Vertical rise: minimal
Hiking time: 6 hours
Maps: USGS 7½' Newton Falls; USGS 7½' Five Ponds
Five Ponds Wilderness Area

The Oswegatchie is canoe country, and, understandably, this northwestern Adirondack river is very popular with canoeists. The long, flat waterway meanders so much that it seems as if, straightened out, it might just stretch completely around the Blue Line of the Adirondack Park. The river's Indian name derives from the phrase for going around a hill. The region is also a favorite with backpackers and trout fishermen and has many, many more miles of trails and interesting destinations than are described here and in the Five Ponds trek (Hike 21).

The broad flood plain of the Oswegatchie has long had a reputation as a great hunting ground. In his *Trappers of New York,* Jeptha R. Simms tells an Oswegatchie tale that is as tall as the pine that dot its plains. Trapper Nat Foster and his younger brother Shubael were hunting along the river shortly before Nat's death, when his eyesight had begun to fail. They cornered a herd of deer against a ledge. Nat's brother shot several before Nat got one, but Nat quickly recovered. He said that if he could get a good piece of venison he would be able to see, and after a meal of his favorite

meat, he proceeded to shoot four more deer. Together that day the two men supposedly killed twenty deer.

The distances on the flat plains between ponds and along the eskers are so great that there are few good day hikes in the area. The trip to the High Falls is an exception. However, you may want to carry a pack in and camp, or use a canoe (see Jamieson's *Adirondack Canoe Waters: North Flow*), for spending the night is the only way you can reasonably continue to Five Ponds and beyond. There are several good campsites within walking or canoeing distance of High Falls, and all are excellent bases for further explorations in the Five Ponds Wilderness.

This easy though long hike describes a journey to the lovely waterfall that breaks the otherwise placid river. The relatively open, level trail makes the 11-mile round trip seem shorter than it really is.

To reach Oswegatchie country, from Cranberry Lake, drive southwest on NY 3 and turn south on the road toward Wanakena. One mile from NY 3, bear right, and then take a second right across a one-lane bridge over the Oswegatchie River. Just beyond, there is a parking

area on the right, immediately past a private dwelling and 50 yards short of the gate that bars the continuing roadway. No vehicular traffic is allowed on this fire truck route that serves as the beginning of the trail.

The edges of the hard-packed sand road are dense with masses of spring and summer blooming flowers, particularly the ones that need a bit of extra sunshine. The road follows a flow, and within fifteen minutes you cross the stream that feeds it. Shortly, you cross a second stream and then come to a pipe that carries water from a good, cold spring, spilling it across the trail. The sandy-bottomed watercourses that you cross are all flowing to the stream valley on your right. You cross two more small streams within a matter of minutes; by now you should be well aware of the area's drainage patterns. A myriad of small sluggish streams flow through the plains, the result of the sandy soil's poor water retention.

In theory, you are walking on a red-marked trail, but the first markers you spot are just before a junction forty minutes and a 1.75 mile walk from the trailhead. Here the red route, the fire truck trail, forks right. Your route, now called the Leary Trail, is along a narrow footpath marked with blue. A variety of ferns, many of them tolerant of dry conditions, covers the higher ground. There are also long wet stretches where sand has been placed in cribs to raise the footpath above the muck. Already a sense of quiet pervades your walk.

After walking for an hour, you cross a bridge over a small stream. Almost imperceptibly, the forest has become taller. There is a second bridge at 3.1 miles. At 4.1 miles, you start to descend to the level of a grassy flow. A short walk along the flow leads to a bridge and a place to pause and enjoy the tamarack, spruce,

and pine. Just beyond, a new portion of trail turns right, avoiding the wet meadow. Beaver have plagued the old section of trail for years, creating a pond that fills part of the meadow and flooding the trail. If you are making the walk in late summer, you will want to stop also to enjoy the fields of bottle gentian and to pick a luscious dessert of blackberries. In another .2 mile, you intersect the truck road at right angles. The intersection is 4.6 miles from Wanakena and can be easily reached within two hours. The blue-marked trail straight ahead leads in under .5 mile to a bridge over the Oswegatchie, near which you will find several good campsites. The best is on the ledge north of the bridge. (The bridge is also the starting point for the Five Ponds hike.)

To reach High Falls, however, turn left and walk the red-marked truck trail for 1.6 miles. I cannot help thinking of it as a blue trail, for it is much more beautifully marked with the purple-blues of gentian, the soft green-blues of tamarack, and the expanse of blue sky that opens up above the broad natural plains beside the trail. The exquisitely lacey giant tamarack are most impressive. A ridge of tall pine and tamarack, a good camping spot, eventually gives way to a black-water swamp. Just beyond, the trail angles to the southwest, and you can begin to see The Plains, which stretch northwest for almost 1 mile. The trail hugs the southern end of The Plains, and just beyond comes another intersection. Continue straight for .6 mile to High Falls, a short walk slowed in midsummer by enticing patches of raspberries.

Shortly you hear the falls. As you approach the pine-covered knoll beside them, several footpaths lead away from the main trail. The first goes to a perch looking up at the falls, and the second to a lean-to. The bridge above the falls as

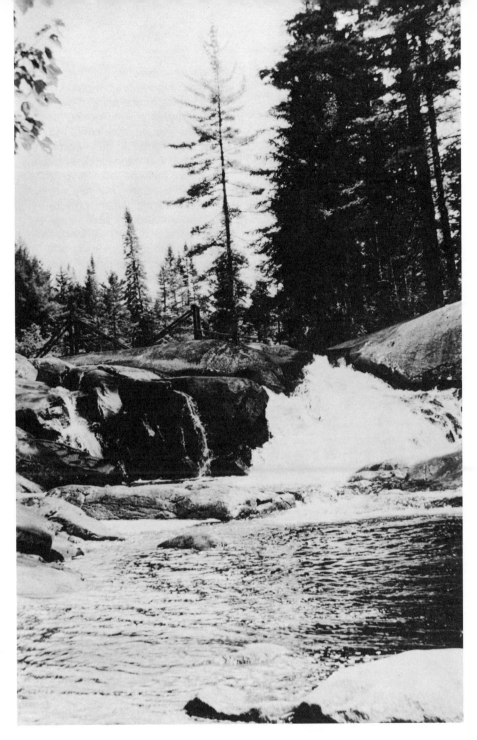

High Falls on the Oswegatchie

well as the lean-to on the south shore have been removed.

A funnel of smooth vertical ledges frames the 15-foot High Falls. You will enjoy the way the water breaks from the smooth stream above, frothing into a wild fury through a deeply channeled course and finally spilling into a deep, rectangular-walled pool where swirls of natural foam trace a pattern of symmetrical white curves on the dark brown water.

While the Oswegatchie abounds in wildlife, you are not likely to see deer in the quantity that Foster did. High Falls, like many other camping destinations in the Adirondacks, has become known for the bear who have learned that careless hiker's packs can be sources of food. If you do camp here, be sure and secure your pack high above the ground, suspending it by a rope from an overhanging tree limb. If you are looking for signs of wildlife, you are more apt to see the rather large footprints of the coyotes that have gradually moved into the Adirondacks from the west. I doubt you will see one of these animals, but they may just spend an evening serenading you, sounding almost like a pack of wolves.

The plains and marshes beside the river are noted also for their birdlife. The Canada or gray jay and the northern three-toed woodpecker both make their way this far south. Be sure to carry your binoculars, for you will see many warblers and water birds.

Five Ponds, Wolf Pond and Sand Lake

Distance (round trip): 14.5 miles
Vertical rise: minimal
Hiking time: 10 hours
Maps: USGS 7½' Five Ponds; USGS 7½' Oswegatchie SE
Five Ponds Wilderness Area

On the hike to Five Ponds you have a chance to examine the effects of the most recent of the Adirondacks' major geological events. As the glaciers of ten to twelve thousand years ago began to melt, channels of water pushed through the ice pack, gradually funneling beneath it. These rivers picked up and moved sand, gravel, and boulders. As the melting slowed, the under-ice rivers deposited their burdens, leaving long, sinuous ridges of stones surmounted by finer and finer sand. The ridges, called eskers, vary from a few feet to over 150 feet in height, and stretch up to several miles in length. The longest eskers in New York developed in the flat lands of the northwestern Adirondack region.

Eskers are usually crowned with white pine, spruce, and hemlock, and in the Five Ponds Wilderness Area those trees exist in towering virgin stands. The tops of eskers vary in width from a few feet to a hundred feet. They can be gently rounded and wide enough to support a road, or they can be as narrow and sharp as a knife-edge, which is the case with one of the Five Ponds eskers.

This hike starts from a campsite on the Oswegatchie River and features a walk past all of the Five Ponds, and then southwest through magnificent forests that stretch in that direction toward Stillwater reservoir in a wilderness broken only by marshes and beaver flows. Best of all, this trek takes you far from other hikers to a world of solitude.

To reach the starting point, you first walk the red truck trail and then the blue hiking trail of Hike 20, then turn south to reach the new bridge over the Oswegatchie after a 5-mile hike. This hike begins at the bridge, 0 mile. If you head south from a campsite there early in the morning, you are apt to find the tall pine and tamarack etched in soft blues against the fog rising from marshes. These marshes line the two outlets of Five Ponds, and the trail generally follows the eastern of the two. After fifteen minutes you cross a small brook and then angle left away from the flow. Small sandy ridges accompany you on each side.

The trail begins to climb gently through a valley, and after forty-five minutes (1.2 miles from the bridge), it turns right to cross the stream. There are enough rocks to hop on, so a bridge is unnecessary. Stop and appreciate the great distances you can see through the open forest, and notice, too, the fantastic understory of blooming plants.

The hill on your right is the northern end of the Five Ponds esker, which you will want to study as you continue walking south beside the stream. The esker becomes steeper and steeper, attaining a forty-five degree angle. The large boulders typical of the lower margins of eskers make difficult footing along this section of trail.

A little under .5 mile beyond the stream crossing, about a fifteen-minute walk, you may be tempted to climb the esker. There are easier places to ascend, but here you can climb to beautiful pine that crown a dip in the ridgeline, just above Little Five Pond.

Return to the trail and continue south for .2 mile to a lean-to a few feet south of the trail on the shore of Big Shallow Pond. West of the lean-to, which is 2 miles from the bridge, an informal path heads up the esker, a climb of over 120 feet. From the top you can see a faint footpath that angles right, back toward the shore of Little Five Pond.

Your path, to the left, winds south along the top of the esker for about 200 yards through a magnificent hemlock grove, before crossing over the ridge and descending in a long southwest traverse to the outlet of Big Five. The path follows that outlet to the pond. The lovely stream exits from the pond over a natural cobblestone spillway of uniformly sized stones, sorted by the glacier. The pond itself is long and thin with swampy shores, much better to look at than walk beside.

Return to the lean-to and head north for 100 feet to the spot where the blue-marked trail crosses the outlet of Big Shallow, fording the stream on another bed of sorted stones. You climb a rise too small to show up on the survey maps, but as you walk south alongside it, you will recognize it as an esker. Just beyond the end of Big Shallow you cross a ridge dense with spruce, and Washbowl, a small cup of a lake rimmed with tamarack, comes into view on your left.

The ridgeline curves around the south end of Washbowl and shortly reaches the end of Little Shallow, another swampy-shored lake, although this one is filled with large stumps. Walk southwest along the shore to a second lean-to. There's a very cold fresh spring below the lean-to, almost at the water's edge.

The lean-to is 2.55 miles from the Oswegatchie as the trail goes, but if you climbed the esker a couple of times and poked about among the giant trees on its ridgeline, you have probably walked for well over three hours. Assuming that you can cover that 2.55 miles in much less time on the return, you might want to continue southwest toward Wolf Pond and Sand Lake, which are an additional 2.2 miles and 4.2 miles along the trail.

Unusually lovely and strange places are few and far between in this vast, unvarying wilderness. You meet one shortly after you continue south, where a new beaver flow backs up a dark and murky pool. The recently constructed long chain footbridge is necessary to traverse the flooded spruce swamp. Otherwise, the 1.7-mile trek south to the side trail to Wolf Pond is rather uniform, if such a dull word could possibly be applied to trees of such significant proportions. The walking is easy, though, and you should reach a trail junction in forty minutes.

At the intersection the yellow-marked trail to the right leads .5 mile into the north shore of Wolf Pond. This detour would take you over a knoll that is covered with some of the best pine and spruce you have yet seen. Your route is left, though, where you begin, for the first time on your Oswegatchie trek, walking a

Giant evergreens on the esker ridge

trail that is hardly used. The narrowness of the footpath increases your sense of wilderness travel. This last 2.5 miles of the blue-marked trail to Sand Lake offers the region's best walking. You cross a knoll and descend through a narrow draw to a beautiful sliding rock falls that separates two flooded meadows.

You continue southwest up and along the side of a small hill, from which you have occasional glimpses of Wolf Pond through the trees. You then drop down to pond level. A short path back to the right allows you to detour to the water's edge, where there's a beautiful bog. Labrador tea and bog rosemary, bog wool and pitcher plants fill the sphagnum mats. You have another hour of walking before you reach Sand Lake, whose sandy shores are more inviting to hikers and swimmers than any of those you have yet encountered.

When you reach Sand Lake you will have walked a minimum of 6.75 miles, even if you have made no side trips, and you might wish you had carried a pack so you could stay put. There are several inviting campsites. As it is, on a day walk you probably will not have time to explore the esker that divides Sand from Rock Lake on the west.

Return the way you came.

Saint Regis Mountain

Distance (round trip): 6 miles
Vertical rise: 1,235 feet
Hiking time: 3½–4 hours
Map: USGS 7½' Metric Saint Regis
Fire Tower; closed Tuesday, Wednesday

Saint Regis Mountain lies in the northwestern quadrant of the Adirondacks, overlooking the Saint Regis Canoe Area. Beautiful chains of ponds stretch south of the mountain. You may very well want to combine a climb up Saint Regis Mountain for an overview of the pond-studded wilderness with an extended canoe camping trip.

If you drive north from Tupper Lake on NY 30, passing Upper Saranac Lake, you will see the entrances to Fish Creek Ponds and Rollins Ponds state campgrounds. Both offer great waterfront camping and access. State maps of the Wilderness Canoe Trail are available from the DEC or campsite headquarters.

As you continue on NY 30 past Lake Clear, you can see the tower on Saint Regis in the northwest. At Lake Clear Junction, where NY 86 continues northeast, you turn north, staying on NY 30. When you reach the town of Paul Smiths, 7.3 miles beyond Lake Clear Junction, turn left off NY 30, and head west past Paul Smith's College for 2.5 miles. Turn left, south, onto a narrow road signposted for the Saint Regis tower, 3.5 miles away. Drive .5 mile to the parking area just outside the gate of the Mer-

riweather Post Estate. In a controversial move, the state sold the buildings and a small piece of land to a private individual. The remaining land is now part of the Forest Preserve.

Saint Regis is not difficult to climb. You should allow about four hours round trip, although you may meet forestry students from Paul Smith's College who regularly run up the mountain in under an hour, starting from the college grounds. The trail has been a laboratory for classes in trail work, and you will appreciate the results as you climb.

The trail, marked with red, makes a short climb into a maple and cherry woods, following the estate boundary. Huge erratics of Marcy anorthosite with large blue crystals of labradorite edge the trail as it begins a short descent and then climbs a small hill. You walk beside the estate line for nearly twenty-five minutes before turning right toward the mountain. Cross a small stream on a new log bridge, pick up the telephone line for the tower, and then head southwest through a mixed woods where the forest floor is wet. You cross some of the wet places on corduroy, some on logs, and a bog on a bridge. The trail is relatively level here, hard-packed, and offers easy walking. After crossing another stream forty minutes and 1.5 miles from your start, you pass a picnic table and out-house to the right of the trail, and to the left, the observer's cabin. The trail continues alongside the little brook and then turns away. You start to climb on stairs built into the side of the hill. The trail has been realigned, and although it is very steep, it is well constructed with water bars for drainage and stairs to prevent erosion.

About twenty minutes from the picnic area the timber becomes much smaller, indicating where the 1876 fires swept the upper slopes of Saint Regis. The summit is bare to this day.

After a level stretch through paper birch and dwarf ginseng, a short climb bypasses an abandoned section of eroded trail. Steep ledges lie to the right. You circle them on newly cut and very steep sections. Gradually you gain glimpses of the lakes below. From an outcrop to the south of the trail you can see Whiteface across the Saint Regis lakes.

After thirty minutes of steep climbing, you emerge above treeline to see the tower ahead on the 2,873-foot summit. A total climbing time of an hour and forty-five minutes reflects a fairly slow pace.

The summit is so exposed there is no need to climb the tower. The mountain seems to stand alone, with broad plains below stretching in almost every direction. Saint Regis is a solitary cone in a huge dish of ponds and lakes, edged with mountains on the horizon. Those to the northwest are low, the foothills of the Adirondacks, but from the north the sweep encompasses the rugged range that includes Whiteface, McKenzie, and the High Peaks through Seward in the south. The High Peaks southeast across Lake Clear are often shrouded in clouds even on a clear day. Saint Regis Pond lies almost due south, with Little Clear Pond to its southeast and Saranac Lake

View toward Whiteface and McKenzie mountains

114 Saint Regis Mountain

stretching to the distant south. Long Pond is visible a little west of south, with Tupper Lake stretching out beyond toward the horizon. Fish, Lydia, and Little Fish ponds, on the Wilderness Canoe Trail, spread out at the foot of the mountain.

East of Saranac Lake, Ampersand Mountain stands in front of Seward and Santanoni, so overwhelmed by those higher peaks that identifying it can be difficult. MacIntyre and Marcy are obvious, with the cone of Colden between them. To the left, north of Marcy, peaks hiked on the Range Trail can be identified, as well as, farther north, Cascade and the Sentinel Range leading around to McKenzie and Moose, which appear from this angle as one long mountain range. Whiteface is just south of east.

The northeast is a patchwork of lakes and fields, some of them the potato fields for which the northern plains are famous. Both the Post estate and Paul Smith's College are visible on the shores of the lakes below you. Sand flats and glacial ridges stretch to the northeastern horizon. Two peaks with fire towers stand out a little east of north: Debar on the left, Loon Lake Mountain on the right. Both towers are closed. Even if you only carry the USGS Saint Regis quadrangle, you can probably name at least two dozen lakes and ponds in view. However, the pleasure of the climb will be enhanced if you also carry the Tupper Lake, Long Lake, Santanoni, Mount Marcy, Saranac Lake, and Lake Placid quadrangles, for most of the area they cover is visible from the summit.

Return the way you came. You will not have much trouble making the trip back in an hour.

Debar Mountain

Distance (round trip): 7 miles
Vertical rise: 1,600 feet
Hiking time: 6 hours
Maps: USGS 7½' Meacham Lake; USGS 7½' Debar Mountain

Debar Mountain is the Adirondacks' northern sentinel, offering sweeping views across its dramatic northwestern slopes to the St. Lawrence Valley and neighboring Canada. Rock outcrops covering the mountain's small summit offer views that adequately compensate for those lost when the fire tower on Debar's peak was closed. Stunted spruce frame the cliffs that drop to steep wooded slopes and finally to the broad plain below, plunging over 1,600 feet in less than a mile.

The entire climb is through a magnificent forest that is as special as the views from the summit. The approach is from the southwest, gentle at first, then steadily uphill, and finally an 800-foot mad scramble up the last .5 mile, the steepest and most arduous climb of any on New York's fire tower trails.

The trail to Debar begins from the Meacham Lake State Campground, a good place to camp before you climb. There, picnic and camping areas surround part of the 2-mile-long lake, whose cool waters washing sandy beaches will welcome you to a refreshing swim after your climb.

The Meacham Lake Campground is about 18 miles south of Malone on NY 30, far enough north so that signs are in both English and French to accommodate visitors from Canada. To reach it from the south also use NY 30. You will pass Paul Smith's College and the new Adirondack Visitors Center. Continue north through level sand plains covered with spruce, pine, birch, tamarack, and poplar typical of the forests in the northern Adirondacks. You will see a sign for McCollums 6.3 miles north of Paul Smith's College. It is the site of an old settlement; today the number of tombstones in the cemetery far exceeds the remaining buildings. An historic marker beside the road bears the legend that in October 1908 Debar Mountain and the surrounding land were burned in the wave of forest fires that struck the Adirondacks that year. The local fire consumed over 6,000 acres.

The sign for the southern access to the Meacham Lake Campground is 9.5 miles north of Paul Smith's College. A marked road angles right, east, paralleling the lake. A northern access is 2.3 miles farther along NY 30 near Clear Pond. The roads meet northwest of Meacham Lake and continue as one .2 mile southwest to

View from Debar Mountain

the main gate for the campground. A day-use fee is charged. Ask the gatekeeper for a campsite map and instructions, because the trailhead to Debar is not shown on the map and signs for it are missing.

Look for a dirt road just west of campsite #48. Take it and turn right at the first intersection in .1 mile. In .4 mile you reach a sand pit where you park. The trail commences along the gated dirt fire road heading east toward Debar. (If you start your walk from the campground, this trailhead is 1 mile from the main entrance.

Walking the soft sand of the fire road is almost like walking on a beach, except that the road is shaded by a tall spruce forest. Beside the road, carpets of Canada mayflowers are punctuated by starflowers, golden thread, wild strawberries, false Solomon's seal, and acres of hayscented fern. As the forest begins a transition to mature hardwoods, you will spot on a huge maple beside the trail, the first of the very few red markers that are supposed to delineate the route. Beneath the hardwoods sarsaparilla and blackberries edge the road.

After you have been walking about twenty minutes, a glacial ridge appears on your right and a spruce bog opens on your left. The bog should be the first of the detours you take to enrich the trip. A true sphagnum bog, it contains most of the typical flowers: the predominant shrub is Labrador tea, which blooms here about the second week in June. Bunchberry in profusion, cinnamon and interrupted ferns, blueberries, and clintonia continue the great carpet of flowers beneath the tall trees.

Unless you spend some time enjoying the bog, it should take you less than a half-hour to walk the first mile to a bridge over a tributary of Winnebago Brook. A barely perceptible woods road heads left from the fire road in the meadow near the brook. Continue on the more obvious road (you will find few markers but you

really do not need them) for 200 yards to a marked fork. Here a sign directs you to turn left and continue on a wide woods road that begins the upward trip so gently you really do not sense you are climbing.

The first perceptible rise begins shortly in a forest of tall, straight hardwoods that cover a lovely woods floor where *dryopteris* ferns, mostly the evergreen wood fern, are interspersed with doll's eyes, lady's slippers, crinkleroot, and jack-in-the-pulpit.

As a few boulders appear beside the route and rocks pop through the roadway, you will realize how few stones there were in the glacial sand at the trail's beginning. For forty-five minutes you follow the road through a forest in which maples become more dominant. Huge boulders edge the route, and a steep hill begins to appear on your right. You will cross several log bridges over a small stream before you reach a height-of-land 1.5 miles from the marked fork. The roadway descends slightly, and a steep valley becomes visible on your right. You will contour around to the head of that valley, which lies between Black Mountain and the peak of Debar Mountain.

As you begin to climb again, ledges are visible on your left, and you reach a lean-to with a fireplace. Beyond, the trees are shorter and noticeably more dense as the road climbs into a small meadow containing the remains of the fire observer's cabin. The state burned the cabin when it closed the tower, leaving a mess of stone and concrete. As you enter the meadow, the summit of Debar looms ahead of you. Cross the meadow and enter the woods to the left of the stone foundations. The trail is now just a narrow footpath.

The final .5 mile makes the first 3 seem dull. Suddenly the route seems to be straight up through a stunted forest. The white of paper birch contrasts with the dark tones of spruce. The mountainside is so steep that stone steps have been built into it. Within 100 yards a stream crosses the trail. For a time it seems as if the trail is through the stream. Rock stairs lead past boulders glistening with outcrops of garnet. Deadfalls block the narrow trail, and the downed telephone wire leading to the fire tower could trip you up. You have to use your hands to pull yourself up some of the small ledges, but don't climb so intently that you fail to stop and look back when the forest opens up. A fine view of Meacham Lake and the mountains to its south and east appears through the trees. You can trace your route on the ridge you crossed during

the lower part of the ascent, and you will be impressed by the steepness of the knob you are climbing.

The trail levels out in a deep ferny glen below a moss-covered ledge marking the last short climb. After you cross the last ledge and a short wet level, the sheer rock face of the tiny knob (elevation 3,320 feet) on which the tower sits seems to block your way. Walk right around the knob to climb it from the north. Fantastic views greet you as you emerge from the forest. Most exciting is the sweep along the mountain's steep-angled northwest face. Only a few more hills break the plain below as it fades into the distance across the St. Lawrence River into Canada. To the southwest you can see Meacham Lake, and in the west a series of small hills barely define the horizon. The view northeast is blocked by a row of small knobs that are a part of Debar itself. The view is less than years ago from the tower, but enough openings remain to compensate for the tower's removal.

There are no other rock outcrops with views, but if you walk around the summit your hollow footsteps will tell you you are walking across exfoliated sheaves, rock slabs that have been broken off by the expansion of ice in cracks in the rock. There is a very small camping spot northeast of the tower. If you climb in June you will also enjoy the bloom of huge clumps of painted trillium brightening the mountain *dryopteris* that covers the wooded parts of the summit with a lush soft background green.

Going down, you find that the mountain is so steep near the summit it requires almost as much time to descend as it did to climb up. Be careful on the stairs and rocks. When you reach the height-of-land between the cabin and the marked fork, pause for a moment to enjoy the magnificent forest around you. Notice how many of the yellow birch seem to be growing from boulders. One beside the trail is perched upon a stone with its roots crossed. It so resembles the caterpillar from Alice in Wonderland with his legs crossed upon a giant toad stool that I almost expected it to ask, "Who are you?"

Catamount Mountain

Distance (round trip): 3.8 miles
Vertical rise: 1,568 feet
Hiking time: 4 hours
Map: USGS 15' Lake Placid

If you like to scramble over ledges and boulders, inch along cracks and crevices on steep rock walls, and do a little non-technical rock climbing, then Catamount is for you. This mountain, one of several with the same name, lies in the north-eastern Adirondacks. The climb is great fun, but it will probably take no more than a half-day, allowing you time to explore some of the area's attractions on the way to the trailhead.

Driving north from Lake Placid on NY 86, your route is along the West Branch of the Ausable River, past High Falls Gorge, a private scenic attraction for which a fee is charged. Next north is the Wilmington Notch Public Campground and Day Use Center, in a very handsome spot near the river. Here there is trout fishing and the best campsites for activities in this area. Beyond Whiteface Ski Center you can stop and walk beside the flume on the Ausable, a wild falls in a deep gorge within sight of the highway. You eventually reach a crossroads where NY 86 turns right toward Wilmington and NY 431 goes left for 2.8 miles to the entrance to the Whiteface Mountain Memorial Highway, a toll road climbing nearly to the summit of Whiteface. That summit,

at 4,867 feet, offers some of the Adirondack's best scenery, but you can get there by car, so for a trek on foot continue straight ahead on the unmarked county highway toward Catamount.

When you reach NY 17, head left, or north, for 1.7 miles, and turn left again, onto Forestdale Road, driving west toward Franklin Falls. In 1 mile you pass an intersection with the old highway. You are now headed southwest with the complex of Catamount on your right and the Wilmington Range on your left. Exactly 4.7 miles from NY 17 a small unmarked path heads to the right into an alder swamp. Easy to miss, it is the beginning of the trail up Catamount. If you are uncertain, continue for 1.25 miles to the Wilford LaHart Farm and turn around. The LaHart property borders the trail, and members of that family laid out the very handsome and well-designed route on Catamount. As you head back, you can enjoy the best view northeast to Catamount's ledges. Watch closely as you descend the small hill just beyond the edge of the posted property line. Now you should be certain the faint opening between the trees is the trailhead. Park off the road.

The narrow footpath follows an old road that is filling in with small balsams. The path is informal and not marked by the state. You should not let the overgrown condition of the first .25 mile deter you. The deadfalls and confusion last only a few minutes, for after .25 mile you come to an orange-painted pipe and cairn indicating the corner of the property. Turn left and follow the property line for .3 mile toward magnetic north. The straight line is marked with orange blazes and is easy to follow.

Hiking here through an old field, you are on one of the most beautiful and unusual stretches of trail you will encounter. Fires in the northern Adirondacks consumed acres of forest land. The burn on Catamount created a wonderful open-rock summit, but the fires in the valley exposed the sterile sandy soil, which is only now becoming reforested. Here the ground is covered in a pastel mosaic of soft limey greens, blues, and lavenders, the lacey growth of lichens turning the ground into a fairyland of tinted hoarfrost and sugar icings. Meadowsweet, hardhack, and blueberry shrubs make a colorful middle range. Pines and balsams grow in isolated clumps with the pure white of birch bark for accents.

You can see the mountain ahead as you cross the field. Near the end where you start down a slight grade, a fairly obvious and well-worn footpath angles to the right and heads into the forest. There are few markings, only some rusted tin can lids and an occasional blue plastic ribbon. The path rises quickly into a lovely birch forest and then angles right and levels off as it crosses a small ridge. Within fifteen minutes you descend into a slight draw with an intermittent stream. After crossing the stream bed at right angles, you head up another incline and cross back to your left.

Near the summit of Catamount

The footpath becomes less clear as it rounds several large boulders, still rising steeply on bedrock. A sharp angle left below an outcrop is indicated by a white blaze on a tree at a confusing turn where some hikers have obviously gone straight ahead. After rounding the ledge, the trail rises sharply, to emerge on the first of the bare rock patches of the summit. Cairns indicate the way across each patch as the path weaves generally to the east between them and thickets of spruce and balsam.

The route turns north toward the summit as you walk across the outcrop. You are facing the sheer rock face of the southern summit, with the principal summit behind and to your left. It is an impressive sight, with the height and steepness of the peak exaggerated by the small size of the trees on the outcrop.

The path heads right to climb the lower summit from the east, first ducking into a thicket of large spruce and then emerging at the foot of the rock knob. It only takes a minute to rise above treeline on the knob, which is almost entirely bare except for patches of luscious blueberries. White arrows guide you across the bare rock in a scramble that leads to a southeast-facing chimney. Pull yourself through. Cairns direct you to turn right and back left to follow a crevice up the steep, smooth face toward the first summit (approximately 2,750 feet elevation).

The principal summit is .4 mile away and 400 feet higher, almost due north across a small valley. The scramble over big boulders down into the col is not easy. Large spruce mark the low point, then the trail rises through a wooded slope to emerge again on open rock. Painted arrows and cairns guide you along a route, which zigzags through patches of woods and over sloping bare rock. It should take less than half an hour to reach the summit.

Your first impression is how small the first summit looks. Beyond it to the right is the sharp cone of Esther, with the summit of Whiteface behind. To the west are Franklin Falls and Union Falls ponds, expansions in the Saranac River; and in the northwest, Cranberry Pond and Silver Lake. Lyon Mountain is almost due north. The Champlain Valley stretches across the eastern landscape.

To spot the row of cairns for the descent, sight from the summit to the left of the lower summit, and retrace your steps.

Pokamoonshine

Distance (round trip): 2 miles
Vertical rise: 1,260 feet
Hiking time: 2 hours
Map: USGS 15' Au Sable Forks
Fire Tower; closed Thursday, Friday

The nearly thousand-foot-high cliff on Pokamoonshine Mountain seems to hang above the Adirondack Northway (I-87) south of Interchange 33. Rockclimbers look very tiny as they challenge the heights of the Adirondack's "most awe-inspiring cliff". This is the way Bradford Van Diver describes the mountain in *Rocks and Routes of the North Country.* Before you climb Pokamoonshine, you should consult Van Diver's book to learn about the mountain's geological history and the thick, dark bands of intrusions, which etch the fault escarpment.

This is a mountain you will appreciate from below as much as from the summit. The best views of the cliff are from the Northway or from NY 9. Because the trail circles behind it to reach the summit, the major cliff is hidden from view; however, the tower on top does provide a spectacular panorama of Lake Champlain and the Green Mountains beyond in Vermont.

Sixty years ago when O'Kane wrote his book *Trails and Summits of the Adirondacks,* he remarked on the unusual display of ferns beside the trail. Today keen observers will be amazed at the variety of ferns that still edge the route. I counted twenty different species, ranging from maidenhair and silvery spleenwort to fragile fern and rusty woodsia. With ferns, views, and cliffs to enjoy, Pokamoonshine is a much more exciting climb that its short trail and low elevation would indicate.

The trailhead is in the Pok-O-Moonshine State Park (the state uses a spelling different from that of the USGS). Settling the spelling of Pokamoonshine seems as unlikely as determining its meaning. No one will probably ever know whether the mountain's peculiar name derives from the will-o'-the-wisp character of its cliffs and crags, or from the Algonquin words for broken and smooth, as proposed by Wm. M. Beauchamp in his 1907 treatise, *Aboriginal Place Names in New York.*

When you drive the three miles south to the park on NY 9 from Exit 33 on the Adirondack Northway, stop and observe the cliffs with their overhanging rocks and columnar structure. There is a day-use fee at the park. The trail begins its steep climb within 100 yards of the southern end of the campground.

The narrow, rooted, and worn trail is marked with very few old red disks, but so many hikers have preceded you that the way is obvious. Tremendous boulders and the ends of ledges rise above the trail. You angle right in a small draw, aiming at a sheer wall, and then turn left below an overhang. The route is fairly steep beneath the cliffs and moss-covered ledges. As the trail turns right along the ridge at about .3 mile, look for a side path that heads to a lovely overlook.

Beyond the overlook, the trail turns north, left, toward the mountain and, after a relatively level .2 mile in deep woods, it becomes steep again. This pitch is fairly short and leads to a level meadow and the site of the fire observer's cabin. An abandoned road heads west in front of the cabin, and there is a lean-to beside it within sight of the trail.

A footpath to the cabin's right leads to a spring on the side of the hill and continues steeply to a chimneylike opening with natural stairs between its walls. Follow it up to a level outcrop and overlook to the east. The path rejoins the red trail about 50 feet farther.

You might not have even noticed the official red trail, which headed away from the clearing about halfway between the cabin and the more obvious footpath. It leads, after rising 50 feet in elevation, to a lovely outlook through the valley to the northwest. Then it continues west to climb the summit ridge by a gentler and slightly longer route, meeting the footpath.

Beyond the junction the trail continues in the woods for 200 yards beside some irresistible blueberries and turns right to approach the tower from the west.

You can appreciate the view east without climbing the tower. From open ledges Lake Champlain stretches from north to south, wrapping around intervening hills, with the Green Mountains defining the eastern horizon. In the southwest and 1.4 miles away is the summit of Deerfield Mountain, which is almost as tall as 2,160-foot Pokamoonshine. Beyond Deerfield is the Jay Range. The fire tower on Hurricane is visible to the left of Jay Range and serves as a guidepost for identifying Nippletop, Giant, and Rocky Peak ridge, which range to Hurricane's left.

Sighting to the north of Deerfield, you

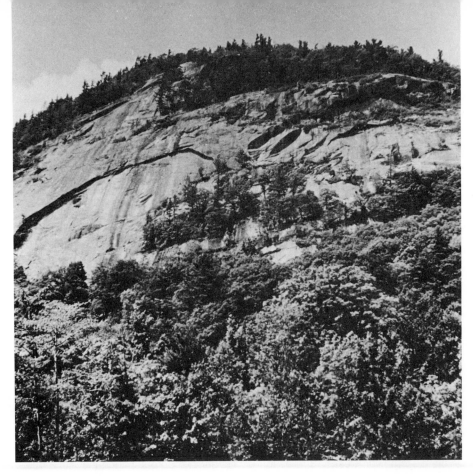

Cliffs on Pokamoonshine

can identify the Sentinel Range, followed by Whiteface, which is due west. Continuing north, the Wilmington Range, the top of Catamount, and Loon Mountain with its fire tower line the horizon. Lyon Mountain, also topped by a tower, is toward magnetic north, 28 miles away.

Rattlesnake Mountain is east of Catamount on the shore of Lake Champlain. Sight toward Lake Champlain, just to the left of Rattlesnake's summit, and you will see Four Brother Island with Willsboro Point reaching north into the lake in the foreground. In the southeast the water of Lake Champlain is interrupted by the cone of Split Rock Mountain. These two mountains should serve to orient the rest of the vast eastern landscape.

Instead of bringing the USGS maps to help you identify the remaining mountains, lakes, bays and points on Lake Champlain, you might want to use the "Adirondack Region Atlas" printed by City Street Publishing Company of Poughkeepsie, New York. That map will be your best help for locating trailheads described in this guide, and it will replace, in this case, several USGS sheets. Most of the quadrangles for Plattsburgh, Willsboro, and Port Henry cover as much of the water of Lake Champlain as the land beside it.

Pharaoh Mountain

Distance (round trip): 6 miles
Vertical rise: 1,474 feet
Hiking time: 3½ hours
Map: USGS 7½' Pharaoh Mountain
Pharaoh Lake Wilderness Area

Few mountains have as much open rock and such beautiful exposures as Pharaoh Mountain, so when the surrounding area was designated Wilderness, forcing the closing of the fire tower atop its summit, the panorama was not lost to hikers. The views encompassing the many ponds and cliff-faced hills of the Pharaoh Lake Wilderness Area are spectacular, and more distant views include a superb one of the eastern High Peaks 30 miles to the north-northwest.

You cannot help noticing Pharaoh Mountain as you drive north along the Adirondack Northway (I-87). From several places on the highway it is visible in the east beyond Schroon Lake, and its profile is most distinctive: the summit slopes south to a ledge, which in turn drops steeply south, ringed by exposed cliffs.

The entire Pharaoh Lake Wilderness is studded with hills and mountains topped by open rock, cliffs, and ledges. Most were laid bare by fires that swept the region at the turn of the century. Tall stands of hemlock mark the few areas the fire spared. The trail to Pharaoh Mountain passes through one extraordinary stand immediately south of Crane Pond and then through a variety of sec-

ond growth as it climbs the mountain's flanks, most of which were burned by those fires.

Several public campgrounds are near the trailhead. Two are accessible from Exit 28 off the Northway and either might serve as your base in the Pharaoh Lake Wilderness. The first is a small campground on Paradox Lake, off NY 74 a short distance east of the exit. A much larger campground is on the shore of Putnam Pond, at the edge of the Pharaoh Lake Wilderness. To reach it, drive east on NY 74 for 12.5 miles to Chilsom and turn south. The campground is 3 miles south of NY 74.

A third state campground, Eagle Point, is nearly at the southern end of the lake off this road and is more easily reached from Exit 26. For private accommodations, follow NY 9 south from Exit 28, paralleling the Northway and the western shore of Schroon Lake.

To approach the trailhead from the Northway's Exit 28, drive south on NY 9 for .6 mile and turn left, east, on Alder Meadow Road. After passing East Shore Road, on the right at 2 miles, the road continues as Crane Pond Road. It is a very pretty drive east, passing a lovely farm shortly before angling south at 4.5 miles. Park on the east side of the road at the turn. People do drive beyond, and motorized access is permitted, though it may shortly be restricted. If you have a four-wheel-drive vehicle you may proceed with caution; if not, you probably should walk. Certainly adding 1.9 miles on a handsome dirt road to the trip is not too much for a day hike, though the total 9.8-mile hike now becomes a full day's outing.

Beyond the parking turnout, the road climbs a small valley beside Alder Creek on a small bridge (3-ton limit) and descends through a terrible washed-out stretch almost to the level of Alder Pond. Near the end of the road, .2 mile from Crane Pond, there is a temporary parking area. Beyond, the road fords a flow created by beaver in Alder Pond and since it may call for a wet crossing, walk north around the flow. Shortly you reach a promontory covered with magnificent pines that borders Crane Pond.

If you prefer wilderness camping, you will find numerous campsites and fire rings along the west shore of Crane Pond, a truly handsome body of water edged with white pine and huge boulders.

The Pharaoh Mountain Trail begins at

Pharaoh Lake

the narrow spit of land separating Crane and Alder ponds. The route, marked with red disks, heads south across a bridge and immediately plunges into a deep woods. Hemlock and pine darken the needle-strewn trail. Even on a bright day, the route can be as dark as night, and the walking may be the best in the Adirondacks. The forest is stately and mature, with pine exceeding three feet in diameter.

Within twenty minutes you reach a junction with another red trail. Turn right to continue south toward Pharaoh Mountain. The sign says the summit is 2.3 miles away. Within a few minutes you pass Glidden Marsh. Stop for a few minutes and walk toward the water to enjoy the reflections in the pond of surrounding tall pine and Pharaoh Mountain.

Boulders and erratics are strewn across the hillside as you continue, but the walking is easy. You pass a picnic table and a campsite and then cross a little stream on a moss-covered bridge. Foamflowers and white violets edge the trail. You soon notice a gentle rise in the trail, and the cover changes from evergreen to birch and maple. The route seems to fork, but you have just reached one of many intersections the trail makes with the telephone line that ran to the tower. The two routes intertwine most of the way up the mountain, the telephone line making the straightest, steepest route and the trail winding about more gently.

Stands of mature hemlock alternate with a hardwood cover of yellow birch and beech. Within an hour you are climbing fairly steeply, and already you will have arrived at sections where the trail has worn through the thin topsoil to bedrock. As the trees become obviously smaller, the dominant evergreen is spruce. After an hour and a half of walking you will notice the trees are quite small, and the trail is very steep and

laced with tangled spruce roots. Ten minutes before reaching the top you will find a welcome spring on the side of the trail where water runs from beneath a rock shelf. The first opening gives you a view back to the High Peaks, with Giant clearly distinguishable. The fire tower, though slated for removal, is still standing beside a small cabin on the 2,556-foot summit where grassy patches and blueberries cling to crevices between the smooth rock.

To enjoy the panorama, you should bring the USGS quadrangles for Schroon Lake, Elizabethtown, Mount Marcy, Lake George, and North Creek. First survey the pond-studded wilderness below you. The largest pond is Pharaoh Lake, which lies southeast below the mountain; Whortleberry Pond is to its right. Whortleberries are not an exotic fruit, just an archaic name for the blueberries that grow so profusely in the area.

Schroon Lake lies to the west, only a portion of its 10-mile length visible. Ranging south of west on the horizon are Gore, Eleventh, and Crane mountains. Continuing on toward south you can see the tops of the mountains that rim Lake George rising in the distance over Pharaoh Lake. The valleys of Lake George and Northwest Bay are obvious, as are Black, Elephant, Erebus, and Buck mountains on the east shore and the Tip of the Tongue on the west shore.

To the west, to the right of Gore, lies Moxon Ridge. Looking to the distant northwest you can see Blue Mountain and Vanderwhacker over the northern tip of Schroon Lake. To their right lie Blue Ridge and Hoffman mountains. Farther right, or north, is Boreas, and then come the High Peaks.

Skylight, Marcy, and Haystack have similar cone-shaped summits from this angle. They range up to 25 miles away. With familiarity you can name Basin, Saddleback, Gothics, Nippletop, McComb, and Dix, which follow next from left to right.

The valley of NY 73 as it cuts through the mountains beside the north forks of Boquet and the Ausable is next, with Giant and Rock Peak Ridge standing isolated to the right. Northeast and close lies Treadway, whose rocky summit can be reached by a trail from Putnam Pond. The Green Mountains of Vermont stretch out in the distance to fill the eastern panorama.

You will find several good places to camp overnight on the mountain, sleeping under the stars. Fireplaces and fire rings mark the best places.

The hour and a half it takes to return to Crane Pond seems remarkably easy, as does the whole day's outing.

Pharaoh Ponds Loop

Distance (around loop): 15 miles
Vertical rise: 1,000 feet
Hiking time: 8½–9 hours
Maps: USGS 7½' Pharaoh Mountain; USGS 7½' Graphite
Pharaoh Lake Wilderness Area

Imagine visiting sixteen ponds in one day! The ponds are connected by a marvelous network of trails in the heart of the Pharaoh Lake Wilderness Area. The map for this area shows only fifteen ponds, but a beaver dam now impounds the waters of a sixteenth, smack in the middle of one of the trails. Beaver have flooded many parts of this wilderness, enlarging ponds, creating new ones, flooding trails, and occasionally making life confusing for the hiker.

There are numerous accesses to the Pharaoh Lake Wilderness Area, but the Crane Pond access, used in the preceding hike for Pharaoh Mountain (Hike 26), provides the shortest entrance to this loop.

Much has been written about the heavy use of the Pharaoh Lake area, but the greatest use is closest to the principal accesses: Crane Pond; the two trailheads on NY 74 in the north; Beaver Pond Road north of Brandt Lake, which is the southern access; and the Putnam Pond State Campground, an excellent base when you hike in the area. On this fantastic loop, you reach the heart of the Wilderness and travel far from the popular area. (Because this route is a loop,

you may begin at other points; a logical alternate is from Putnam Pond, although the hike then is slightly longer.)

Starting from Crane Pond, your first steps take you over the bridge across the outlet from Crane Pond, which flows into Alder Pond. The contrast between those two ponds is typical of what you experience throughout this hike. Crane Pond is fairly deep and has a high, dry shoreline dotted with paper birch; Alder Pond is a marsh with alders, reeds, and grasses crowding its wet shoreline.

The trail bears red markers for .7 mile, following the same route as the Pharaoh Mountain hike. The wide, needle-strewn trail through tall hemlock provides easy walking.

Within fifteen minutes, you reach the first junction, where the red-marked trail heads to the right toward Pharaoh Mountain. Take the left fork, marked with blue, straight into a small clearing and then back into deep forest on a narrow path. The signs here indicate that Crab Pond is 2 miles away, that Pharaoh Lake is 3.2 miles away, and that Putnam Pond is 8.3 miles away. There are inconsistencies on many of the signs in the Wilderness, and this one is no exception. Crab Pond is barely over 1 mile from the junction.

The route runs past huge boulders and glacial erratics, and into a deep hemlock valley where you cross a stream on a good hiker's bridge. It continues beside a small boggy marsh with corduroy stretches helping to keep the trail dry. Within ten minutes you cover the .4-mile distance to Glidden Marsh, a long, thin, shallow watercourse filled with lily pads and reflecting the tall pines surrounding it. A few steps past your first approach to the marsh you reach another trail intersection with confusing distance notations. A sign indicates correctly that the right fork, which climbs the hill northeast of the marsh, leads in 1.7 miles to Horseshoe Pond. You will use this route when you return much later in the day. It is not true, however, that any part of Pharaoh Lake is only 2.2 miles south, as posted, and it is obvious that 2.2 and .4 do not add up to the 3.2 miles the sign at the very first intersection indicated. Ignore the discrepancies and simply enjoy the diversity of ponds you meet.

At this junction, head south, now on the yellow trail, along the shore of Glidden Marsh. The trail, a narrow footpath showing little sign of use, winds through a mixed forest of birch, pine, and striped maple, a forest only fires could have created. It contrasts sharply with the huge hemlock of the first part of the trip. As you round a big boulder you have a fine view back the length of the marsh. Continue past the long, thick meadow of cattails, reeds, cedars, and spectacular paper birch whose reflections glisten in the narrow watercourse flowing through the marsh.

After crossing the inlet stream on a slippery three-log bridge, turn away from the flow. The trail climbs into a very dense hemlock thicket, where you should spot one of the forest's giants, a spruce with a diameter exceeding 2½ feet.

Again the forest changes, this time to mature hardwoods with tall straight birch and maple. An understory of horse nettles crowds the trail. You should learn to recognize these plants, for although their sting persists no more than a couple of hours, it is still uncomfortable.

You quickly reach an intersection where a red-marked trail heads back left, northeast, .4 mile to Crab Pond. Your route is straight ahead on the yellow trail, where the sign points optimistically to Pharaoh Lake just "1.5 miles" away. As the trail climbs the lower slopes of Pharaoh Mountain, a deep valley opens to your left. Beech die-back has caused a number of trees to fall across the trail, obscuring it slightly.

After walking for an hour and ten minutes from Crane Pond, you will find the trail detouring right around a beaver flow. This is a good example of the impediments hikers meet in this wilderness, for just a few years ago, they flooded the trail causing this realignment. All the valleys here are at about the same elevation. They were scoured by glaciers, and until recently held glacial ponds. This makes it easy for beaver to enlarge or create new ponds, which they do every few years.

Beyond the flow, the trail crosses its inlet stream. You then continue high on the hillside in an area where dead beech have so opened the forest floor that underbrush is filling the trail. You continue beside the stream and a rather eerie little swamp filled with huge clumps of all the osmunda ferns: royal, cinnamon, and interrupted. Stumps covered with lichens and mosses are rotting in the algae-filled water. Beyond it, you begin a fairly steep descent of over 300 feet to Pharaoh Lake, 3.6 miles.

You first approach the lake near a small inlet stream and then head east along the sinuous shoreline, reaching a lean-to within twenty minutes. On the way, you cross a small hemlock-covered ridge dotted with paper birch. The east side of the ridge overlooks Split Rock Bay, which serves as a reflecing pool for a group of nature's more handsome sculptures, boulders worn smooth by the last glacier. As you round the bay you find a sign for a spring and a pipe spewing cold, clear water. Beyond it three split-log bridges cross the marsh at the head of the bay, and the trail leads to the hemlock- and pine-covered promontory where the lean-to is located.

The lean-to has one of the world's better settings: views of the pond and, overhanging it, Pharaoh Mountain, with its rock slides clearly visible. If you are lucky you may spot great blue heron nesting nearby. You surely should stop here for a rest and lunch. The lean-to is just under 4 miles from Crane Pond, and a candidate for a camping stop if you wish to break the hike into segments.

The yellow trail continues behind the lean-to up a small ridge covered with hemlock. The trail is so unused that little foot tread is visible. As you approach another of Pharaoh's swampy bays, look for a short waterfall on a small stream entering from the left. The trail continues just east of south to still another bay, this one with a long view of the lake. You reach a major trail junction at 4.8 miles on the bay's shore less than twenty minutes from the lean-to. Here a sign directs you back along the shore of the bays to Wintergreen Point or Split Rock Bay, straight south along the lakeshore, or east toward Grizzle Ocean. The last route is the one you want. It is a narrow trail up a small hill. Within ten minutes you reach the end of Wolf Pond, a swampy-bordered, dying pond filled with water lilies and pond weeds and framed with high evergreens. Some of the tallest pines in this Wilderness grow on its far shore.

The trail continues along the flow, making a hairpin turn north to avoid swamps. In this vicinity you encounter several peculiar ridges, long thin sinuous chains. Because the trail stays high and dry on top of most, and runs up and down and across a few, you enjoy pleasant walking. The ridges, "roche moutonee," or sheep backs, were sculptured by glaciers. The residual hummocks of bedrock lying in the direction of the ice flow have smooth curved edges parallel to the movement of the ice. At the northern end of the hairpin turn you descend to the level of the swamps and then cross a part of them under a moss-covered ledge. As you climb the shoulder of a small hill, the marsh continues to accompany you on your right, now west.

You now begin to climb the hill east of the swamp, realizing that the hairpin detour took you nearly 1 mile, and ninety minutes, out of your way. First turn sharply left away from the swamp and follow a small stream on a trail that hardly appears to have been used. It passes through a tall and stately hardwood forest, very gradually gaining elevation. You are walking through the long thin valley between Grizzle Ocean Mountain and Thunderbolt Mountain. The stretch is probably the least exciting in the entire loop, a dull walk through what develops into an interminable draw. You need about an hour and a half to walk from the eastern bay of Pharaoh Lake to Grizzle Ocean. Perhaps you can enjoy spending part of the time speculating on the origin of Grizzle Ocean's name. It is certainly one of the Adirondacks' most inventive. One Adirondack historian claims the name derives from the wild bragging of a fisherman named Tom Grizzle. His tales so astounded his listeners that they began to refer to his secret pond as Grizzle's Ocean.

Your first glimpse of Grizzle Ocean at

7.5 miles, 2.7 miles from the intersection at Pharaoh Lake, is at the edge of a narrow swampy finger of the pond where a forest of evergreen stumps gives a ragged look to the shoreline. A sign by a trail with blue markers (the state brochure shows them as red) notes, "trail around pond." Take that trail a short distance to the right, south, for a better look at the entire pond with its pine- and birch-covered shoreline, but with so many miles to go, you will probably want to go back to the sign and take the left trail for the shortest trek. A loop around the pond would add at least .5 mile to the planned route.

Bearing left keeps you on the yellow-marked trail, which almost immediately turns across a moss-filled swamp on a sinking and decrepit log bridge. It brings you into a forest of hemlock so dense it can seem as dark as night. You encounter another marked intersection in about .2 mile. Here the right fork leads to the east side of Grizzle Ocean and its lean-to, ".15 miles" away. The sign that says it is 6.6 miles to Crane Pond is incorrect.

Stay on the yellow trail, heading north. The trail shows a lot of use and can even be muddy. It descends steeply beside the outlet of Grizzle Ocean through a deep and handsome valley, crosses the stream, and continues beside it to a marked intersection, a distance of .8 mile from your first approach to Grizzle Ocean. You could walk to Putnam Pond and the campsite there by following the right fork on a blue-marked trail. For the route past ponds less frequently visited, stay left on the yellow trail. Within a few hundred feet you glimpse a marshy end of Putnam Pond. Within fifteen minutes, approximately .4 mile, your trail intersects one that leads from a boat landing on the shore of Putnam Pond to the summit of Treadway Mountain.

The loop walk is full of lovely places,

and one appears in the next 200 yards, where the trail follows the outlet of Mud Pond. Another marshy lake, it offers lovely views across to part of Treadway Mountain.

The trail continues beside a stream after leaving Mud Pond, this time the outlet of Clear Pond at 8.2 miles. Just south of Clear Pond a red trail forks left across the stream and heads around the west side of the pond. There you may choose either fork, for distance is no factor. However, the right fork, on the pond's east side, passes a lean-to, a perfect place to rest. It is perched on a small ledge above the pond, which has deep clear water and views of Big Clear Pond Mountain. Swimming is good from the ledge. A trail with yellow markers heads east behind the lean-to to another boat launching site on Putnam Pond. The access accounts for the signs of heavier use at Clear Pond.

The route north along Clear Pond has blue markers, and within ten minutes it intersects the red trail from the west side of the pond. The route north climbs through a deep valley with ledges on either side, facing the long round-topped ridges that characterize this Wilderness. The trail emerges on a saddle in a white birch thicket and then turns right to descend toward Rock Pond. As the trail turns, you can see Rock Pond down to the north through the trees, but the trail reaches it by a roundabout route, heading first almost to the shore of Little Rock Pond. Within thirty minutes from Clear Pond you reach at 9.3 miles another trail intersection. The intersection is 1.1 miles from the Clear Pond lean-to. The trail that continues north here, eventually leading to NY 74, may be used to reach a lean-to on the northeast shore of Little Rock Pond. Leave the trail and walk east to inspect Little Rock Pond, with its lovely reflections.

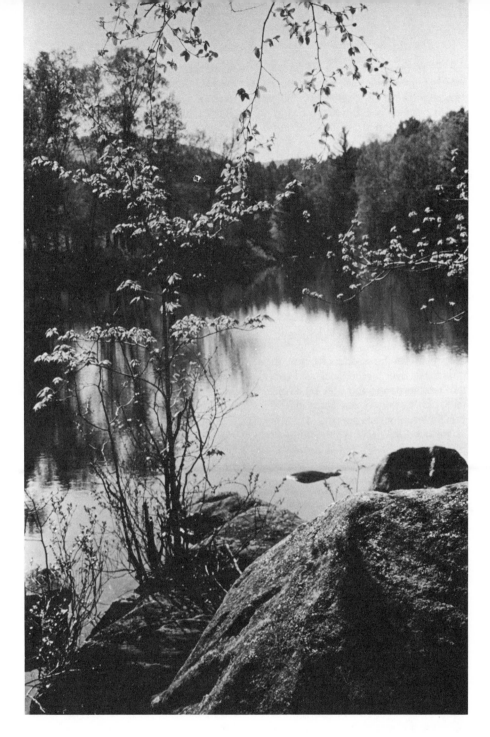

Crane Pond

For the loop, however, you turn left, west, at the intersection, on a red trail heading toward Lily Pad Pond. The stated distance of 5.5 miles to Crane Pond on the sign at the intersection is accurate.

After the trail passes the marshy end of Rock Pond, it follows closely the pond's southwest lobe. What a surprise the pond is, with rocks and boulders edging and emerging from it. Everywhere, smooth light gray ledges rise from the water. The trail is dry and little used, shaded with tall maple and white birch. The ledges are the best places on the entire loop from which to swim. After you cross a small inlet stream on the pond's southwest corner, you head north where the trail presents views northeast to ledges on Bear Pond Mountain. Small cliffs rise above you on the west shore, and huge pine tower over the hemlock and birch that rim the pond. You walk on ledges thick with carpets of needles and bunchberry, and an opening with a view of the pond may entice you into a short break.

A sign near the outlet states that Lily Pad Pond is 1.1 miles away. By this time you may have solved the mystery of the lost miles. Someone has calculated the distances between ponds as if they were point sources, forgetting that the trails often follow the pond's shorelines for quite a distance. The walk beside Rock Pond alone occupies twenty-five minutes.

The trail heads west near the outlet, and within ten minutes you should see an intermittent stream entering from the left, south. In wet times, it tumbles in a waterfall from the high ledges that face Peaked Hill. A short distance farther, less than a five-minute walk, you hear a waterfall on your right on the outlet of Rock Pond. This one should be explored, so leave the trail and walk below a small cliff from which the outlet emerges in a series of vertical drops, forming a cascade nearly 50 feet high. Be careful walking on the talus-strewn base of the cliff that leads to the edge of a small pool into which one chute of the waterfall plunges.

Return to the trail, and continue downhill to a marsh on your right. Another of the strange stump forests, it has recently been flooded and is full of birds. You should be able to spot Potter Mountain north across the swamp. The walking here is rough, for a new footpath has been worn to avoid the flooded marshes. You leave the marsh, heading southwest, beside a small stream along a trail choked with maple starts and viburnum, the new growth on the forest floor filling the open spaces created by dead beech, a few of which lie across the trail. The relatively obscure trail from the outlet of Rock Pond to Lily Pad lean-to requires thirty-five or forty minutes of walking. You may want to stop at the lean-to for a brief rest. Just remember to keep at least two more hours of daylight to walk the remaining distance. Lily Pad Pond is minute, choked with lily pads, but nevertheless it is a beautiful camping place.

The red trail ends at 11.3 miles, .1 mile from Lily Pad Pond, within sight of the pond's outlet. Here it intersects a blue trail. The right fork heads north toward NY 74. The sign points to Tubmill Pond, which you will not find on your map. It is another of the Wilderness's newcomers, a beaver pond filling the huge marsh east of Crane Pond. The area is shown as a marsh in the 1954 USGS 15-minute series, and as a real, but unnamed, flow on the newer 7½-minute series. Take the left fork, continuing southwest up a short steep pitch through a low scrub on a trail that could become more overgrown in the future as the beech that cover it continue to fall.

The trail crosses a high pine-covered

ledge with a crunchy lichen tread. Fires have opened the hillside, and a sign on the ledge points toward 2,248-foot-high Treadway Mountain and toward 2,551-foot-high Pharaoh Mountan. As the trail descends around a marsh you begin to notice steep ledges below on your left and a stream, which flows toward Crab Pond. If you are making the walk in summer you can enjoy a few blueberries on the ridge before descending to Horseshoe Pond.

Horseshoe is a half-hour walk from Lily Pad. A small rock promontory jutting into the pond from the west gives it its horseshoe shape. The peninsula has been used for camping. The trail zigzags down a sharp, almost vertical, drop beside the rock wall over which the outlet flows. Immediately at 12.2 miles you see Crab Pond, for only a stone's throw separates the two ponds.

Crab Pond's picturesque shoreline hosts the trail for over .5 mile. Giant pines topping rounded boulders that seem to rise from the water provide delightful companions. But, before you walk beside its shores, you have to cross its inlet, and there is no bridge. In low water you may not believe this could ever be a problem. Suitable stepping stones can be found, even in high water, but you may have to walk away from the trail to do so.

All of the ponds are lovely, in their distinctive ways, but Crab is especially beautiful. Cliffs and ledges on its northern shore are accentuated with pine and white birch. You will spot at least one beaver house. This marvelously handsome section of trail is sometimes close to the pond and sometimes above it on a hemlock-covered knoll overlooking a new beaver flow. You will find a lovely rocky knoll for a brief rest about halfway along the shore, this one surmounted with red

pine and white birch, lady's slippers and lichen, and within sight of the sheer rock face of Peaked Hill.

For a time the trail takes a course transverse to the ledges, so the route is up and over and down and up again. There is a short spur trail that continues southwest, but the signpost may be missing. In any event, you should continue around the western end of Crab, heading west toward Oxshoe. This route takes you through a mixed forest and past another unnamed swamp with a pine-covered knoll. Within twenty minutes you reach the southern end of Oxshoe Pond, at just over 13.4 miles, where a lean-to caps a ledge covered with enormous white pine. There is a beautiful view up the pond's length across to wonderful ledges.

From here it should not take ten minutes to climb over a height-of-land west-southwest to the lean-to, and to drop over 100 feet, the last of it fairly steep, to Glidden Marsh. Here you take the right fork, the blue trail, north. You only have .4 mile to go on this trail before reaching the wide and easy .7-mile stretch that takes you to Crane Pond. It is surprising how muddy stretches and a little corduroy can trip you up at the end of a long walk. However, retracing the last .7 mile is so easy that you will almost feel refreshed as the trail emerges at Crane Pond with birches glistening and reflecting the setting sun.

You certainly can break this 15-mile day hike into a camping trip of at least three nights, using some of the lean-tos noted; but the easy, relatively gentle route makes a fantastic one-day hike. And when the road to Crane Pond is closed, the additional 3.8 miles will make this too long for a day hike.

Severance Hill

Distance (round trip): 2 miles
Vertical rise: 880 feet
Hiking time: 1¼ hours
Map: USGS 15' Schroon Lake

The walk up Severance Hill is so short and gentle that you can easily make it your first climb in the Adirondacks even after a long day's drive. If you are planning several days of hiking in the eastern Adirondacks, this small mountain is an ideal place to become acquainted with the region's hills.

The summit of Severance Hill offers several rocky open perches with commanding views of Schroon Lake and the Pharaoh Lake Wilderness to the east. The 880-foot climb to the 1,693-foot summit is scarcely more than 1 mile long and takes forty-five minutes at most. The summit is a perfect place for a picnic, perhaps over an early evening campfire to watch the rays of the setting sun play across the normally dark summit of Pharaoh Mountain. From here you can understand why that mountain was first known by Indians as Ondewa, or the Black One.

From Severance, Schroon Lake stretches out to the south between the hills. The origin of that lake's name is still shrouded in mystery. Donaldson in *The History of the Adirondacks* wrote that early French settlers at Crown Point "named it in honor of Madame Scarron,

young and beautiful wife of the famous wild and comic writer Paul Scarron . . . I am not alone in wishing the story might be true—that this humble but fascinating goose-girl, who became wife of a physically misshapen poet, and later, as Madame de Maintenon, the wife of a morally misshapen king, had given the imprint of her memory to a lovely lake in the American wilderness."

Severance itself bears the name of settlers who reached the area in the early 1820s. Walking the hills in the Adirondacks you cannot help but be fascinated by the origins of the names, and the histories of the families who once lived in what is now the Forest Preserve. Most of the early nineteenth-century settlers were loggers and lumbermen. The few farmers eked out a meager subsistence in the cold north. Many early families in the Schroon Lake area were attracted by work in the iron mines north of Paradox Lake.

The beginning of the trail up Severance is unusual. The Adirondack Northway (I-87) cut direct access from Schroon Lake to the range of hills west of the lake and NY 9, so a hikers' underpass was constructed beneath the highway. Take

Beyond a hikers' bridge you come out of the cedar swamp thicket to begin climbing again, this time into a forest of magnificent tall trees with huge pine and hemlock shading ground cedars and other lycopodia on the forest floor. You may want to stop and study the pines spared by early loggers. Most of the largest have double or triple trunks, which were spurned by loggers, but a few significant single trunks can be found. The route seems straight up through evergreens and immense paper birch. You cross a second level, angling south, then zigzag back to the north and begin to climb again. The trees, now mostly oak and considerably smaller, open out to rock ledges from which the views begin.

The first lovely promontory you reach looks across to Pharaoh Mountain and down the full length of Schroon Lake. Patches of wild columbine grow beneath the scrub oak that cover the summit. You will find several stone fireplaces on the open rock. Walk north to a second opening that overlooks Paradox Lake and the mountains to its north. High water brings Paradox Lake two outlets, hence the name, to explain that peculiar phenomenon.

The summit in early spring seems to be a choice place for watching migrating warblers. Within a half-hour I identified the Blackburnian, the blackpoll, the yellowthroat, and an ovenbird.

Because the walk is so short, consider combining it with a visit to the Natural Stone Bridge and Caves at Pottersville, west of the south end of Schroon Lake. The caves are a privately owned tourist attraction, and an entrance fee is charged. Plenty of signs direct you from NY 9 at Exit 26 off the Northway, west 1.7 miles to the caves and adjacent lunch and picnic facilities. More than enough signs point out the scenic wonders along the self-guided tour

the Northway's Exit 28 at NY 74, north of Schroon Lake village, and head south on NY 9 toward town. Driving less than .6 mile south you pass Alder Meadow Road on the left. Immediately beyond that road turn right into a parking area.

Before starting make sure you have water, for the summit is very dry. The trail, denoted by yellow markers, begins at the western edge of the parking area. Your first steps take you through a narrow culvert under the Northway and then through a flat area on a broad trail covered with pine needles and shaded by a low forest of pine, maple, birch, spruce, balsam, and popple. After five minutes you start to head gradually up into a tall cedar forest. The broad, smooth trail soon becomes steeper. A small stream gurgles in the valley to your right, and you may notice an old roadway entering from that side. Continue straight, and within twenty minutes the trail briefly levels out. Here the forest is open enough for you to see the top of Severance Hill ahead. You may still hear traffic noises from the highway below as you enter a patch of wet woods that throbs with bird songs. I spotted a scarlet tanager and a black-throated blue warbler, both at the side of the trail.

View from Severance Hill, with Pharaoh Mountain in the distance

through the site. The path winds past caves cut out in the Grenville bedrock and beside huge potholes scoured out in the stream bed by giant grindstones. Trout Brook, whose waters created the caves, disappears into clefts in the rock, reappearing again in the gorge below to provide reflecting pools for the handsomely sculptured rock walls.

The Pottersville caves are a great place to begin learning the geology of the Adirondacks, and the owners can tell you much about the area's more common minerals. Their gift shop has a range of literature on geologic subjects to enhance all your walks through the mountains.

Crane Mountain

Distance (around loop): 4.8 miles
Vertical rise: 1,300 feet
Hiking time: 4 hours
Map: USGS 15' North Creek

Crane Mountain is my favorite Adirondack peak. I have introduced many people to its trails, and because they share my enthusiasm, they, too, return almost yearly to enjoy this perfect hike.

Crane is a massive mountain, isolated from surrounding peaks and commanding great views in all directions. Its steep slopes offer a challenging climb, and its bare rocks provide unrestricted overlooks.

If you are coming from the north or west to climb Crane, which lies in the middle of the southeastern Adirondacks, you will find the easiest approach is from NY 8. Turn south at Johnsburg onto South Johnsburg Road and drive to Thurman. There, take Garnet Lake Road, which is marked with a sign for Crane Mountain.

There is no easy route from the south and east. You could take the Adirondack Northway (I-87) to Exit 25 and head southwest on NY 8 through Chestertown to Johnsburg. Or, you could pull out a road map and improvise a route through Luzerne or Warrensburg. The major roads trend north-south, so winding east toward Thurman by way of Stony Creek or Thurman Station inevitably involves a

circuitous route on a number of back roads. You never know what you will discover along them, so allow a little extra traveling time if you choose a complicated approach.

Shortly after turning onto Garnet Lake Road you are treated to a lovely view of Crane. Drive west from Thurman 1.2 miles to a fork and bear right, continuing west on a newly widened dirt road whose condition depends on the amount of recent rainfall, despite constant care. After 1.5 miles the road turns sharply left toward the Ski Hi Lodge, but you continue straight for just under .5 mile to the marked trailhead.

Were you to continue on Garnet Lake Road to circle Crane Mountain by car, you would have a dozen places to view its sheer rock faces and its companion peak to the north, Huckleberry Mountain, which appears to have been split off Crane by some giant cleaver. The name Huckleberry should be your clue to plan your trip in midsummer, for some of the best blueberrying in the Adirondacks is on Crane and Huckleberry mountains.

The trees near the trailhead are reminders that Crane, like so many Adirondack mountains, was ravaged by fierce fires. Aspen, maple, and birch saplings are sprinkled with white pine, all pioneering trees. Both ends of your loop meet at this trailhead. By the northern route, on which you start this hike, it is 1.9 miles to the summit. You return on the western spur, a trail that bypasses the private land and leads quickly to Putnam Farm Road and another trail up the mountain. By this route, which takes you past Crane Mountain Pond, it is 2.9 miles from the summit to the trailhead. You may, of course, walk the loop in the opposite direction.

Following the red disks of the northern, or right-hand trail, you soon enter a forest with a deep canopy cover of white and yellow birch interspersed with beech and maple. Within ten minutes, the grade becomes quite steep. You are about to climb 700 vertical feet in .4 mile.

As the grade steepens, the trees become smaller, with pine emerging dominant. Many rock outcrops appear, and very early on you come to openings with views back to the southwest.

After a forty-minute walk and a climb of about 600 feet, the trail approaches ledges of anorthosite gneiss, where you find good views to the west. Within another five minutes you reach a second large rock outcrop, where the continuing trail is poorly marked. Walk about halfway out on the open rock before heading up across it. You should see a marker a little east of north on a dead pine. Within another three minutes you reach a trail junction. The left fork is a spur trail leading .4 mile west to Crane Mountain Pond.

Turn right for the .8-mile continuing climb to the just over 3,200-foot summit.

Your route is toward the east, moderately uphill at first, but steep enough in one place to require use of a new 6-foot ladder. The trail enters a balsam and spruce thicket and heads almost southeast below the cliffs that face the summit, trending northwest to southeast. Less than fifteen minutes from the junction, you will have covered most of the distance to the summit, leaving only a bit more than a 100-foot scramble up the cliff. The trail turns sharply left, climbing on almost bare rock. There are almost no wires left holding a 15-foot ladder to the rock wall. They may be replaced, but if the ladder appears shaky it is definitely safer to climb using the good handholds in the rock ledge to the right of the ladder. As you reach the uppermost rock ledge, head left about 100 yards to the actual summit.

You will find views from almost every point along the summit ridge. The first view east stretches all the way to the southern end of the Green Mountains, with the mountains on the east shore of Lake George clearly identifiable in between. To the south Moose and Baldhead almost conceal the summit of Hadley. Walking west along the ridge you can enjoy the view across the valley defined by Garnet Lake Road. Garnet Lake is southwest, and the string of sharp hills on its western shore lead to the rocky cone of Mount Blue.

Views to the west and north improve as you continue west. The best are from a large outcrop at the end of a short spur path branching south, left, .2 mile from the summit. So many hikers have walked this part that you should have no difficulty finding the unmarked turn, which is just before the trail descends steeply into the woods. The outcrop overlooks Crane Mountain Pond. Across the pond, in the northeast, lies massive Eleventh Mountain. Use it to orient the distant horizon. Over it and 24 miles away lies Snowy, the knob and cliff face of its summit always easy to identify. To its left is Speculator Mountain; Pillsbury is a little north of east, between Speculator and Snowy on the horizon. North of Snowy and 7 miles farther is the summit of Blue Mountain. To the right of Eleventh Mountain is the steep and unmistakable cone of Height of Land Mountain, and next, toward magnetic north, is Gore.

In the small angle between Gore and due north, the High Peaks are visible. It was easier to name individual peaks before the new tree growth began to crowd the vista, but Santanoni on the west and Nippletop on the east offer the easiest profiles to identify. Dix and Giant are to the right of Nippletop. Marcy, Haystack, Basin, and Gothics are prominent between Santanoni and Nippletop. If you want to be certain about the peaks you see, you will need the USGS quadrangles for the area and good binoculars.

Continue descending the main trail toward Crane Pond. When you reach a muddy stretch at pond level, turn left to continue the loop. The intersection is frequently flooded. (If you are adventurous, turn right on the unmarked path, which dwindles out as it approaches a small knob north of the pond. You can easily wind between rock outcrops to a point on the southern side of the knob that has a special view across Crane Mountain Pond to the outlet, with the summits of several distant mountains unexpectedly rising over treetops in the south.) Heading generally west on the trail around the southern edge of the pond, you pass the intersection with the spur trail, several places campers have used, and a smooth rock that leads to a good swimming spot.

There is no mystery about the name Crane, for old-timers tell stories of crane nesting in the vicinity of the pond. However, the mountain's namesake pond, which lies nestled on a shelf west of the summit, has provoked comment. There are rumors that it has no outlet and that it has two outlets. There is some truth to both. Midsummer droughts can so reduce water draining into the pond that no water flows from it along the principal outlet to the southwest, which you will soon cross. A swamp on the north of the pond drains into Crystal Brook, and in high water times water sometimes also flows into the brook, seeping from the swamp as if from a hidden outlet of the lake.

It is 1 mile from the summit to the outlet of the pond, which you cross to begin the steep descent toward Putnam Farm.

Across the outlet of Crane Pond

Again, if you are adventurous, you can easily make your way north-northwest along the top of Crane's western summit ridge toward several other outcrops with good vantages south and west.

Crane, like all the mountains west of the Hudson, was scoured by a glacier, which left a gentler slope on the northwest but scraped smooth the cliffs on the southeastern flanks. And, like many neighboring mountains, Crane was ravaged by forest fires so intense that the thin organic topsoils that had accumulated since the last glacier were also consumed. The pattern of open rock interwoven with pockets of shallow mineral soils is typical. From the pockets spread the pioneering lichens and mosses that slowly create soil to support scrub balsam, spruce, and birch. In June, pink lady's slippers thrive beneath the evergreens. And along the sunny edges, blueberries produce abundant crops.

Stay on the trail beyond the outlet crossing, for the smooth, rounded slopes are deceptively steep. This trail is steeper than the route up, dropping nearly 900 feet in little more than .5 mile. It heads east-southeast, generally following the outlet and crossing it again after about a 200-foot drop in elevation from the pond.

This is the only place you may have problems on the descent. Stay close to the stream and do not venture out on the escarpment. The trail reenters the woods just a few feet from the stream.

After .4 mile the trail heads south, away from the stream, to intersect Putnam Farm Road. Just before reaching the road, about .8 mile from the pond, the trail crosses a stream on a natural stone bridge. The tiny stream disappears into a cave of Precambrian marble, and re-emerges about 50 feet away, only to disappear again in a still larger cave. The cap of granitic gneiss that constitutes the bulk of Crane Mountain overlays a belt of marble. There is a second layer of marble and easily eroded rock at the level of the pond; it has been worn away to create the bench that contains the pond and gives Crane its distinctive stepped profile.

Beyond the cave, turn left to follow the old road toward your car. Both the roadway and a bypass, .2 mile from the parking area, are marked. The bypass circles private land to reach the trailhead.

You can make the circuit described in four hours, but I have never spent less than six hours on the mountain. There is so much to see and enjoy that you may want to plan an even longer trip.

Siamese Ponds

Distance (round trip): 13.2 miles
Vertical rise: 600 feet
Hiking time: 7 hours
Map: USGS 15' Thirteenth Lake
Siamese Ponds Wilderness Area

The Siamese Ponds are a favorite southern Adirondack camping destination. They lie at the heart of the Siamese Ponds Wilderness Area, a region so remote that the trails to them are the only break in some fifty square miles of surrounding forest.

The Siamese Ponds access trails are among the few marked, state-maintained trails in the Wilderness Area. Most other destinations in this forest are reached by either informal paths or bushwhacks (see *Discover the South Central Adirondacks* for details of over ninety nearby trips).

Hikers carrying a pack for overnight camping need as much as four hours for the roughly 6.6-mile trek into the ponds, but day hikers can make the 13.2-mile round trip in seven hours. That is just walking time, though. You should add at least three more hours for exploring, swimming, and picnicking.

This hike follows the East Branch of the Sacandaga access trail, which begins on NY 8 between Wells and Wevertown. If you are traveling from the south or west, turn east on NY 8 at the intersections of NY 8 and NY 30 north of Wells, and drive 13.5 miles northeast. That section of highway follows the East Branch of the

Sacandaga River and is one of the prettiest drives in the mountains. Coming from the east or north, the trailhead is 4 miles southwest of Bakers Mills on NY 8, south of Wevertown. The trailhead is designated by a state historical marker, and the trail is marked with both the blue hiking and yellow ski-touring disks used on state-maintained trails.

You begin by climbing 200 feet up the shoulder of Eleventh Mountain in .5 mile and then dropping 400 feet to the valley of the East Branch of the Sacandaga at 1.2 miles. The short pitch on the latter rise always seems formidable to tired hikers on their return.

The trail reaches the confluence of Diamond Brook and the Sacandaga in a most attractive beaver meadow. From the flow you can see the cliffs on Diamond Mountain on the north, those on Square Falls Mountain in the southwest, and the highest of all, those ranging across Eleventh Mountain back to the southeast.

The trail continues east-northeast beside the river for a little over 2 miles to a junction. Occasionally, where the valley is very narrow, you walk close to the water, but most of the time the route is back from the river on slightly higher ground.

The trail you are following was once a principal route north, used by loggers and tan-barkers to transport logs and hemlock bark from the interior to mills along the river at Oregon and Griffin or east to settlements in the Town of Johnsburg. The trail was thus designed for practicability, not for the scenery.

You see few signs of the early settlers; only their names survive. Big and Little Hopkins mountains to the west were named for two brothers who joined the settlement near the Curtis Clearing. That clearing was named for Norman and William Curtis, who settled in the area after 1865 and whose sisters, Eliza and Electra, married the Hopkins brothers. Later, John Sawyer harvested timber in the area now called Burnt Shanty Clearing, which is halfway between the Diamond Brook crossing and the intersection.

At the trail junction, at 3.4 miles, the right fork heads due north toward Thirteenth Lake. You want the left fork, which continues near the river for .5 mile to a lean-to by an enormous modern hikers' bridge, a few feet upstream from the ford used by outfitters who transported hunters and their camping gear into the wilderness via horse and wagon.

The trail to the ponds heads west, circling the southern edge of the flows that edge Siamese Brook, and then swinging north around Siamese Mountain. After the trail crosses Siamese Brook, it begins to climb toward the west-southwest, rising 300 feet to a plateau before dropping to the shore of the eastern pond. You will probably notice the climb only if you are carrying a heavy pack.

Several campsites edge the trail and the eastern lake's western shore. Another choice camping spot can be found on the spit of land separating the ponds.

Diamond Brook Flow on the East Branch of the Sacandaga Trail

152 *Siamese Ponds*

Occasionally, you will find a rowboat on the eastern lake suitable for the trip across to the western lake. Many campers bring inflatable boats to Siamese Ponds, a wise move for those who wish to fish or simply to get away from other campers.

As you explore the ponds, you may find it hard to believe that the area was once heavily logged, and that not too many years ago a guest cabin for hunters was maintained on the eastern lake shore. If you are spending the night, you may have to share the lakes with other campers, but it is usually possible to find a camping spot in a hidden cove or bay, away from everyone else.

Chimney Mountain

Distance (round trip): 2.5 miles
Vertical rise: 900 feet
Hiking time: 4 hours
Map: USGS 15' Thirteenth Lake
Siamese Ponds Wilderness Area

Chimney Mountain serves as an excellent introduction to the story of the rock mass that underlies the Adirondack landscape. Nowhere is that geological tale more vividly depicted. Hiking Chimney Mountain takes you back millions of years to the birth of these mountains and allows you to confront directly the results of many of the forces that shaped today's Adirondacks. This adventure to columns, caves, and crevices is as exciting as any climb up a "big" mountain.

Beginning about 2.3 billion years ago, limestone and sandstone sediments were deposited in an area known as the Grenville Sea, a shallow body of water. Slowly, throughout the Precambrian period, sediments accumulated in the sea until about 1.4 billion years ago.

In the next 200 million years, there followed a period of mountain building known as the Grenville Orogeny. Some speculate that its cause was the collision of continental plates. Whatever the reason, the event changed all the area's rock. The sediments were intruded by magma which cooled into syenite, gabbro, and granite. The entire mass lay several miles below the surface of the earth and the resulting heat and pres-

sures metamorphosed any rocks that predated the Grenville Sea as well as the sediments and the intrusions. The metamorphism produced syenite gneiss, granite gneiss, and metagabbro (or metanorthosite, as the feldspar-rich variety of Adirondack metagabbro is known).

These are among the rocks visible in the Adirondack dome today. Only the rocks persist from this ancient time, for the landscape is new. Erosion gradually carried away the overburden. About 400 million years ago, a period of upheaval created faults in the rock mass. Further erosion deepened the northeast-trending faults into the valleys and lakes we see today. Indian and Thirteenth lakes were created in just this way. Finally, the period of glaciation sculpted the landscape into its present form.

It is possible that a part of Chimney Mountain, composed of Grenville rocks, took on its present form as recently as the retreat of the last ice age, a mere 10,000 years ago. It is theorized that in the period of erosion that culminated in the last ice age a layer of resistant rock was stripped from the mountain, revealing an upturned sandwich of syenite gneiss, metamorphosed Grenville sediments or marbles, and a topping of layered granite gneiss. As the overburden was worn away, the release of pressures created fractures in the top layer. Erosion of the exposed surfaces was most rapid in the relatively softer middle layer; and as the top was undercut, a huge triangular block broke away, creating the rift on the mountain. Smaller blocks were moved along the fracture zones by ice and by the collapse of the triangular block, creating caves in the rift and in its western wall.

The rift valley is 600 feet long, ranging in width up to 250 feet and in depth to 200 feet. The Chimney itself rises 35 feet above the eastern rim, which falls beneath the Chimney, presenting a vertical drop of over 80 feet. Some of the openings are only cracks and crevices but others are true caves and should be explored only by those with spelunking experience and equipment. A detailed map of the caves and paths through the valley is given in my *Discover the South Central Adirondacks.*

To reach Chimney Mountain, you drive south on NY 30 from Indian Lake village for .6 mile to Big Brook Road, on the left. Approaching from the south on NY 30, you drive along Indian Lake, one of the Adirondacks' longest lake-filled fault valleys. From this direction Big Brook Road is a sharp right turn at the bottom of the hill below the marked scenic overlook. You will be disappointed if you stop there for a look east to Chimney, because the Chimney barely rises above the mountain's profile. The view is great, nonetheless.

Driving southeast on Big Brook Road, you cross the Abanakee Causeway. At 1.5 miles, turn right, or south, continuing on Big Brook Road. There is a second, unmarked, right turn about 2.2 miles farther. Continue 2.5 miles from that fork to the end of the road at Kings Flow, by a former Scout Camp. Hikers are still permitted to park for a fee, currently $1, in a designated area and cross the campgrounds to the trail on state land. Remember camping, fishing, and hunting are prohibited on the private lands. Be very respectful of the property so that the owners will continue to extend this privilege of access to the public.

Walk east through the field beside a large barn that occupies the camp's northeast corner. The trail leads east-northeast into the forest and continues relatively level for a five-minute walk to a sign-in register beside a small stream. Cross the stream by hopping rocks and continue uphill. The 900-foot, 1.25-mile climb takes less than an hour.

At 1.1 miles, you reach the first overlook, just south of the rift valley, with views back across Kings Flow. At the overlook, the trail goes straight ahead, steeply uphill to the east rim and the Chimney. A path left becomes indistinct and branching; it leads to various caves and can be followed part way to the west rim. There is currently no good single route to the west rim; in fact, the whole area is a maze of paths. If you continue to the Chimney and study the landscape, you should be able to plot a route that will enable you to explore the rift as well as find your way to the west rim.

So, stay straight and in less than ten minutes from the intersection you enter a walled corridor beneath ledges that extend from 8 to 15 feet above the path. Just as you enter this draw, note the small path heading down into the rift on your left, for you return here after inspecting the Chimney and absorbing the view. For starters, climb now to the top of the ledges on your right, from their northern end. From here the views of the mountains north of NY 28 are spectacular, with Vanderwhacker's cone silhouetted against the High Peaks.

Return to the end of the draw and make the 8-foot climb over the ledge to the left. It leads to an outcrop that overlooks both the valley below and the Chimney above. Be careful near the cliff edge. If you walk around the Chimney on its eastern side, by first descending from your outcrop directly to the Chimney's base, you find a window in the boulders that artfully frames the view of the western rim.

When you return to the draw to find the path into the rift, be careful. Although it is not quite as steep as others, it is still a precipitous drop to the rift floor. Diverse paths lead through the valley, and you will want to poke about as much as time and ability allow. In summer, blasts of cold air emerge from the deeper crevices, and sometimes bursts of fog alert you to their presence. The walking is very rough, and it is easy to jam a foot in a crack between rocks.

The north end of the rift is a jumble of broken rock and talus rising about 18 feet from the valley. You can climb its western corner and find several large holes and a cave with ice in early July. If you walk across the valley floor on any of the many footpaths to the southwest corner, you will pass several large openings. Shine a flashlight into them. One cave has a distinctive round opening about 4 feet in diameter facing north at the edge of a huge free-standing boulder. It drops 6 feet to a ledge from which you can almost always see ice and icicles in the late summer.

After you have explored the valley, continue southwest, walking behind the rock that shields that ledge-cave, to find the unmarked path up the west wall. (Remember, all of this is really bushwhacking, improvising your own route, for no path in the valley is marked. It is a small area so you are not apt to lose your way, but do watch your footing at every step.)

As you climb out of the valley toward the west wall, a narrow spine of rock, look for a clearly defined, but still unmarked footpath. Turn right, uphill, on it to find the highest overlook along the

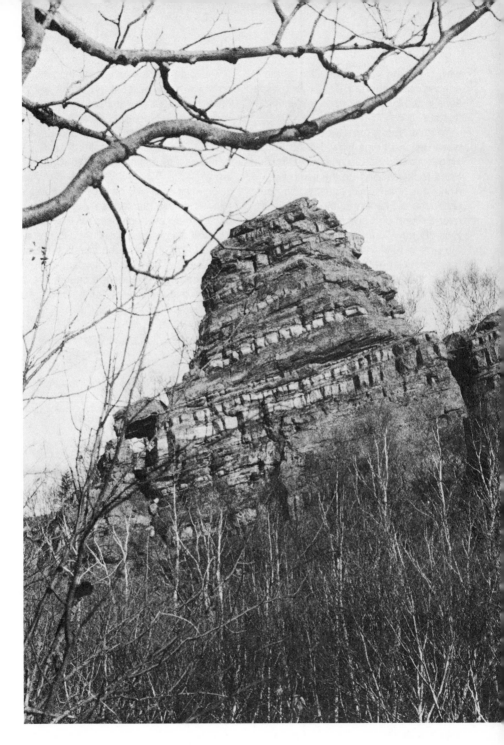

The Chimney

wall. Here, the view of the Chimney is spectacular, with the lines showing variations in the Grenville deposits clearly defined.

There is also a great view to the southwest. Beyond Kings Flow, Round Pond is visible, flanked on the north by Crotched Pond Mountain and on the south by Kunjamuk Mountain. Farther south, the split cone of Humphrey Mountain rises over the end of Kings Flow. Only the tops of Snowy and Squaw mountains on the west side of Indian Lake show above the intervening range. From the northern end of the west wall, you see a panorama of the High Peaks that ranges from Santanoni to Giant.

The path leads south along the west rim for a quick descent to the fork above the first lookout. Several paths diverge from it, some leading back along the west face of that rim to deep and usually ice-filled crevices. You continue angling to the east to rejoin the path to Kings Flow.

Only the main footpath up the mountain is formally marked, so you should have a map and compass for this trip. You will also want a flashlight. Do not attempt to go in any of the caves without proper equipment, and knowledgeable and experienced leaders. I cannot stress enough that the majority of the caves are for experts only.

Pillsbury Mountain

Distance (round trip): 5.6 miles
Vertical rise: 1,677 feet
Hiking time: 4 hours
Maps: USGS 15' West Canada Lakes; USGS 15' Indian Lake

The hike to Pillsbury Mountain has been shortened significantly by a land swap between International Paper Company and the state. This exchange straightened out the ownership pattern, which had resembled a checkerboard. IP's holdings have been consolidated on the eastern side of their holdings. The state has acquired two ponds and the remaining private land on one of the larger lakes in the West Canada Lakes Wilderness. By the terms of the swap, IP will allow the public to use the principal road through its property. This leads to a new parking area in a gravel pit that was once known as Sled Harbor. This parking area, at the western border of IP's property, allows hikers to drive 1.7 miles closer to both Pillsbury and the West Canada Lakes.

Pillsbury's tower has been open in some of the most recent years; and the land classification given the part of the newly acquired state land that includes the tower is Wild Forest, so the tower will not have to be removed. However, there is no guarantee that it will be maintained in the future. (If it is, the observer's days off are Wednesday and Thursday.)

The summit gives an intimate view of one of the Adirondacks' most remote, inaccessible, and hidden lakes and forest regions. Hikes and camping trips in this wilderness core are described in *Discover the West Central Adirondacks*. There are five gateways to the West Canada Wilderness: a long trail from the north that begins after a tedious drive along a dirt road into the Moose River plains; the Northville-Placid Trail from the northeast starting at the Cedar River Flow; the Northville-Placid Trail from the south starting at Piseco; the Sled Harbor access from the east through IP lands; and a connector to the Northville-Placid Trail from the southern extension of the road to Sled Harbor.

Inaccessibility has always enhanced the romantic aura surrounding the West Canadas, but the exploits of one of the region's former inhabitants, the trapper French Louie, have added spice to that image. French Louie's trap lines were strung between the region's lakes, circling the interior wilds. He knew every fishing hole in the wilderness and harvested hundreds of deer, bear, martin, beaver, mink, and otter skins. Each year, using part of the route you will follow on your trek to Pillsbury Mountain, he walked from his home on West Lake to Newton Corners, now Speculator, pulling a sled piled high with skins. These he exchanged for money, which in turn was exchanged for the whiskey that fueled some of the north woods' most notorious drinking bouts. Stories of his excesses and antics survive in tales contemporaries related to Harvey L. Dunham. His book, *French Louie, Early Life in the North Woods,* is your best introduction to the West Canada Lakes Wilderness, as well as a most amusing account of nineteenth-century life in the backwoods.

The road north from Speculator to Indian Lake originally passed through Perkins Clearing before heading west into the wilderness. Beyond Sled Harbor, the roads were so bad that wagon loads had to be shifted to sleds or sledges before continuing to distant lumber camps. Then the road, following precisely the road laid out in the War of 1812 to transport men and munitions from Albany to Sackett's Harbor, headed north through the Miami River valley between Pillsbury and Page mountains.

To reach Sled Harbor, drive north on NY 30 for 8.4 miles from Speculator. Just after you pass Mason Lake, turn west along the shore of the lake on a dirt road that heads back south and southwest. There are a number of camping places along the lake, all very popular and often full. The road angles south and at 2.4 miles traverses a swamp dominated to the west by views of Page Mountain. Turn right, west, at the intersection at 3.4 miles. This is Perkins Clearing.

The logging road, which is easily passable to ordinary cars, heads due west, crosses the Miami River at 4.4 miles, and reaches the parking area—an old gravel pit—at 5.1 miles. This was Sled Harbor. You can park here or further along at a new parking area. The main road bends left past the gravel pit; the Old Military Road, which is now the trail to Pillsbury immediately forks right, steeply uphill. You can drive along it to the new parking area, but the roadway is more suitable for four-wheel-drive vehicles, so walking is preferable.

The road/trail heads uphill and you begin to hear the Miami River. Shortly the trail swings close to the river, following it through a lovely valley. The way is now gently uphill. At 1.1 miles from Sled Harbor, you pass a small field on the right, which is the new parking area. Just beyond, at 1.2 miles, the trail to the tower is a left turn. The intersection is marked with a guideboard and the trail has red markers.

You descend nearly 100 feet to cross the Miami River, here no more than a small stream. Then you immediately begin to climb, for you have over 1,500 feet to go in 1.6 miles.

The handsome woods surrounding the Miami River soon give way to groves of beech that have been decimated by the die-back. At first the trail does relatively little traversing across the hillside. It just heads straight up. Within thirty minutes you notice many blowdowns, the beech of course, but also good-sized birch and striped maples, making the mountainside a scene of desolation. As the trail begins to zigzag up the slopes, you may tangle with the fallen telephone line which used to serve the tower. Along the steady climb, you pass a few erratics perched on the hillside. You may want to pause beside the stump of a huge yellow birch that once grew from a boulder beside the trail. Beyond this large boulder, the trail levels in a fern meadow, remarkable for the lack of forest cover. Grasses, sorrel, and hay scented ferns grow beneath the few spruces.

The trail becomes steep again, and on the next rise is worn to bedrock with seepage, so the footing is slippery. The worst of the climbing ends as the trail levels, then dips slightly, before rising again, a last, sharp pitch. Suddenly the cover opens, providing a spectacular view northeast past Indian Lake to the High Peaks. A little more climbing brings takes you through a narrow trail beneath stunted spruce to the tower. The summit elevation is 3,597 feet.

As of this writing, you could still climb to the lower levels of the tower, though the lookout cabin has been vandalized. Many points on the horizon should be obvious. Due north lies Wakely, and to the left, west-northwest of its tower, Manbury and Little Moose mountains rise above portions of the Cedar Lakes. Both mountains have open rock slides. To the right of Wakely, Blue Mountain presents its rocky southern slopes. In the foreground to the northeast, Blue Ridge and Cellar mountains lead to cone-shaped Lewey Mountain. Panther is the peak to the right of Lewey, and next, Snowy's unmistakable profile rises above the valley of Indian Lake.

To the right of Snowy, over the north end of Indian Lake, stretches one of the most exciting views in the Adirondacks. The eastern High Peaks, 50 miles distant in the northeast, are clearly visible above the lowland valleys of Indian Lake and the Boreas River. Only a couple of intervening mountains interrupt the string of summits.

Rock faces, scars, and slides present clearly recognizable patterns on the distant peaks. To the left of Indian Lake the mountain with two big open rock patches flanking its bare summit is Gothics. Between it and Snowy, but hardly obvious, lie Mount Marcy and Haystack. To the right of the foot of Indian Lake lies Vanderwhacker, and to its right on the horizon the outline of a range of mountains traces the shape of a bracket pointing skyward. The apex of the bracket is Hough, with McComb and Dix flanking it, each baring rock slides that appear nearly identical at this distance.

Closer to Pillsbury the mountains east of Indian Lake are readily identified. These include Bullhead, Puffer, and Gore with its rock cut. Crane Mountain lies due east on the horizon, almost in line with Dug Mountain. Whitaker Lake is visible

Pillsbury fire tower

162 *Pillsbury Mountain*

southwest of Dug's summit, and the Kunjamuk Valley is outlined beyond it. A little east of south, Speculator Mountain rises behind Lake Pleasant. Much of Sacandaga Lake is also visible. Southeast from the lakes lies the valley of Piseco Lake, and you should be able to recognize the mountains on its western shore.

In the west you can see the valley of the West Canada Creek stretching to the horizon. Nearer the tower you can spot a corner of Pillsbury Lake, with Noisey Ridge beside it. Mountains behind West Canada Lakes have more open rock ledges. Kitty Cobble is the highest peak to the north of "Big West" Mountain, the peak with cliffs that guards the lakes' northern shores.

Snowy Mountain

Distance (round trip): 7.5 miles
Vertical rise: 2,100 feet
Hiking time: 6 hours
Map: USGS 15' Indian Lake
West Canada Lakes Wilderness Area

Some trails require and deserve rich and detailed descriptions. Others need only be located, for the route is obvious once you have arrived. The trail to Snowy Mountain is of the latter kind. The mountain is, after all, the Mount Marcy of the southern Adirondacks—it is the tallest and the most popular, with an overly worn trail to prove it. However, while this guide omits the trail up Mount Marcy on the grounds that it is often "as busy as a walk down 42nd Street," Snowy cannot be overlooked. Its views are too spectacular, and its striking profile too important as a reference from every other mountain in the southern and eastern Adirondacks. You have only to see its angular summit or its cliffs reflecting white in the sun from NY 30 driving north from Speculator and you know you must climb it. And even though you can no longer climb Snowy's closed fire tower, you will be able to pick out a vast number of the Adirondacks' mountaintops from Snowy's clifftop vantages.

So, choose a brilliant day, in mid-week if possible, and be rewarded with a solitary walk to this magnificent peak. Though long, and precipitously steep

near the summit, the trail is easy enough to follow. The trailhead is opposite a parking turnout 17 miles north of Speculator and 7 miles south of Indian Lake Village. A new sign marks the trailhead at the road, but you will find a sign-in register about .2 mile from the highway along the red-marked trail.

Rising 2,100 feet in just 3.7 miles, the trail is the most challenging in the southern Adirondacks, so allow plenty of time.

The first 2.5 miles is over rolling terrain, and the climb is gentle, as you only gain 800 feet in that distance. The trail has recently received a lot of work done by ADK crews. Most of the mud wallows are fixed.

The trail heads northwest at first, through a mature forest of aspen; white and yellow birch; striped, red, and sugar maple; and beech interspersed with balsam, spruce, and hemlock. Within 1.1 miles you approach Beaver Brook, which accompanies the trail at varying distances for another 1.5 miles. The trail crosses it twice. After the second crossing at 1.9 miles, the trail continues close to one of its tributaries for .6 mile.

It is in the last 1.2 miles or so that you

encounter steep pitches, with the last .5 mile so steep that you have to use your hands.

The summit of Snowy is so steep that little realignment of the trail would even be possible, in spite of considerable erosion. The trail is worn to bedrock, deeply cut through the soil in places, but fairly stable. In wet weather, danger exists both for the trail and hikers, however, for then you are forced off the slippery rock to the sides. Pulling at trees and roots for support further erodes the trail sides.

In the last .5 mile, the forest changes dramatically from tall to scrub trees, mostly balsam, mountain ash, white birch, and striped maple. Long before you reach the summit, you can enjoy glimpses of the mountains on the east side of Indian Lake. The trail climbs through a draw between two cliffs and emerges on the top of the eastern cliff beside the fire observer's abandoned cabin with its northerly views.

You should be able to pick out Crotched Pond and Kunjamuk mountains a little south of east, across Indian Lake. Behind them range Bullhead, Puffer, and Humphrey, the latter a distinctive, regular cone. On the horizon between Crotched Pond and Kunjamuk mountains, the slash of the Barton garnet mine clearly identifies Gore Mountain. Farther to the south, right, is the broad summit of Eleventh Mountain, and beyond, to the right, is Crane Mountain, whose summit is 24 miles distant. You may be confused by the jumble of hills farther south; the view of them was better from the tower.

Walk west from the cabin to an open rock ledge on the west side of the summit. Narrow footpaths winding across the scrub covering the summit lead you to it. The rock surmounts a cliff, so wooded that it is scarcely noticeable from western vantages; however, the opening provides my favorite vista from Snowy. The dense row of hills, in which Snowy is almost central, is cut with a deep cleft valley trending northeast to southwest. The heavily wooded and remote valley is really not obvious from many other points, but it is one of the Adirondacks' deeper ones. Two brooks rise in the valley, Squaw, which flows northeast into Indian Lake, and Little Squaw, which flows southwest into the Cedar River Flow. The valley is bordered on the east by Squaw, Snowy, and Lewey mountains; on the west by a steep little knob called Onion

Hill on the USGS map; and by Buck, Buell, and Panther mountains ranging to the north. The latter's summit is only 34 feet lower than Snowy's almost 3,900-foot elevation. Panther's peak is toward magnetic north from Snowy, and to its right is Burgess Mountain.

Beyond Lewey Mountain is a chain of mountains. Cellar is to its left, south, with Blue Ridge Mountain between them. Farther to the right of Cellar you can spot Pillsbury Mountain, which lies, as does Snowy, on the edge of the West Canada Wilderness.

Farther to the south you can see Lewey Lake, and the long finger of Indian Lake that fills the valley through which the Jessup River once flowed. To the east of south, Dug Mountain is obvious.

Returning to Panther, look to its south for Buell Mountain. Immediately south of Buell, in the distance, is Wakely, which also has a fire tower (see Hike 34). To its right on the horizon you should be able

to spot West Mountain exactly 20 miles distant.

You need a really clear day and good binoculars to pick out the High Peaks. While views from the north summit both east and west are marvelous, the tower certainly did enhance the most distant views.

To name the High Peaks, start again with Panther. To its right and 12 miles away lies the top of Blue Mountain. Moving around to the right, on the distant horizon, you should be able to identify the Seward Range, in which Seymour presents the most obvious shape, a steep cone. Santanoni is next, a huge mountain on the horizon. It is reported that the top of Whiteface can be seen above the right side of Santanoni, but it is 51 miles away and requires a perfectly clear day. I have never been certain that I could see it.

Moving to the east, right, MacIntyre is obvious, as is the cleft of Indian Pass that precedes it. The sharp valley to the right of MacIntyre is Avalanche Pass, and

Indian Lake from Snowy

to its right range Colden, Marcy, and Haystack, 36 miles away. The jagged summits that follow are the Gothics and Sawteeth, then Nippletop. Vander-whacker is the isolated mountain in the mid-distance; it lies between the Hudson Valley and the High Peaks, in line with the eastern range of the High Peaks and the end of Indian Lake. In all, 32 of the 46 High Peaks are visible from Snowy Mountain, though without the tower, you have to move about the summit to find openings that duplicate the tower's views.

Even with this outline and the appropriate USGS maps, you may at first have trouble recognizing the profiles of distant mountains. In your climbs you will find that the change in perspective from one crest to another completely alters the distant profiles, so it may take several trips before the mountains become familiar. Snowy is a marvelous place to begin to make their acquaintance.

Wakely Mountain

Distance (round trip): 6.4 miles
Vertical rise: 1,636 feet
Hiking time: 3 hours
Maps: USGS 15′ West Canada Lakes; USGS 15′ Indian Lake
Fire Tower; closed Mondays, Tuesdays

In 1978 only 200 visitors made the climb to Wakely, while 5,200 made the trek up Blue Mountain, just 11 miles away. Perhaps the long drive to the trailhead on Cedar River Road deters some people, but that trek is part of the fun of discovering Wakely, whose fire tower is still manned.

The Cedar River Flow, a long lake, begins .3 mile beyond the Wakely trailhead, and it is a popular camping spot as well as a gateway to the Moose River Plains (Hike 15). Consider camping there when you climb Wakely. You will find details of many adventures in the area in *Discover the West Central Adirondacks.*

Hikers who become acquainted with the Adirondacks by approaches from the south and east are often unaware of Wakely's existence, because from that direction it is hidden by the range of mountains west of Indian Lake. However, if you hike the low hills in the northern and western Adirondacks, you soon discover how commanding a position Wakely holds. The panorama from its summit includes the only overview of the Moose River Plains, which reach to the southwestern horizon.

The fact that Little Moose and Manbury

mountains block the view to the southwest and to Cedar and West Canada lakes, is more than compensated for by the view to the east over the Cedar River Flow and valley, which leads up to the western profiles of Panther and Snowy mountains. Best of all, the Cedar River Valley opens out to permit a view northnortheast to the High Peaks.

To reach the trailhead, drive west from Indian Lake village of NY 30-NY 28. You cross the Cedar River in just under 2 miles. Cedar River Road is a left, west, turn at the point the highway turns north .2 mile beyond the bridge.

William D. Wakeley, a British-born hotelkeeper, pushed this road through to Cedar River Falls, where in the 1870s he built a dam, a sawmill, and a hotel. His Cedar Falls Hotel was "so remote that each night bonfires were required during his first season to keep the wolves from his tethered oxen. The impressive hotel had a three-story main building, with two-story wings, and sported a bar." According to his advertisements in *Wallace's Guide to the Adirondacks* of 1878, his hotel was located in the finest sporting grounds of the Adirondacks, and his table abounded with game and fish. The hotel burned in 1878 and was rebuilt on a smaller scale, only to burn again in 1884. Wakeley apparently spelled his name with a second e although the USGS map spells the pond and mountain named for him without it.

Throughout the late 1880s Wakeley ran a stage from North Creek to Blue Mountain, with connecting coaches to the Cedar Falls Hotel. At that time, the main road from Indian Lake followed the Cedar River Road south to a dirt road that is now the route of the Northville-Placid Trail between McCanes and Lake Durant.

Cedar River Road changes from macadam to dirt within 3 miles from NY 30, and it is so rough you need at least forty-five minutes to drive the 12 miles to the Cedar River Flow. On the way west the road intersects the Northville-Placid Trail at McCanes. From McCanes south the trail follows the road for the 7.1 miles to the flow. Near McCanes the handsome view southwest across nearby fields is of Burgess and Panther mountains.

With the exception of a short stretch within 1 mile of NY 28-NY 30, the Cedar River is just out of sight. The guideposts along the road are a series of short hills to the west; Round Top is first in the north; Sugarloaf with its dramatic rock face is next, and Water Barrel is just north of Wakely Pond. Sugarloaf's resemblance to an old-fashioned cone of sugar is so striking that the mountain actually looks like a miniature of its Brazilian counterpart. Your best view of it is looking north from the road, 2 miles north of Wakely Dam.

You will cross the outlet of Wakely Pond 5.5 miles south of the Northville-Placid trailhead. Pause a moment on the causeway to view Wakely and its tower, and then continue a little over .6 mile to a dirt road on the right. This tote road, at 12 miles from NY 28, is marked as the trailhead for Wakely Mountain. At present you can drive west along the road for just over a mile. However the surrounding land was recently acquired by the state from International Paper Company

View from Wakely

and it is questionable just how much maintenance even this first mile of IP's old logging road will receive in the future. At present it is passable to four-wheel-drive vehicles. Land on both sides of the road and even up the steep lower slopes of Wakely were logged in 1986 and 1987, just before the sale to the state.

Note that the state purchase included Wakely Pond and a portion of the Cedar River downstream from Wakely dam. Both have good fishing.

The roadway is sparsely marked with red trail disks and heads west from Cedar River Road through a scrub forest of popple interspersed with spruce thickets. The road fords a small stream at .2 mile and continues with the stream close on the left, or south. As you walk

you have occasional glimpses of Wakely. Some of the surroundings appear to be fields returning to the forest, and you will spot the remains of several buildings. The trees beside the road are uniformly small and dense, with several unusual patches of cherry saplings. The road begins to climb gradually past a swamp, and as it makes a long curve to the left, another road enters from the right at an acute angle. All this occurs within the first mile and twenty minutes.

At 1.1 miles, a logging bridge has been replaced by a narrow hikers' bridge, so you can no longer drive any farther. The trail now follows the stream you have just crossed. You continue to the right of it and its merry tumbling course. As you continue gently uphill you can see the tower ahead. You cross a second, smaller stream without benefit of bridge and begin a gentle climb.

You cross a brook on a washed-out bridge. A logging road branches right, but your way left is the obvious route even if there are no markers here. Within ten more minutes you reach a sign pointing right to the tower. Here, at elevation 2,530 feet, you have climbed about 400 feet from Cedar River Road, but you have over 1,200 feet left to climb in under a mile. Before you begin that climb, walk a few feet farther along the main logging road and enjoy the tranquil view across a lovely series of beaver dams.

The next couple hundred yards of Wakely's trail has been used as a skid way for the logging operation. The trail immediately begins its relentless climb, which does not moderate until you reach the summit.

Red markers guide your way on the narrow footpath, a dry, hard-packed trail up the heavily logged hillside. A few old stumps indicate the size of the forests that once covered the mountain, but the walk is one of the longest through a scrub forest in the Adirondacks.

A mixture of beech, maple, and yellow birch gradually gives way to spruce, and finally balsam. A cherry railing helps to keep you on track when, forty-five minutes past the intersection, you find the trail becomes very steep, rocky, and washed out. More railings guide you along the zigzag path through a largely evergreen forest, but in general the trail is not in the best shape and climbing is slow.

Just past half way to the summit, the mountain is so steep that the trail begins to zigzag back and forth across the straight course of the telephone line which lies coiled on the ground and could trip you up when you cross it. A sign indicating the trail marks a couple of the crossings, but there is one where you will certainly take the steeper route of the telephone line if you do not watch carefully. The trees become smaller, mostly balsam. Finally the grade eases and you can see an opening to your left with the helicopter pad that serves the tower.

You should reach the tower on the 3,744-foot summit after walking two to two and a half hours from Cedar River Road. You have to climb the tower for the view, for the broad summit is mostly tree-covered. The tower is ninety-two feet tall, the tallest in the Adirondacks. The fire observer is off on Monday and Tuesday, but on other days he will be able to help you orient landmarks.

Blue Mountain lies beyond the helicopter pad north of the tower. If you are lucky enough to have climbed on a really clear day, you should spot Whiteface in the distant north to its right. The eastern High Peaks range farther to the right, and you can name Santanoni, MacIntyre,

Colden, Marcy, Haystack, Gothics, Giant, and Big Slide.

The view east is not as distant, for the range of mountains west of Indian Lake valley block the horizon. From north to south they are Panther, Snowy with its tower, Lewey, Cellar, and Blue Ridge. Directly south lies Pillsbury Mountain, also topped by a tower.

The view west and northwest encompasses many lakes, with Fourth Lake, the largest of the Fulton Chain, beyond Lake Kora; Sagamore Lake north of Kora; and Raquette Lake to its north. West Mountain is visible across Raquette. The wooded summit of the Blue Ridge, the second group so named and visible from Wakely, shuts out a view of Blue Mountain Lake, but the tower on Blue is clearly visible. Rondaxe tower on Bald Mountain is visible on the rocky ledge overlooking Fourth Lake, and Goodnow tower can be seen in front of the High Peaks.

For the first part of your descent, you will find you are walking almost as slowly as you climbed, for the way is really steep. Still, a half-hour should see you past the worst, and forty-five minutes suffices for the descent to the main logging road. You should be able to make the return trip to your car in under another hour.

Rock, Cascade and Stephens Ponds

Distance (one way): 7.5 miles
Vertical rise: 370 feet
Hiking time: 4 hours
Map: USGS 15' Blue Mountain
Blue Ridge Wilderness Area

Lake Durant Campground is an ideal location from which to discover the heart of the Adirondacks near Blue Mountain. If the weather is not clear enough for a mountain hike, you will enjoy the variety provided by a visit to three remote ponds. A handsome loop connects Rock, Cascade, and Stephens ponds, all in the wilderness just south of Lake Durant. The eastern end of the loop terminates at the Lake Durant Campground. The western end is at the opposite end of the lake. If you do not have two cars, one to leave at each end of the loop, you can make a full circuit by walking back along the highway between the two trailheads, adding 2.2 miles to the trip.

The entrance to the Lake Durant Campground is on NY 30, 8.5 miles north of Indian Lake Village and 2.5 miles southeast of Blue Mountain Lake and the junction of NY 30 and NY 28. On part of the loop you follow the North-ville-Placid Trail, New York's famous trail that winds along both footpaths and roads, from Northville in the south, through wilderness areas and villages, to Lake Placid in the north, a distance of 119 miles. A parking area for the North-ville-Placid Trail is immediately west of

the entrance to Lake Durant Campground, and day hikers may wish to begin there to avoid the campground's day-use parking fee.

Otherwise drive or walk west beside Lake Durant for 2 miles to Durant Road and bear left .2 mile to the trailhead. The trail begins by following a dirt road alongside a cemetery. The road goes to a picnic spot on the shore of Lake Durant, passing a big glacial erratic and an outhouse. The trail turns south opposite the outhouse. The intersection is not well marked, although there are some informal red blazes to indicate the trail, which immediately crosses a small stream on a footbridge. Now you see the first of the official red trail markers.

It is only .8 mile to the long bridge separating Rock Pond from Lake Durant. From the bridge Blue Mountain appears to loom over the water. Across the bridge the trail becomes a narrow footpath heading up and over a ridge. The route is so little used you really need the red markers here. As you cross the ridge you see a second hill across a small valley. A short, steep descent into that valley takes you to a small stream. Cross it and turn right to parallel it, climbing through the valley along the prettiest section of the day's hike. Tall, straight hardwoods make a forest so open you can see the hills on both sides.

At the head of the valley the trail turns left for the short climb southwest over the end of the ridge. A long, almost level stretch through a hemlock thicket follows before you reach a trail junction. The right fork is unmarked, but the left is designated as being .9 mile from Cascade Pond. The sign says it is 1.8 miles back to Rock Pond and 2.3 miles to Blue Mountain. The mileages on signs you see on this trip do not quite add up, but the walking time to this point is about an hour and fifteen minutes.

Bear left. The trail turns southeast to follow an obvious old road walled in with tall, straight hemlock and spruce. As you first approach Cascade Pond a path forks right to an evergreen-covered promontory with a good camping spot. The

trail continues to a lean-to at the foot of the pond and there crosses the outlet on a collapsed bridge. Struggle across on the log remains. Beaver work has flooded the stream below the bridge, creating a new trout pond.

Southeast of Cascade Pond the trail is good and broad, offering a lovely twenty-minute walk through a forest with many white birch and lots of spring flowers. Then, for the next fifteen minutes, you descend slightly to an intersection 1 mile from the Cascade Pond lean-to, and .6 mile from the Stephens Pond lean-to to the right via the blue-marked Northville-Placid Trail. The left fork, also marked blue, heads 2.5 miles northeast to the Lake Durant Campground.

Bear right to Stephens Pond. The walk is very pretty, heading east and then southeast down a long hill to the lean-to. You often find nesting loons and sometimes good fishing in the pond, though

View across Lake Durant to Blue Mountain

reputedly not as good as at Cascade Pond. Much of the shoreline is swampy, but there are several good campsites near the southwestern corner.

As you head back to the intersection and then on toward Lake Durant, you will be impressed by the width of the Northville-Placid Trail. The route northeast from the intersection runs moderately downhill a short distance and then slopes more gently the rest of the way to the campsite. Here the forest is less exciting, and the trail is fairly heavily used. It is typical of that trail's passage through the Adirondacks; in comparison, nearby routes are often much more fun.

Rock, Cascade and Stephens Ponds **175**

Blue Mountain

Distance (round trip): 4 miles
Vertical rise: 1,560 feet
Hiking time: 3½ hours
Map: USGS 15' Blue Mountain
Fire Tower; closed Thursday, Friday

A combination of extraordinary views and easy accessibility attract thousands of hikers yearly to the 3,759 foot summit of Blue Mountain. The 2-mile climb of 1,750 feet requires less than two hours and is not overly strenuous. The walk down usually takes only an hour and a half, so even with a picnic to top, exploring Blue Mountain is a half-day outing, allowing you plenty of time to visit the nearby Adirondack Museum at Blue Mountain Lake. The museum is 1.1 miles north of the intersection of NY 28N and NY 30 and the trailhead is .4 miles north of the museum on NY 30.

If you make the climb in the early morning you can enjoy the play of sunlight across the Eckford Chain of lakes that stretch west from Blue Mountain to the distant horizon. If you visit the museum first and then climb the mountain, the western sun will best illuminate the distant crest of the eastern High Peaks. Either way, the museum is a good introduction to the Adirondacks. Hikers will find the museum's large relief map of the region especially appealing. Lights can be switched on to indicate many of the more famous mountains.

The Blue Mountain region was almost

the first area in the Adirondacks to be developed as a resort. The first hotel was started on the lake's shores in 1874 by John Holland. The principal developer of this part of the Adirondack interior, however, was William West Durant, the son of the Union Pacific railroad baron who was also responsible for getting the first tracks to North Creek. The younger Durant invested his time and enthusiasm for the North Woods in acquiring huge tracts of land, including all of Township 34, in which the Eckford Chain of lakes lies. Blue Mountain Lake is the northernmost in that chain; Eagle and Utowana stretch to the southwest and are connected, via the Marion River and its famous carry, to Raquette Lake. Durant built for himself the magnificent Camp Pine Knot on Raquette Lake as well as several homes in the style the noted Adirondack writer Donaldson calls "Camp Beautiful" on nearby lakes, among them Uncas on the lake that now bears that name.

Durant also encouraged the development of Blue Mountain Lake. But while Raquette Lake was "dominated by the camp beautiful idea, Blue Mountain succumbed, structurally, to the hotel horrible." The lake's original hotel took its name from the mountain that rises to the lake's east, and Blue Mountain became the dominant feature of the landscape in name as well as fact.

The mountain looms over the surrounding countryside, almost always appearing in shades of blue, a dark, imposing hulk, scarred on its southern face with rock slides and presenting a distinctive silhouette as a reference from almost every direction.

There is a new trailhead, at the height of land north of the museum, replacing the traditional beginning which crossed private lands. This new route, slightly longer than the original, saves about 200 feet of climbing. It commences from the same point as the trail to Tirrell Pond.

The trail still crosses private lands, those of Finch Pruyn Company, who have granted public access. The beginning follows a logging road for 300 yards to a sign-in booth. Land on both sides of the road is posted. The newly cut trail heads generally east and already shows signs of being rutted and eroded by hikers' boots. You cross a stream on a half log bridge, then begin a fairly steep climb. After twenty minutes, the route levels out beneath huge paper birch with a lush fern understory. In the next few minutes you will cross two streams and shortly beyond turn steeply uphill. This pitch leads to a level in an especially beautiful wooded area. As you wind in a southeast direction across the saddle you encounter another stream. After a forty-minute walk climbing 600 feet in 1.1 miles, you turn east to join the old route. You have nearly a thousand feet to climb in less than a mile.

Blue Mountain's famous steep pitches begin almost immediately. The route is worn to bedrock, smooth slabs that at times seem like an almost vertical sidewalk. The route is so steep the sky seems to emerge deceptively through the evergreens, prematurely alerting you to the summit. The cover has shrunk to scrubby balsam and birch, dense growth clinging to the steep mountainside. Look for the intrusion of quartz crystals in the rock beneath your feet. The steep section levels out after a half hour of puffing, unless you rest to catch your breath. New and old corduroy line the trail through a sphagnum area on the level summit. Forty minutes from the intersection, you should see the tower.

The best views are from the tower. The sweep of ponds and lakes fading into the distant west is amazing. Blue Mountain's isolation from surrounding hills means the views are especially good. The closest summit that exceeds it in height is more than 12 miles away. Most spectacular is the vista northeast across Tirrell Pond to the outcrops of Tirrell Mountain. Beyond them rise Dun Brook Mountain on the right and Fishing Brook Range on the left, with many of the High Peaks recognizable on that distant horizon.

To the east you have the lovely view across Blue Mountain Lake and its sisters in the Eckford Chain. "Sisters" is appropriate, for originally all three lakes were named by the surveyor Emmons for the daughters of Henry Eckford: Janet, Marion, and Catherine. Eckford first visited the lakes while participating in the 1811 State waterway survey.

You need the USGS Santanoni, Mount Marcy, and Lake Placid maps and a good pair of binoculars to help identify individual mountains. From right to left beyond the north side of Dun Brook Mountain are Dix, Colvin, Marcy, Colden, the MacIntyre Mountains, and Santanoni. The most distant identifiable peak is Whiteface, which appears behind Sawtooth, with Seward, Kempshall, and Ampersand filling out the row of significant summits to the north.

You would need quite a map folder to

show all the peaks within Blue Mountain's viewing range. South of Dun Brook Mountain you can pick out Vanderwhacker, and if conditions are right, Pharaoh Mountain on the far eastern edge of the Adirondacks. In the south, Wakely is obvious, but Snowy is harder to spot because you see only a small portion of it behind Panther. Immediately south lies Lake Durant, with Stephens Pond visible behind it. Completing the panorama back to Eagle and Utowana lakes are the Metcalf Mountains and the Blue Ridge.

Looking northwest across South Pond with its several islands, the double summit of Owls Head, with Mount Sabattis to its north and a little closer, completes the view back to the north and Kempshall. Once you have picked out the major peaks, you can more easily name the numerous bodies of water.

The northeast face of the summit is bare, so it offers good views without climbing the tower. There is a picnic table north of the tower, and several other places along the ridge are ideal for a pic-

nic, offering a panorama of the sweep of mountains beyond Tirrell Mountain and Tirrell Pond. In 1853, Irish immigrants were brought to the shores of Tirrell Pond from Ticonderoga by a Catholic priest, Father Olivetti. The rigors of the woods proved too much for them, and they quickly moved on, abandoning the sixteen log cabins they had erected, but leaving the name of their foreman, Pat Tirrell.

To the north of the summit rises a radio relay tower, but there are no good views from the exposed rock that covers the summit in that direction. The slides you see while driving north on NY 30 are all well below the summit on the south face and fairly difficult to reach.

Almost exactly 100 years ago, the summit of Blue Mountain was the center of surveying efforts to produce an accurate map of the Adirondacks. Much of the top was cleared to gain a view of distant peaks, but scrub spruce have reestablished themselves in the thin soil, effectively blocking most of the views. One

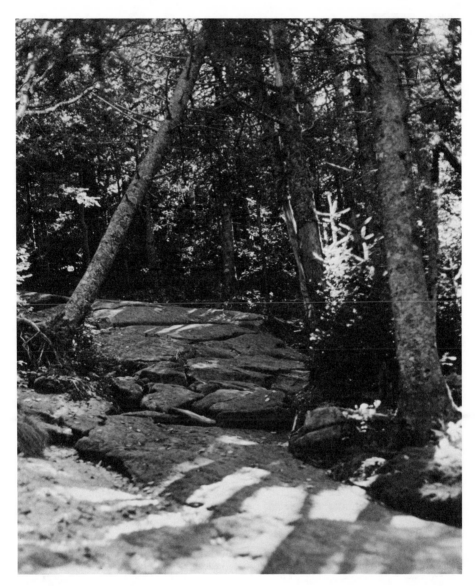

Along the Blue Mountain Trail

of the more amazing happenings in the preparation of the survey was the way in which observations were synchronized: each night at nine a charge of gun powder was set off to alert observers on distant summits and coordinate their efforts.

Return by the same route. For the first half-hour of your descent, watch your footing, for the trail is steep and rugged.

Owls Head Mountain

Distance (round trip): 7.2 miles
Hiking time: 3½ hours
Vertical rise: 1,060 feet
Map: USGS 15' Blue Mountain

From NY 30 along the eastern shore of Long Lake you can spot the double peak that inspired the name of Owls Head Mountain. Owls Head overlooks the southern end of that 14-mile long lake, which is really just a widened section of the Raquette River. South of the lake on the river is Buttermilk Falls, one of the Adirondacks' choicest spots. Since the climb up the mountain should take no more than five hours, plan a morning visit to the falls before you reach the trailhead and an afternoon trek from the mountain trail to Lake Eaton for a swim (that 1-mile detour is included in the hike total above). With all these opportunities you are sure to remember the day as one of your great ones in the Adirondacks.

If you are coming from the south, certainly visit the falls first. Drive north on NY 30 from Blue Mountain Lake for nearly 8 miles, where the highway angles right and another road turns sharply left. A state sign designates the road as the access to the Forked Lake Campground, a good base for explorations near Long Lake. The sign that indicates the road also leads to Buttermilk Falls is visible only if you are driving south from Long Lake village, 3.5 miles to the north.

In 2.1 miles there is a small unmarked parking turnout, which is not even 100 yards from the falls. No camping is allowed in the vicinity, but there are picnic tables and fireplaces. The light in the early morning, shining through the pines, is especially good for photographing the falls, whose roar is evident even at the parking turnout. The falls are so handsome you may want to return for a picnic after you climb Owls Head.

To reach the trailhead, drive back north to NY 30 and follow it for 3.5 miles to Long Lake village. Continue on for .6 mile past the bridge over Long Lake to Endion Road and turn left, southwest, on it. Follow it for 1.5 miles to a parking turnout on the right where the trailhead sign indicates distances on the red-marked hiking trail to Owls head and to several destinations reached by snowmobile trails, which intersect the hiking trail at several points.

The trail, narrow at first, climbs to a trail register (a five-minute walk). Five minutes beyond, a snowmobile trail from NY 30, comes in on the right. The joined trails continue along an old road-way, only to split again and rejoin within a hundred yards. After twenty-five minutes, at 1 mile, you reach a three-way intersection. The way right is the yellow-marked route to Lake Eaton, along which you will return if you make a detour to the lake. You go left (the sign says 2.1 miles to Owls Head) and in 200 yards, another trail, this one currently overgrown, forks right toward Lake Eaton. In another two or three minutes the snowmobile trail forks back left, headed toward Forked Lake Campground (this route is not currently maintained and is officially closed at the Forked Lake end, nearly 8 miles away.)

There are no more snowmobile markers along the red-marked route straight ahead. It continues through a good, deep forest of yellow birch, spruce, hemlock, and maple. The trail is generally level for a bit longer; it's a great, dry route, hard-packed and smooth through a mixed forest of mature trees and smaller saplings.

Forty-five minutes into your walk, the trail starts uphill, gently at first, then more steeply. The trail enters a little draw with a small stream.

Follow the stream on its right bank; perhaps you will spot signs of both bear and deer. You walk for another twenty minutes before you notice you are really beginning to climb. Fifteen minutes later you encounter the first rock-strewn section of trail as the old logging road joins an intermittent stream bed. A deep valley begins to appear on your right and a small one on the left. The trail becomes noticeably steeper with a water-washed, rubbly base. Stay left of the watercourse, in a shallow draw, for the trail disappears in a section of deadfalls. A few huge maples and beech have fallen across it, and higher up there has been a significant blowdown of striped maples.

As you emerge from the draw you will see high ground on your left. You cross a height-of-land and descend nearly 100 feet in elevation to a valley that lies below the summit of Owls Head with the abandoned tower. The remains of the ranger's cabin occupies a portion of the meadow of hay-scented fern that fills the valley.

Immediately beyond the cabin site you climb again, now on a much narrower

View from Owls Head

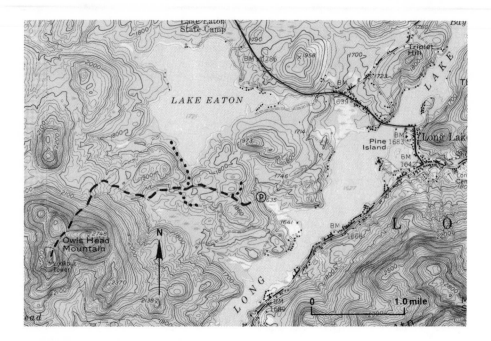

and steeper trail. The footpath zigzags across the steep face of the summit knoll. A few of the rock stairs and ledges constructed by the tower's first ranger survive, although all the railings are gone. The route is just steep enough for you to need an occasional handhold.

As the trail swings west just below the summit, you catch glimpses through the trees of the watery panorama that stretches to the southwest, including Raquette and Forked lakes. You should be able to climb the small summit knob in twenty minutes or less, in spite of the route's steepness.

The fire tower is still standing, minus its lower staircases, but the tower is not necessary to take in the spectacular view to the east. A cliff faces the mountain's eastern side, keeping the vista open through more than 180 degrees of the compass. To the southeast you can see Blue Mountain across South Pond. Owls Head Pond is the dark emerald gem a little

west of south just below. Due south, Snowy and the mountains adjacent to Indian Lake stand out on the horizon.

Not much of Long Lake is visible from the 2,780-foot summit, for the lake is narrow and tucked between mountains that range to the northeast. A little south of east, East Inlet and Sabattis mountains rise above one of the few parts of the lake that can be seen. Over it in the northeast you can spot Kempshall Mountain, with Santanoni in the distance beyond. Just to the right of Santanoni you should be able to discern Marcy and the eastern High Peaks fading into the distance.

The northern spur of Owls Head bisects the range of the High Peaks in the northeast. To the left of the spur lies Seymour, then the Seward Range.

These views from the cliffs are the best the 2,687-foot summit has to offer, for there are no really good vantages from which to survey the sweep of lakes that lie to the southwest. The drop below the tower summit is several hundred feet, a distance that provides a marvelous updraft for soaring hawks and a windswept perch to keep the bugs away.

When you descend, even if the day is not warm enough for swimming, consider visiting Lake Eaton. Within three minutes from the marked junction, you intersect a snowmobile trail from Endion Road (you use a shortcut to this route on the return). It hardly takes ten minutes to reach the lake, so the .5-mile distance stated on the sign must be a bit exaggerated.

The road approaches the lake and then turns west to round it. Walk to the first opening you see, a lovely grass-covered spot below tall spruce. The lake's sandy shores invite you to swim. The opening is a landing site and access to the trail for boaters from the Lake Eaton Campground that could also serve as a base for hiking in the Long Lake area. The campground is off a right fork from NY 30, 1.4 miles northwest of Endion Road.

On your return to the Owls Head trail, bear left on the more obvious fork. (If you were climbing to the summit from Lake Eaton, you would probably miss the right fork completely.) You will intersect the trail that takes you back to Endion Road in less than ten minutes. Without the detour to Lake Eaton, the descent should take little more than an hour and a half.

Nehasane Preserve

Distance (round trip): 9.4 miles
Vertical rise: 460 feet
Hiking time: 5 hours
Maps: USGS 15' Tupper Lake; USGS 7½' Wolf Mountain;
  USGS 15' Big Moose

Since 1894 land that the state has acquired for the Forest Preserve of the Adirondack Park has come from many sources. A few parcels have been outright gifts and some have been purchased by conservation groups, but the vast majority have been bought with state funds. In the early years of the Forest Preserve, most of the Adirondacks had been heavily logged so that huge tracts with depleted value were often offered for sale to the state or taken by the state to cover back taxes. Over the years, though, the most exciting purchases have been the huge tracts of land, encompassing thousands of acres, amassed by private clubs or wealthy individuals during the second half of the nineteenth century. One such acquisition by the state is Nehasane Preserve, once the private park of Dr. William Seward Webb.

This major addition places within the public domain the largest wholly state-owned lake in the Adirondacks and a huge preserve that offers great opportunities for hiking, camping, canoeing, and fishing. The walk described here only introduces you to the area; I am certain that once you have visited Nehasane

you will want to return for a longer stay to explore other parts of the preserve.

Nehasane originally encompassed over 140,000 acres and even with the sale years ago of 50,000 acres in what is now the Five Ponds Wilderness Area, Nehasane was still larger than either Litchfield or Whitney parks. The lands around Lake Lila have not been logged for over fifty years, so this addition is a true wilderness gem.

Dr. Webb was the builder of the Adirondack & St. Lawrence Railroad. It stretched across the Adirondacks, connecting Utica on the south with Malone on the north. That railroad once carried Webb's guests by private railcar from New York City to his personal station just north of the lodge.

At Nehasane, you can enjoy the woods as the railroad baron might have, for parking restrictions limit the total number of hikers and campers in the area to approximately the number of guests Webb could entertain at one time at his huge, twenty-bedroom lodge and a cluster of guest houses on the shore of Lake Lila.

Before you start, you should note two things. First, the three USGS Maps listed show you the principal routes described,

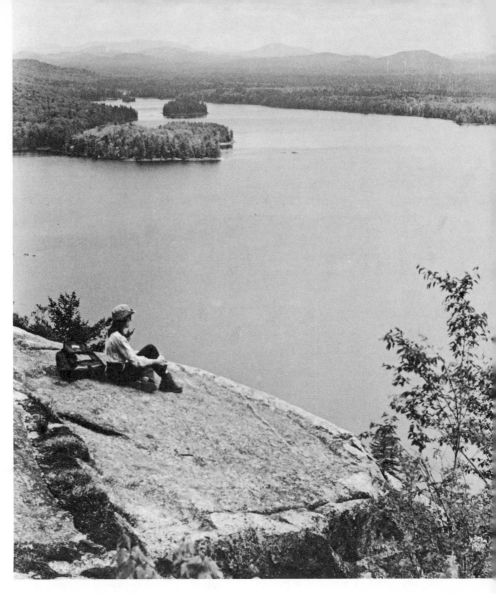

Lake Lila from Frederica Mountain

but not all of the new acquisition. For that you also want the Five Ponds and Raquette Lake quadrangles, both available in the 15-minutes series. Second, the land around Lake Lila has been classified Primitive, while the rest of the estate has been given Wilderness protection. This means that no motorboats are allowed on the lake and only DEC vehicles are permitted on the road that is the principal access trail to the area. Further, special rules govern use of the estate. Parking is permitted only at the designated area, not along the access road. Where the road passes through private lands still held by Webb's heirs, you must stay on

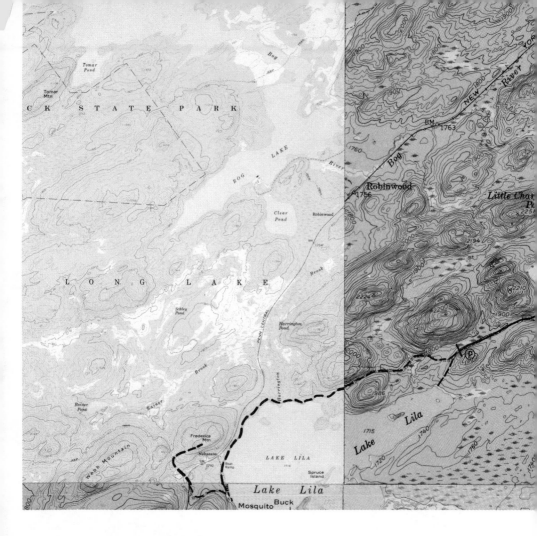

the road. No trailers are permitted, and you may not camp within .25 mile of the parking area. You must camp at designated sites only or at sites at least 150 feet from water.

To reach Nehasane, turn west from NY 30 on County Route 10 a little over 6 miles north of Long Lake village. A second road, similarly designated, also heads west from NY 30 farther north, approximately 11 miles south of Tupper Lake village. The roads intersect near Little Tupper Lake and continue west past Whitney Headquarters toward Sabbatis.

County Route 10 is good macadam and fairly attractive, for it follows part of Little Tupper Lake's shores after crossing its inlet.

In 7.5 miles a sign points left to "Access Road to Lake Lila 5.8 miles." This dirt road leads southwest across private land. It is closed during part of the winter and is apt to be muddy in very early spring. If you are planning a trip then, check with the DEC ranger in Long Lake to see if it is usable. The road ends in the designated parking area, which accommodates twenty-five cars. If it is filled you will have to return to County Route 10 to park, and then walk in.

The roadway continues southwest to Lake Lila, but it is barred to vehicles. You start your walk here, but first remember to sign in at the registration booth. If you plan any canoeing, notice the path heading south from the trailhead. The shortest portage to Lake Lila, it takes you in .3 mile to a northeastern arm of the lake.

Your hike is an easy 3.2 mile walk along the roadway to the lodge site. Part of the time you see the lake through a

screen of hemlock, spruce, and yellow birch. To vary the tempo, look for a large boulder on the right side of the road with a red marking "Sta. 230" a bit more than 1 mile from the parking lot. Beyond it the trail starts to descend to lake level, but instead, climb the ledges on the shoulder of Harrington Mountain. As you walk along them, parallel to the roadway, enjoy the excellent views of the lake. Return to the roadway by following the ledge tops as they descend toward Lake Lila.

The road first approaches the lake at 1.5 miles. Note that distance if you want to return and use a hand-wheeled carrier for portaging a boat or canoe. The road's hard gravel surface is ideal for these contraptions.

You cross Harrington Brook about 2 miles from the trailhead. This very pretty little brook drops over a series of large boulders in its final rush to reach the lake. About 400 yards beyond the brook an old logging road forks north, right. It is typical of the many logging roads that lace the estate, allowing you to explore the preserve's recesses.

At the first main intersection, just before the lodge, a road forks right, north, to the old railroad station. The lodge site faces east, commanding a fine view of 3-mile-long Lake Lila, named for Webb's wife, who was the daughter of William Vanderbilt. The estate's inclusion in the Forest Preserve meant that all the buildings were removed, even the fireplace of the main lodge with its stones nearly a yard square.

Many of the lake's sandy beaches are suitable for swimming. The fishing is as good as in any of the Adirondacks' rapidly acidifying lakes. There is an excellent stock of lake trout as well as land-locked salmon and brook trout. Be sure to bring binoculars, for the lake's remoteness makes it a good spot for viewing the bald eagles and osprey that nest in the area. There are many loons as well as other shore and water birds.

For the best view of the estate, continue south along the gravel road. At the intersection just beyond the lodge site,

bear right. This roadway heads west, crosses the railroad tracks, and then swings north into the draw between Webb and Frederica mountains.

Climb into the draw to the height-of-land, about 1 mile from the lodge. A pile of stones beside a skidway should alert you to an unmarked path (scheduled for trail designation) on the right that climbs east for under .5 mile. It should take you only forty-five minutes from the lodge site to reach the crest of open ledges that face the south side of Frederica Mountain. Older maps designate that mountain with the name Smith, after the region's first settler, a trapper who arrived about 1830.

The view is outstanding from the southeast through the southwest, encompassing all of Lake Lila and the Beaver River Valley through to Nehasane Lake. You should spot the fire tower on Mount Electra a little south of magnetic west.

Notice the open ledges on many of the surrounding mountains. All are the result of fires that swept the area in 1903 and 1908, after the period of heaviest logging. Those fires created another unusual feature on the Nehasane estate, one that has few counterparts in the normally heavily wooded Adirondacks. Many huge, open fields dot the preserve, and you will want to return another day to visit the larger ones. They stretch north of Frederica Mountain beyond Rainer Brook and are most easily reached from the old railroad track.

Ampersand Mountain

Distance (round trip): 5.6 miles
Vertical rise: 1,790 feet
Hiking time: 3¾ hours
Maps: USGS 7½' Metric Saranac Lake; USGS 7½' Metric
  Ampersand Lake
High Peaks Wilderness Area

Ampersand stands almost isolated from other mountains in the center of one of the Adirondacks' great expanses of mountains and water. To the north and west, ponds and lakes stretch to the horizon; to the east, the High Peaks range north to Whiteface; and to the south beyond Ampersand Lake, Seward, Seymour, and Santanoni form an impressive chain. Ampersand is a mountain to enjoy as you would a great painting or savor leisurely as you would sip a rare vintage wine. Walking up it is as beautiful and special as the views from the summit.

Its 3,352-foot summit is entirely bare. That clearing is the work of man: in 1873, when Colvin was making his mountain survey, he had paths cut to expose triangulation lines to other mountain tops. Erosion did the rest. The removal of the fire tower does not limit in any way the full panorama you can enjoy from Ampersand's bald crest.

Trailhead parking is on the north side of NY 3, east of Tupper Lake and precisely 7 miles east of the intersection of NY 30 and NY 3. The turnout is just over 8 miles southwest of Saranac village. The trailhead itself is on the south side. NY 3

has become a very busy highway, so cross carefully. The sounds of the highway may pursue you most of the way to the summit.

The trail enters the woods on an old roadway blocked by a barrier. The barrier seems to provide an immediate separation from the civilized world, for crossing it you enter a deep, quiet woods. Large and stately hemlock mingle with maple and yellow birch to shade the rich understory of oak fern, long beech fern, golden thread, sarsaparilla, and almost the complete array of the spring-blooming flowers typical of eastern forests. Moss-covered rocks edge the rolling trail with its soft root-free tread.

Within a few minutes you cross a sandy-bottomed stream flowing from the right. A stretch of old corduroy leads you to a fantastic hemlock grove with a view of the mountain through the trees. No trail markers guide your way, and none are needed. A long section of corduroy elevates you above the muck of a thriving deep spruce swamp. Huge spruce tower over an understory of ferns and bunchberry growing in the sphagnum bog. You may find yourself walking more slowly than usual, in spite of the easy

View from Ampersand

trail, for the woods are worthy of an observer's pace.

The old 15′ USGS quadrangle showed the trail incorrectly; the new metric map is still wrong, but the mistakes are different. You begin to climb gradually and cross several intermittent streams. You cross a larger stream, this one not shown on the USGS, and continue east of south. Within forty minutes, you notice you are really climbing. A section of corduroy may lead you to believe you are on one of the more carefully built Adirondack trails. Just wait!

At fifty minutes, after climbing a steep pitch, you enter a minute clearing, the site of the fire observer's cabin, 1.4 miles from the highway. From here an abandoned trail heads straight across McKenna Brook, which is very small at this point, and then angles up the mountain. The trail was maintained by the fire observer, Walter Channing Rice, who earned the nickname the "Hermit of Ampersand." Wooden steps and railings, log and earthen risers, and stone stairs once provided an easy way to mount the nearly 1,500 feet remaining.

Today, the trail makes a ninety-degree turn to the right and then swings left toward the brook, crossing it above the cabin site. Shortly the way becomes very steep; sections here have been called the worst in the Adirondacks. Strangely, they do not detract from the walk. Some trail work is certainly necessary, though the uniform abruptness of the mountain precludes much effective rerouting. The trail is now a narrow footpath, rooted and rutty, with slippery muck in a few precipitous sections. The steep pitch is compounded by blowdowns, some old, some quite new. At times the trail is a scene of destruction, at others it takes on the romantic aura of wilderness that pervades some early Adirondack photographs. The trail reminds me of early pictures of mountain gorges, with a jumble of trees lying across huge boulders. It only needs a few women in long skirts, their escorts encumbered with wicker packs, to complete the illusion.

The trail enters a narrow gorge with a moss-covered wall on the right, ferns dotting the ledges. You will probably have to pause for breath, leaving plenty of time to enjoy the scene. Beyond the top of the gorge, a view opens through the trees, glimpses of island-studded waters hinting at what is to come.

The forest cover shrinks and becomes predominantly spruce as you approach the summit, but the narrow, washed-out trail continues. In several places blowdowns have forced hikers to develop new footpaths. None of the detours are more than 100 feet long, but the nearly vertical slopes make you pause and question the proper route. In most cases your choice will not matter, for you have to scramble in any case. By this time you have stared at enough eye-level mud-covered ledges so that the thousands of hikers' footsteps that preceded you have destroyed any notions that this could be a pristine wilderness.

Just about the time you despair, in a terrible, steep section where the average slope must exceed forty-five degrees, you emerge in a level valley filled with exquisite paper birch and ferns. Even huff-and-puff hikers should take no more than an hour to reach this spot from the cabin site, a distance of 1 mile. The 1,000-foot climb is excuse enough for the slow pace.

A few spruce and balsam dot the glen, which is edged on the left by the cliffs that ring Ampersand's summit and on the right by an unbelievably large boulder. "Boulder" is hardly adequate; the rock might better be called a miniature mountain. Moss clings to its nearly vertical sides, ferns fill its crevices and fissures,

Clearing: site of
old fire observer
cabin

N

0   1.0 mile

and spruce perched on the top have managed to grow to mature size. If you are planning a full day on the summit, wait until your return to photograph the birch glen, for then afternoon sun highlights the trees against the grey cliff walls.

The trail continues through the glen, rising to pass under an overhanging velvet moss-covered rock. If you are curious, look just before the overhang for a footpath heading to the right around a massive pile of boulders. Follow it to explore a cave concealed in the rocks; a razor-thin shard of rock is wedged above it between overhanging boulders. Cold air emerges from this and several other openings, hinting at deeper crevices. Take time to clamber around the rock, looking for little caves and openings.

Continuing, you walk under another overhanging rock, dip into a small cleft, and emerge from the woods facing a

sheer, smooth rock wall. A gentle alternate path swings right, but your exuberance should carry you up and over the ledge, following yellow arrows painted on the rock.

You arrive at the summit on the westernmost of three knobs, each of which offers different exposures. The truly great emerging views reward you for your climb of two hours and fifteen minutes. Turn around first to look back the way you have come, past a series of ledges to a cone that is a part of the flank of Ampersand and then to Stony Creek Mountain. To the south, at the foot of the mountain, Ampersand Lake is nestled in the center of a giant handful of mountains.

Everyone who writes of Ampersand Lake reminds you of the brief role it played in the life of a distinguished group of Boston scholars that included Ralph

Waldo Emerson, James Russell Lowell, and Louis Agassiz. The story of their choice of Ampersand for an Adirondack camp, the "philosopher's camp," is beautifully told in Donaldson's *The History of the Adirondacks*. Donaldson also discusses the origin of Ampersand's name as deriving from a corruption of Ambersand Lake, which in turn was inspired by the "bright yellow sandy shores and islands which make it truly Amber-sand Lake."

You should have with you at least the following USGS maps, all in the 15-minute series, to assist in identifying distant mountains: Saint Regis, Lake Placid, Mount Marcy, and Long Lake. Directly south across Ampersand Lake, the Seward Mountains climb impressively skyward, rising 1,000 feet higher than your perch, but nowhere commanding a finer view. To the right of Seward lies Kempshall, its long and rounded summit in the distance beside Long Lake. Between the two, on the horizon, lies Blue Mountain, its profile a narrower one than is usually seen from other vantages. To the west of Long Lake lies a mountain that appears so large from this perspective its lack of name is peculiar.

In the distance, immediately left of Stony Creek Mountain, lies Mount Morris, topped by a fire tower; Buck is the long mountain to its left and farther away.

Looking back again beyond Ampersand Lake, a narrow cleft separates Seward and Seymour mountains. In front of them, extending from the lake, a valley stretches southeast toward the Duck Hole. On the far side of the valley, Santanoni stands next to Seymour to the east, with Henderson beyond it. Continuing to your left, Mount Adams is the small peak in the distance next in line.

East, between Ampersand and its pond, lies Van Dorrien Mountain, and if you follow beyond its summit you see the Sawtooth Mountains, whose peaks dip down to border the northern edge of the valley leading to the Duck Hole. On the horizon beyond Sawtooth range Nye Mountain in the north; Street Mountain next, south or right; and then, overshadowing everything and blocking farther views east, the MacIntyre Mountains.

Walk east along Ampersand's summit to the middle knob, from which the views north are best. Immediately below the mountain is Middle Saranac. Upper Saranac begins on its left and curves around it to the north, with Boot Bay Mountain in between. Lake Clear is due north, with Saint Regis and its tower to its left. You can see only a little of Tupper Lake in the west, with Raquette Pond to its north. Mount Arab, also a fire tower mountain, can be spotted west of Tupper.

The best eastern views are from the farthest perch, beyond the knob that once held the tower. As you walk across the summit, you will enjoy the magnificent feeling that the mountain drops away, with cliffs facing all exposures.

Lower Saranac Lake is just east of north, with Kiwassa and Oseetah lakes ranging east. Over Lake Oseetah lies McKenzie Mountain, with Whiteface and its distinctive white slide behind it. Slide, Hurricane, and Cascade complete the eastern skyline back to Nye. With binoculars and a clear day, you can spot three more fire tower mountains in the north, from left to right, Debar (Hike 32), Loon, and Lyon.

The huge dark crystals of labradorite imbedded in the anorthosite exposed on the peak are fascinating to geologists, but to ordinary mountain climbers, the mountain is a gem by itself. You see so much: water expanses to the north and west, impressive peaks to the south and east, and all so separate from your perch, as if placed to form a perfect panorama. None of the higher peaks with their barer summits are as open and expansive as this.

As you start back across the summit to return, look for the plaque erected to the memory of Ampersand's hermit facing the ledge below the tower knob. Be careful to retrace your steps all the way west across the summit ridge to pick up the trail. The ranger reports a few hikers have headed north through the draw and become seriously lost as they enter the woods just a few feet from the summit rocks.

McKenzie Mountain

Distance (round trip): 10.6 miles
Vertical rise: 1,221 feet
Hiking time: 6 hours
Map: USGS 7½' Metric Saranac Lake
McKenzie Wilderness Area

McKenzie is an isolated peak rising north of the High Peaks between Saranac Lake and Lake Placid. Its wooded summits do not permit a single complete panorama, but overlooks on the east and west sides of the northern summit cover a surprising portion of the compass. Moose Mountain, a slightly taller peak, lies in the northeast blocking views and creating the impression that the two are part of one long mountain range. From the overlook west of McKenzie's summit, the panorama extends from Moose Mountain through the north with low hills, fields, and ponds; the west with Saint Regis Mountain; and the southwest across the Saranac lakes to Ampersand and Scarface mountains. The views from the second overlook, on the east, encompass Whiteface, the Sentinel Range across Lake Placid, and the High Peaks. That view includes the MacIntyre Mountains and ends with the eastern flanks of Scarface.

The beginning of the trail, which crossed private land, has been rerouted, adding considerably to the distance to the north summit.

The relocated McKenzie trailhead is on the north side of NY 86, 1.6 miles east of the DEC office in Ray Brook. The new route adds 1.1 miles to the round trip and relatively little pleasure.

The new trail is well marked with blue disks and since a foot tread is barely visible, the markings are sometimes necessary. The first half-mile heads generally a little east of north, first through a reforestation area, around a small wetland, then up hill to change to a more westerly course just before crossing a small stream on a rock ledge bridge. The next half-mile or so is relatively level, contouring a little north of west on the side of Little Burn Mountain. A gentle descent due west follows. The cover of mostly small white birch is broken by occasional glacial erratics. A forty-minute walk takes you to a split log bridge at 1.5 miles. Beyond, the trail angles along the top of a ridge line of a small esker and reaches a rock outcrop with through-the-trees views of Scarface to the south. The trail curves north to northeast following the contour of the hillside and descends to meet the old trail at 1.8 miles after a fifty-minute walk.

The trail, following an old road, continues northeast beginning a gentle rise along the valley of Little Ray Brook. Much new trailwork makes the walking easy. Small waterfalls and rapids mark the stream, which tumbles through a very handsome gorge, covered with tall hemlock and a sprinkling of huge yellow birch and cedar.

Ten minutes later, at 2.4 miles, you reach a fork. Blue disks now mark the left turn to Haystack. Stay straight ahead, on the red-marked route, uphill for a time, but continuing through the valley on an almost level stretch. At 2.6 miles you cross one stream; 100 yards farther, a second; and at 3.4 miles, a third. Here you meet a bad stretch of trail, rocky and washed, with exposed roots.

The snowmobile trail from Whiteface Inn to McKenzie Pond crosses your route .2 mile farther. Continue straight on a gentle rise for ten more minutes. Then, at 3.8 miles, the trail appears to hit a sheer wall. You start climbing, straight up and then angling across bare rock and mucky slides in a slow zigzag pattern. To

scramble up the long slope to the northwest as far as the first overlook will take you over thirty minutes, but you will have climbed nearly 900 feet in .6 mile.

Walk to the right of the trail at the overlook and then turn left to follow the trail below more ledges, descending a few feet into a deep, ferny glen. This walk along the wooded summit ridge is McKenzie's most attractive feature. Stands of sorrel and mountain dryopteris fill every niche below the open balsam cover. The top of McKenzie has one of the state's most handsome stands of mountain woodfern, a lacey gem that is among our most ornamental ferns. This dryopteris is common from the subartic through Canada and into northern New York State, but it is rarely seen and even then only at high elevations south of the northernmost Adirondacks. The species constitutes most of the tall fern cover on McKenzie. You can identify it by its

Climbing McKenzie

broadly triangular form (and by the fact that the lower subleaflets are obliquely triangular).

The trail winds northeast through the fern woods, climbing two short rises before reaching a path that leads a few feet left to an overlook atop a cliff. The northern summit is visible on the right, still over .4 mile away.

The trail ducks back into deep woods, climbing a few feet in .1 mile across the narrow ridge line to the southern summit, which has a limited view southeast to Scarface. Then at 4.9 miles the trail slides down a steep pitch into a col, reaching the bottom in .1 mile and crossing a second beautiful wooded glen. You encounter two steep pitches on the climb to the north summit.

At 5.2 miles, about 100 feet past the last rock scramble, a path turns left for the western overlook. In the foreground the view of McKenzie Pond is neatly framed by Little McKenzie, Baker, and Haystack mountains. You will probably want the Saint Regis and Santanoni USGS maps to help you identify the distant mountains.

The second overlook is scarcely 100 feet to the north. That intriguing sharp cone to the right of Whiteface is Moss Cliff Mountain. The Lake Placid and Mount Marcy USGS maps will help you identify the rest. From both outlooks you will marvel at the way the mountain drops steeply away from the summit ridge, which is 3,860 feet in elevation.

Your return trip should take you just a bit less time than the ascent.

41

Pitchoff Mountain

Distance (one way): 5.2 miles
Vertical rise: 1,440 feet
Hiking time: 5 hours
Maps: USGS 7¹/₂' Metric Lake Placid; USGS 7¹/₂' Metric Keene
  Valley
Sentinel Range Wilderness Area

Pitchoff Mountain lies immediately north of the High Peaks Wilderness Area between Lake Placid and Keene and offers some great views south to the High Peaks and north to the Sentinel Range. Pitchoff is not a simple mountain; it is actually a series of small summits, which are connected by a range trail as varied and exciting as you could wish. That trail begins and ends on NY 73 in the Cascade valley; the two trailheads are 2.6 miles apart. The best way to enjoy Pitchoff is to walk the full length of the trail, leaving a car at each end; you will have nearly 300 feet fewer to climb if you begin at the western end.

The western trailhead, on NY 73, is 4.4 miles east of Heart Lake Road, directly opposite the trail to Cascade and Porter mountains. The eastern trailhead is a little over 4 miles west of Keene; this end of the trail starts on a bridge over an unnamed tributary of Cascade Brook. The tributary rises in a spring on the side of Pitchoff near the end of the trail. Unfortunately, it is the only water you encounter on the trip. You will need water long before you reach the spring, so be sure to carry plenty.

The upper, western, trailhead is less

than .5 mile west of Upper Cascade Lake. One of the rewards of this climb is the rapidity with which you gain the first views of the Cascade lakes and the sheer cliff faces of the Cascade Range bordering them on the southeast.

The trail is marked by red disks and begins by traversing the steep bank of the road cut. Then there is a steep pitch through a forest cover that indicates the area burned perhaps seventy-five years ago: small spruce and balsam are filling the spaces between striped and red maples, and white birch. The short pitch north for .2 mile is followed by a level trek northeast along a ridge parallel to the road. You drop down into a spruce thicket and then climb gently over rock outcrops to reach the first overlook, a boulder, .8 mile from the highway and less than a twenty-five-minute walk from your start.

Standing out on the boulder here, the sheer drop makes you feel as though you could easily jump into Upper Cascade Lake. From this spot you can see the spit of land that separates it from Lower Cascade Lake. This overlook also offers the most dramatic view of the cliff behind them. Even though you've barely begun your hike, take time now to enjoy this view.

The trail clings to the side of the hill around the boulder, climbing a small pitch, then a modest rise, and then another pitch above steep ledges to the right. Birch, balsam, bracken, and dry, scrubby growth mark the way. A second outcrop appears within five minutes, offering another beautiful excuse to pause.

As you descend from this outcrop, a wall of rock rises ahead of you across a small, damp woods with large red baneberries. The trail heads almost straight up, and it is slippery with loose dirt. You angle left, below a ledge, and then climb, steeply again, on an almost polished marble base.

About an hour into your hike (if you have stopped to enjoy the views) and 1 mile from the start, the trail angles west. The trail used to go straight up the rock ahead, on a dangerous route that is now closed. The new route to the left will take you to the same vantages as the steeper one. The new trail, a narrow footpath, hugs the outcrop, heading almost west, then north, and after descending a little, finally northeast again. You pass under an overhanging rock that looks like the entrance to a cave. Here the trail climbs again. A smooth, vertical rock rises above you as you traverse the wooded back side of the ridge. In fifteen minutes you intersect the older route.

Turn right across the ridge on the old trail for a detour to one of the day's best promontories. Stepping on parts of a giant jigsaw puzzle made of huge, angular, flat slabs of interlocking rock, some with deep crevices between, walk west to three huge reddish boulders. Glacial erratics, they are precariously perched on a beaklike rock. To the south, the views west from the shoulder of Cascade include Basin, Haystack, and Marcy, Colden, and Avalanche Pass. The MacIntyre Mountains are to the right of the pass, with Santanoni, the Sawtooth Range and Ampersand filling the horizon around through the west.

A half-hour will suffice for the detour, unless it is blueberry season, when you will just have to stop every other step for another handful. Your trip will have covered about 1.7 miles when you duck back into the woods and pick up the trail again. It continues northeast between scrubby patches and open rock, circling left around a bare outcrop and then angling right on open rock. Intervening clumps of balsam have a good, rich, spicy smell. You walk through a birch glen with a fern meadow beneath and then rise through mountain maples and taller spruce. As you climb between two boulders, you reach a wooded height-of-land, the highest point on the range walk. You have to leave the trail, walking to the left, for even limited views, which begin to include the Sentinel Range to the north. In spite of a leisurely pace, it has probably taken you less than two hours to walk the over-2.2-mile route to the summit, which is just over 3,600 feet in elevation.

Continue northeast along the ridge, descending a little through a fern glen and then ascending .2 mile to a rock ledge with a spectacular overlook to the north. What a drop to the valley below! There is a big slash on Slide Mountain to the north. Pitchoff's ridge is so narrow that you can see most of its length, a series of knobs and summits that appear as high as your perch.

Blueberries, ledges, balsam, and gorgeous views continue before the trail drops into a wooded glen. Within a half-hour of the wooded summit you reach a narrow spine of open rock. The trail turns left at 2.9 miles to climb the highest rock along the spine. Now you can enjoy the view back, past the spectacular ridges

View of the High Peaks from Pitchoff Mountain

you have traversed, to the summit of Cascade. The knobs ahead are equally impressive. The view north is across the deep valley to Black Mountain and North and South Notch mountains, which are about as tall as Pitchoff.

Again you descend, but the roller-coaster trail immediately climbs to follow a cairn-marked route across open rock at 3.3 miles. In the northeast another summit in the chain appears; and to its right, across Cascade valley, range Hurricane Mountain and, on a clear day, the Green Mountains of Vermont rising above Lake Champlain. Farther right, just to the left of Cascade, Giant and its distinctive slides are clearly visible.

Northern views continue as you walk across ledges that hang steeply above

the valley on the north. Prostrate spruce and tall blueberries cling to the thin soil on the summit. At 3.6 miles, you should glimpse a small, steep knob in the valley that separates you from the last summit. Walk about 15 feet to the left, off the trail, to enjoy the view of the last summit across the peculiar knob.

Next, yellow arrows painted on the rock guide you into a steep gully below and north of the ledge. Be careful; it is slippery! After dropping to the col, turn sharply left, below the outcrop, then climb through a cleft, head down a slide, and cut sharply up a ridge for a view northeast to the last summit in the range. It takes fifteen minutes to cover the distance from the col, just over .2 mile.

You are climbing on bare rock now,

guided by more yellow arrows. Do not forget to look back; those views are great, too. You approach the last summit from its northern side: the south and west are too steep. You reach it just short of 4 miles from your start and after three hours and fifteen minutes of walking. Stop, rest, and enjoy the curious rock formation below you to the south; it is easy to see why it was named the Sleeping Elephant. You have a slightly different perspective on the eastern views you enjoyed from the previous summit; this last knob is only a little more than 300 feet below the highest one. You will marvel at the steep drop to the south and east to Cascade Valley, with Owls Head Mountain a little north of east across it.

Your route down is as steep as the way up. To find the continuing trail, walk a short way northeast, following arrows and cairns on the open rock. A few of the signs are concealed by the spruce and balsam that fill the crevices. The trail makes a sharp, hairpin turn to the right, dropping below the ledge and doubling back southwest beneath ledges into a draw below the summit. Rocks and rub-

ble fill the steep and difficult trail. It is really a scramble to descend through the birch-covered slope. Erratics cover the hillside and boulders fill the trail. It is so steep that you probably need an hour to cover the final 1.25 miles to the highway.

About halfway down, you cross an intermittent stream, and within a few feet you can hear the spring emerging from below a boulder about 50 feet east of the trail.

Below this point, the slope is noticeably gentler. Your route is close by a small stream on the right, across it, and then across the main stream. Following a fairly steep section, you cross and recross the stream. Finally the route levels out, just before emerging from the woods on the bridge by NY 73, where you have left your second car.

You will agree that this is not a long or difficult trail, but there is a fair amount of climbing between the summits. Be sure you have allowed at least an hour a mile for the trek and extra time for picking blueberries and enjoying the changing views.

Blue Ledge on the Hudson

Distance (round trip): 5 miles
Vertical rise: 230 feet
Hiking time: 3 hours
Map: USGS 15' Newcomb

The Hudson, New York's mightiest river, has more beautiful vistas than the fabled and historic rivers of Europe. But from its birth at Lake Tear of the Clouds high in the Adirondacks, to its passage through the Hudson Highlands, and then to its mouth below the skyscrapers of New York City, no more inviting place exists than the narrows of Blue Ledge in the heart of the Adirondacks. The towering cliffs that give the gorge its name rise above one of the river's wildest stretches of rapids. The boiling white foam contrasts with the deep blue shadows of the rock. On a sand beach opposite the ledges you can picnic and in spring watch the noisy antics of a pair of nesting ravens. Their nest is usually secreted in a dark niche high on the cliffs, and the black young birds would be totally concealed if they did not reveal themselves with gaping brilliant red mouths, screeching for food.

The 5-mile, round-trip walk to Blue Ledge can be made in less than three hours, but you should allow twice as long to appreciate the gorge's uniqueness. The walk begins after a long drive on the handsome but rugged North Woods Club Road in a high, open forest typical of this part of the Forest Preserve. The easiest access to the dirt road is from NY 28N, driving north from its intersection in North Creek with NY 28. By this route you pass a lovely view of Moxham's slide 3.5 miles above North Creek and go through the hamlet of Minerva at about 7 miles. At 9.4 miles turn left, west, on North Woods Club Road. The road bridges Deer Creek, heads west, and then swings south through the valley between Kellogg and Venison mountains.

The road descends a steep side hill to a one-lane bridge over the Boreas River 3.8 miles from NY 28N. There is a picnic area at the bridge from which several informal fishermen's paths head along the river.

Beyond the bridge you cross railroad tracks that serve the titanium mine at Tahawus. In the early nineteenth century iron was the raison d'être for the mine's existence. It was the failure to build a good road or railroad that prevented the mine's development then, and impurities, namely titanium, made the mine a marginal operation. In 1871, Dr. Thomas Clark Durant completed the Adirondack Railroad, which was first chartered in 1839, from Saratoga to North Creek; however, it was not until the early years of World War II that the road was extended all the way to Tahawus to ship out the titanium, which turned out to have greater value than the Adirondacks' fabled iron.

From here the dirt road can be rugged; you have to drive so slowly you can easily spot some of the lovely clumps of wildflowers that edge the road. The trailhead is exactly 3 miles from the bridge over the Boreas. Park at the marked turnout at the east edge of Huntly Pond.

The first part of the trail south crosses a boggy area covered with huge yellow birch and hemlock. Blue trail markers denote the route, which heads up and away from the pond along a dry and narrow footpath. The easy, gradual climb through mixed forest is followed by a gentle descent into a little valley through a sort of natural gate formed by two huge boulders and two huge yellow birch. The valley is filled with many

spring-blooming plants, which form a multi-colored carpet of wild oats, dog-tooth violets, and spring beauties.

After crossing a small stream you continue generally southwest to an area of low scrub and brush beside an old shanty, all signs of logging. The place is about 1.2 miles in, and here the footpath intersects an old roadway with a stone-work base. The trail continues on the roadway toward the Hudson, passing to the south of a long beaver flow with extensive signs of both old and new beaver work. The high open canopy of huge trees (through which the old road passes) creates a parklike setting. The Hudson was used to flood logs to sawmills throughout the last seventy years of the nineteenth century and into the twentieth century, and this road was undoubtedly a principal route for dragging logs to the river.

Just about the time you first hear the Hudson, the trail reaches a section with

Blue Ledge

206 *Blue Ledge on the Hudson*

posted signs designating North Woods Club property. You cross the property line and head straight up a narrow pathway that traverses a knoll bearing old blazes on the trees as well as the blue markers. The low shoulder of a hill separates you from the Hudson. As the roar of the river grows louder, the trail turns due south to wind along the nose of the ridge. You are approaching the area opposite Blue Ledge. The trail is covered with the tall white pine that rim the entire gorge here. The route is up and down along the ledge, past a pine point that affords a small glimpse of the crest of Blue Ledge on the opposite shore. The crest rises higher than your perch on the north shore. You will have walked for no more than an hour, but pause to enjoy sounds from the promontory overlooking the Hudson: the wind in the tall pines and the din of the rapids. With the exception of the Harris Rift west of the confluence with the Boreas, the most violent of the Hudson's rapids are the ones you hear. They churn and boil the river both above and below Blue Ledge.

Now the trail drops rapidly to the Hudson, past rattlesnake fern, boulders and ledges, right down to the sandy banks. Blue Ledge rises 300 feet above you on the opposite shore. The blue cliffs are surrounded with other ledges colored gray and green and even various hues of orange and salmon. Pines and cedars cling to tiny crevices in the cliff faces. The marvelous colors and the variously eroded bands reflect Blue Ledge's geological structure: a series of banded gneiss beneath bands of schist interstratified with gneiss and limestone.

Short informal paths head both east and west along the riverbank. Cedars rim the shoreline, which is barely flat enough for a picnic site, though it is obvious that several places have attracted campers. The Hudson is only 150 feet wide just below the cliffs. Huge rocks break the water into swirling rapids and crests of foam, both upstream and downstream. The deep pools for swimming are deceptive, for the Hudson can have a mighty current. Be careful if you do enjoy the cooling waters.

In spring, in high water, you may glimpse a kayak or rubber raft shooting the rapids. Eagles and hawks are often sighted riding the updrafts above Blue Ledge. And, of course, this is one of the few places in the Adirondacks where in spring you can expect to see ravens.

Allow at least a full day for the trip to Blue Ledge even though you will spend no more than three hours of it walking. The drive in and out may take another hour and a half, and you will want plenty of time to picnic and admire the cliffs.

Vanderwhacker Mountain

Distance (round trip): 5.8 miles
Vertical rise: 1,700 feet
Hiking time: 5 hours
Map: USGS 15' Newcomb

Vanderwhacker Mountain stands alone, the only peak in a rough rectangle of Wild Forest land outlined by the Hudson River on the south, west, and a portion of the north, and the Boreas River on the east. Neither river is visible from the summit of Vanderwhacker, but the broad expanse they define separates the mountain from any other that approaches its height. Enormous Vanderwhacker sits in isolated splendor, offering commanding views of distant summits in all directions.

The tower is not manned at present, and its lower flight of stairs may be removed, although there are no current plans to remove the tower. If the stairs are there, permitting you to climb the tower safely, you can enjoy all the distant views described; but if not, you may have to scramble about the summit to obtain all the views. You can enjoy the spectacular panorama of the High Peaks to the north, framed by stunted spruce trees, without climbing the tower.

Vanderwhacker is very steep, rising sharply 1,700 feet from the surrounding valleys. The trail generally follows a long narrow ridge that leads to the small summit cone. The 2.9-mile climb is strenuous

enough to make a good one-day hike.

To find the trailhead, drive north from North Creek on NY 28N, which is also called the Theodore Roosevelt Highway. A sign beside a deserted frame building 14.6 miles north of NY 28 relates the events of September 4, 1901, when then–Vice President Theodore Roosevelt heard that President William McKinley was on his deathbed. Roosevelt stopped at the inn here on his wild dash from Mount Marcy, where he had been vacationing, to North Creek, where he caught a train to Buffalo to be sworn in as President of the United States.

You cross the Boreas River at 16.2 miles, and if you are not in a hurry, you might enjoy walking .5 mile south on an informal path that follows the eastern shore of that river past rapids and a small falls. Other destinations along the Boreas and NY 28N are described in *Discover the Central Adirondacks*.

Immediately north of the bridge, an unmarked dirt road heads west. Even in early spring, its firm gravel base makes it safe for ordinary vehicles, though there may be washouts, so use caution. A parking area is on the left near the start, and many camping places are tucked

View from Vanderwhacker Mountain

beneath the tall pines lining the road. Huge hemlock stand out in the dense mixed forest off to the sides. The dirt road is so beautiful that you might enjoy walking along this stretch. Particularly good camping spots are 1.1 miles in and 1.5 miles in, near Vanderwhacker Brook. Just beyond, you cross the railroad track from Tahawus mine, which trains use at irregular intervals, so look before you cross. The road continues west, more interesting than many trails in the Adirondacks. Beyond the tracks it climbs a small spruce-covered bank bordered with bunchberry, blueberry, and pipsissiwa. The road winds about and reaches a fork at just over 2.6 miles from the highway. The way left leads to a private club at Moose Pond. Your route is to the right.

There is a parking spot 150 feet along the right fork, but the road is not good, so a safer parking turnout is on the north, 200 yards east of the fork. The trail's beginning is marked with a sign giving Vanderwhacker's elevation, 3,385 feet, but no mileage. Orange snowmobile disks and red trail disks mark the trail which begins by following an old road that leads to the fire observer's cabins.

Because the tower was manned for a few years prior to 1986, much trailwork has been done. The first 1.5 miles to the cabin site is much improved. Shortly after the beginning, the trail angles right away from the roadbed to higher, dryer ground. You are following a small stream and .3 mile from the trailhead there is a lovely spot where the water slides over a small ledge and tumbles into a sheltered pool. Chains of logs make dry crossings over the few wet places on the new route, which climbs up and over a couple of knolls before rejoining the roadway. Good bridges span the streams that flow from the north.

In fifteen minutes you see a lovely wetland to the right of the trail and a few

minutes later you approach a large drying marsh whose stumps frame views of the mountain to the northwest. The trail, now a narrow route again, skirts the marsh to the north. Only those who have walked the route before will be aware of the fact that the trail strays from the old roadway which used to circle south of the marsh. Beyond the marsh, you cross a small stream flowing into it, then begin to climb. There is a larger stream to your left. Another stream joins the trail and makes it wet. Here you see the cabins ahead of you. After forty-five minutes, you reach the cabin sites, elevation about 2,050 feet. A large sign warns there is no camping here.

Walk between the cabins uphill to begin the strenuous climb up the lower, and much steeper flanks of Vanderwhacker. You are headed more northerly on a narrow but well marked route that traverses the almost-vertical slopes. A twenty-minute struggle suffices to reach the first crest, and the gradient eases. You cross a draw and a small stream flowing to your right, and shortly other small streams join the trail. It is wet going as you traverse the southern slopes for nearly thirty minutes. The moderately steep climb is straight up through a narrow defile, walled by spruce and balsam. Much of the route is on bedrock. It may take you an hour to climb a mile from the cabin site and reach the next crest where the trail is dryer and the climb becomes more gentle. Soft mosses line the corridor and host golden thread, bunchberry, and sorrel. You continue west along the south slopes below the narrow ridgeline, still climbing. The mountain continues to drop steeply away from the trail to your left. The narrow passageway is really pretty, and it even smells good; but it does seem interminable.

As you descend from a small rock ledge (the only noticeable descent on the climb) walk south to an opening just a few feet from the trail with a view to the south. The spot overlooks Moose Pond down on the left. The trail is now on the top of the knife-edge ridgeline, going up only slightly through trees that are progressively smaller, when suddenly, you are at the tower.

When you reach the summit, your first impression of the view north is of the looming, massive hulk of Santanoni and the enormous spread of the MacIntyre Mountains. If you can climb the tower, you can see west to Kempshall and the mountains that line Long Lake. To their south is Blue Mountain. You will need binoculars to pick out Goodnow's tower as it is silhouetted against Kempshall.

The rest of the panorama to the north is visible from the rocks below the tower or from the tower. Straight below lies the village of Newcomb, identified by the town's water tower, with Lake Harris to the west of it. Santanoni, with its long, curved slide, is beyond Newcomb and to the left of Santanoni lie the Seward Mountains, with Couchsachraga and Little Santanoni between. To the right of Santanoni on the horizon lie Sawtooth Mountain and Henderson, and beyond them are flat-topped MacMaughton and Wallface, with its cliff bordering Indian Pass and leading up to the broad sweep of MacIntyre Mountains. Continuing to the right, the cone of Colden is impressive behind Mount Adams, whose rock outcrops can be seen with field glasses. Next is Redfield, with Marcy peeping over it and then Skylight and Haystack on the horizon. In the foreground, the North River Mountains lead up to Allen and on to Haystack.

Farther east range Colvin and Nippletop, then the cleft of Hunters Pass, with Dix, Hough, and McComb rising behind Boreas Mountain. You feel you are on top of the world, surveying the broad valley to the north and the sweep up to the Adirondacks' most impressive range.

To the east, you can spot Texas Ridge and Hoffman Notch with Hoffman Mountain beyond. Pharaoh Mountain can be seen over Hoffman's right flank.

From the tower, you can see south all the way to Indian Lake and the mountain on its western shore. Immediately below the tower lies Moose Pond and spotting clockwise (west) from Moose Pond, you can identify Little Beaver Mountain in the foreground, and Beaver and Split Rock ponds. Directly over them lies Panther Mountain, with Wakely to the west. Panther defines the western side of the Squaw Brook Valley, which you look straight through from this angle. Snowy Mountain with its sharp profile punctuates the eastern side of that valley. Next is Indian Lake, and to the east, or left, lies the heart-shaped summit of Humphrey, then Puffer, and finally Bullhead. Between the latter two, and closer, is one of the rare views of the chimney on Chimney Mountain. The dominant mountain in the south-southeast is Moxham, which appears like the back of a closed fist, its string of summits ranging off to the left. From the stairs on the tower, you can easily identify the mountains to the southeast. Gore, with its tower, is clearly defined a little east of south over Moose Pond. On a really clear day, you can even discern the mountains edging Lake George.

You will need about an hour and forty minutes for the descent. The way across the ridgeline is so gently downhill that you seem to fly along, but watch the slippery, wet places as you descend through the walled corridor. After you cross the draw, you may even catch a through-the-trees glimpse of the marsh that seems very close below as you approach the crest of the steep flank. The short descent along that flank is so steep you will need to proceed slowly down to the observer's cabin. The newly marked trail beyond makes the rest of the hike seem very easy.

Goodnow Mountain

Distance (round trip): 3 miles
Vertical rise: 1,050 feet
Hiking time: 2 hours
Map: USGS 15' Newcomb

Goodnow is a nice little mountain (elevation 2,685 feet) just south of the High Peaks with a great view. It is accessible to state campsites and close to the new satellite Adirondack Visitors Interpretive Center with its lovely nature trails. In short it is the best way to become acquainted with the region near Newcomb, which has many attractions for hikers.

Goodnow Mountain is owned by Syracuse University and although the DEC no longer maintains the fire tower there, the University still allows access to the mountain. You can enjoy the wonderful views north to the High Peaks from the exposed rocks at the tower site.

Goodnow lies south of NY 28N. The trailhead is 3.4 miles west of the Newcomb Town Hall and 10.4 miles east of the intersection of NY 28N and NY 30 in Long Lake village. Closer at hand, the trailhead is just west of the Syracuse University Ecology Center and 1.4 miles west of the Huntington Nature Preserve. You might want to add to the day's outing a walk through the preserve on the labeled nature trail, which takes you past marshes, bogs, and forest sites. You should also explore trails at the VIC a

bit farther east at Rich Lake.

The trail to Goodnow, marked with red disks and older red blazes, follows an old logging road through a clearing into second growth forest. The road becomes fairly steep almost immediately, winding beneath a new telephone line. An unmarked turn right takes you away from the line, but the road quickly swings back east to rejoin it.

Logging has greatly disturbed the surroundings, but the trail itself is a pleasure to walk because it demonstrates how good a trail can be with proper maintenance. Recent additions of ditched culverts, waterbars, and split-log stringers keep the trail dry and relatively mud-free even with heavy use. The work allows spring carpets of dogtooth violets to mass beside the trail.

Within fifty minutes the trail levels off in the col west of the summit. To the right of the trail there is a covered springhouse and, just beyond it, a small old stable. The trail, now only a footpath, turns east up the narrow ridge. The route is handsome through an enclosing cover of spruce and balsam. A rock ledge offers a vista of Gore and surrounding mountains to the south and a second opening gives a glimpse north to Rich Lake.

Shortly, the tower comes into view at the end of the evergreen-covered tunnel that traverses the last pitch to the summit. The climb, of just over a thousand feet, should take no more than an hour and fifteen minutes.

Goodnow surveys the southern panorama of the High Peaks and the most impressive part of the view is to the northeast, through Indian Pass (see Hike 49). Wallface and the MacIntyre Mountains clearly define the pass. Following along to the right, east, Avalanche Pass is also outlined, with the MacIntyre peaks on the left and Colden on the right. Next,

View south from Goodnow

Marcy, Skylight, and Haystack define the horizon, with Marcy almost hidden behind Redfield and Skylight. The jagged crest of Sawteeth leads up to a part of the series of peaks that Adirondackers call the Range Trail. That route connects the summits of Basin, Saddleback, Gothics, Armstrong, and Upper and Lower Wolfjaw. Here the eastern peaks of the Range Trail lead around to Giant, which is barely visible. To the right of Giant, Colvin, Nippletop, and Dix are easily spotted.

A little north of east lies Boreas Mountain, and south of east is Vanderwhacker, both with fire towers. Goodnow River flows south along the western edge of the mountain, and beyond its flow lie the little-known and rugged slopes of Dun Brook Mountain and the Fishing Brook Range.

Following around to the south, Snowy, 21 miles away on the shore of Indian Lake, is unmistakable. In the south beyond the small hills that rim the Hudson River Valley, Humphrey, Puffer, and Bull-head range east on the horizon, with the mine cut on Gore making that mountain most distinctive in the south-southeast.

Looking back north, Mount Adams, topped by a tower, rises south of the MacIntyre Mountains. To the left, west, of Indian Pass you can see Henderson and then Santanoni. To the west of Santanoni, and over several intervening hills, lie Couchsachraga and Little Santanoni mountains. Farther left, the Seward Mountains define the northern horizon. To the northwest, Kempshall Mountain lies between you and Long Lake. Harris Lake, with its state campground, is visible in the northeastern foreground, just beyond Newcomb. Due north, below Goodnow, is Rich Lake.

After your return, a forty-five minute walk, you should have time to drive east 1.5 miles toward Newcomb and visit the satellite VIC. Trails lead to the sandy shores of Rich Lake where the northern cedar that rim the lake handsomely frame a view of Goodnow and the tower.

Santanoni Preserve

Distance (round trip): 10.2 miles
Vertical rise: minimal
Hiking time: 4 hours
Maps: USGS 15' Newcomb; USGS 15' Santanoni
High Peaks Wilderness Area

Picture yourself camping near or canoeing on a remote lake surrounded by beautiful mountains and having the spot almost to yourself. You can arrange to do it in the Santanoni Preserve, and you may not even have to carry your own canoe.

Santanoni Preserve was once a huge private estate. Now it is managed as a wilderness retreat, with no motorized vehicles permitted along its access road. Both hikers and campers must sign in at the trailhead registration booth. Camping is limited to a couple of lean-tos and a few isolated and primitive tent sites around the shores of Newcomb Lake. Campers rarely fill the designated campsites, whose number is limited. In spring and fall it is possible to enjoy the handsome lake in almost complete solitude.

It is possible to arrange with local drivers to have your canoe transported to the lake on horse-drawn carts for a nominal charge. This will let you explore the islands and bays of Newcomb Lake.

Hunting, in season, is permitted, subject to the usual state regulations. Fishing for both brook and lake trout is limited to artificial lures only, with a minimum size of twelve and twenty-one inches, respec-

tively, and a day limit of three brook trout and one lake trout.

Day hikers and canoeists can easily make the 5.1 mile walk to the estate boathouse in two hours. The trail follows the old estate road that is broad and fairly level and still used by DEC. You should plan a fairly early start in order to spend a full day on the lake, and then walk out after a picnic supper. That way you can enjoy birding both in early morning and late evening, when it is best.

Campers find walking with a pack takes a bit longer. They may resent the fact that they are carrying packs when the road appears to be suitable for vehicular traffic; in fact the road is in such good shape that bicyclists can and do use it.

To reach the entrance to the preserve from the east, use either Blue Ridge Road from the Adirondack Northway (Exit 29 off I-87) or NY 28N northwest from North Creek. It is about a forty-minute drive along either road to their intersection. Continue on NY 28N west, passing the Harris Lake Campsite in 3.1 miles and crossing the Hudson River in 3.4 miles. The entrance to the preserve is in Newcomb, 5.2 miles from the intersec-

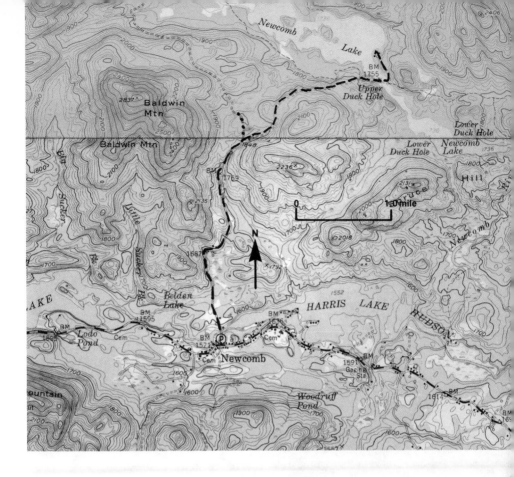

tion. If you are driving from the south or west along NY 30, turn east onto NY 28N at Long Lake, and drive 14.7 miles to the entrance. Drive north along the entrance road across the Hudson to the gatehouse near a farmhouse, one of the oldest buildings in the village of Newcomb. Dark brown shingles with red trim and fieldstone distinguish all the estate's buildings, including the magnificent home that still stands on the shore of Newcomb Lake.

A sign near the parking area tells the estate's history. The late Robert C. Pruyn, one of the state's wealthier foresters, assembled the Santanoni Preserve from several smaller parcels in the late 1800s and early 1900s. He used the property

until 1953, when it was sold to the Melville family. Through efforts of the Nature Conservancy, the DEC, the Federal Bureau of Outdoor Recreation, and anonymous donors, the land was acquired and given to the state to manage as a wilderness retreat.

From the entrance many foot and horse trails emanate into the preserve and on into the High Peaks area. All routes begin along the estate road.

A parklike area greets you just beyond the gatehouse, a forest of large hemlock, spruce, tamarack, cedar, and birch. Down on your right you can spot a beaver flow through a spruce thicket. Within a half-hour you pass the shingled barns and silo of an old farmsite. Stone walls

View to Santanoni across Newcomb Lake

still edge the fields, which lead east to an open flow. The meadow beside the flow is a good place to watch for birds.

The roadway winds past other field-stone buildings through woods to open fields, across which you can see a small hill to the north; you will circle it to reach the lake. Watch for hawks and owls near the fields. If you make the walk in spring, say late May, you should be able to spot a dozen different warblers. They migrate into the area before the leaves are fully out, making it easy to spot them in the mature forests that edge the road.

The road follows a stream on the right for a time, crossing it on a beautiful stone bridge, passing a wet meadow, and rising a gentle incline to a fork 2.1 miles and less than an hour's walk from the gate. The way left heads to Moose Pond, but you keep straight on the principal road toward Newcomb Lake, 2.7 miles away. The road begins a very pleasant and gentle descent around the hillside. In very little time you see the lake through the trees. Keep circling, now to the east, above the lake, crossing two stone bridges. At 3.7 miles, a red-marked trail heads left through the woods to a lean-to. The road now descends to a promontory where a picnic table overlooks the lake. Beyond, the bridge carries you over a narrow neck of the lake. The bridge separates the flows called the Upper and Lower Duck Holes from the western principal part of the lake. Continue along the road, which turns west, past numbered campsites along the lakeshore for .4 mile to the estate and boathouse. The most beautiful campsites are beyond the buildings.

The high open forest along the eastern shores appears undisturbed by any logging. Most of the western shoreline and all of the islands are densely covered with cedars. The islands range in size from .3 mile long to tree-covered boulders. Even if you are not a fisherman, you will enjoy exploring the lake's bays and coves. You can easily spend nearly four hours paddling around Newcomb Lake and the Duck Holes, all of which abound with birdlife. The shoreline is partly edged with boulders, often with huge pine capping the rocks' promontories, and the lake bottom is generally sandy and perfect for swimming. Standing at the boathouse, you can see Moose Mountain in the west, with Baldwin on the left and Santanoni peaking over the trees on your right. As you move out into the western end of the lake, Santanoni becomes most impressive with its long, thin, curved slide glistening in the sunlight.

You will certainly want to poke about the buildings of the estate. They are massive log structures connected by wide porches and covered breezeways, which seem to attract the slightest winds from the lake. The doors, inlaid with rustic logs in a variety of geometric patterns, are truly fascinating. Huge fieldstone fireplaces warmed every room of this lodge, which was typical of the Adirondacks retreats built in the late nineteenth and early twentieth century by those whose wealth permitted "camping" in such a grand style. Efforts to preserve the buildings as examples of the Great Camps, which these are not, have failed. Over the years the buildings have deteriorated and been vandalized. Since they are now part of the Forest Preserve it is only a matter of time until they are removed.

You can follow a yellow-marked trail to the north beyond the buildings, around the eastern end of Newcomb Lake. It passes a number of campsites situated behind some of the most beautiful sand beaches found anywhere in the Adirondacks. Huge, old, gnarled and twisted cedars rim the shore, providing a lovely backdrop for a refreshing swim that is free from the leeches that inhabit the water nearer the bridge.

The return seems a bit steeper than the trip in because of the height-of-land on the shoulder of the hill, less than half-way back to the gatehouse. It is mostly an illusion, for the road never rises more than 200 feet above the level of the lake. Maybe the fact that you notice a climb and the length of the trip out reflects displeasure at leaving so beautiful a spot.

Hoffman Notch

Distance (one way): 7.5 miles
Vertical rise: 300 feet
Hiking time: 6 hours
Map: USGS 15' Schroon Lake
Hoffman Notch Wilderness Area

The Hoffman Notch trail is a beautiful and little-used route through a high mountain pass. Handsome streams, waterfalls, and upland marshes edge the trail its entire length. You can walk into the Notch from either end of the trail and then simply retrace your route, but if you want a full day of great hiking, walk it all at once, traveling from south to north. The logistics of leaving cars at both ends are time-consuming, but not impossible.

The northern trailhead, where you leave your second vehicle, is on the south side of Blue Ridge Road, the western spur of the road at Interchange 29 of the Adirondack Northway (I-87). Here, Blue Ridge Road follows The Branch, which flows south from Elk Lake and then east to the Schroon River. In 2.5 miles you reach the small settlement of Blue Ridge, where lodgings and campsites on private property overlook a set of falls you will certainly want to stop to view. Continuing west, you pass the marked turn for Elk Lake Road in 1.8 miles and 1.5 miles farther come to a small parking area just beyond the bridge over The Branch. Here an abandoned road heads south along The Branch. Although there are no signposts,

the road and the continuing route south are marked by new yellow DEC disks.

Finding the southern trailhead is an adventure in itself. From the Northway, exit onto the parallel highway, NY 9, and drive to Schroon Lake village, about halfway between Interchanges 27 and 28. There take Hoffman Road west, climbing steeply away from the highways. In just over 5 miles it crosses Trout Brook, just beyond which a road forks left to Olmstedville. Less than .2 mile farther, Potash Road forks right. You could turn here, but natives warn that its condition can be marginal. Instead, turn right at the Loch Mueller sign, .8 mile beyond. Loch Mueller Road intersects Potash and continues north past the Dimick Farm to a farmhouse beneath a giant pine.

Pause a moment here to enjoy the view north through Hoffman Notch, to search for bluebirds in the old apple orchard, and to read the sign affixed to the pine: "On this spot in 1845, a sapling of 12 years was transplanted by me. I have watched and protected it in my advancing years. It has given me rest and comfort. Woodsman spare that tree, touch not a single branch. In youth it sheltered me and I'll protect it now. Signed, Paschal P. Warren, June 1, 1920, age 87."

Your route north follows some of the roads early settlers used as they moved into the mountains to harvest the virgin timber and farm the rugged countryside. This isolated and remote valley has been settled since the early nineteenth century.

Continue another 200 yards into a draw and turn right about 100 yards up its far side. The spot is poorly marked but leads into a large open field that serves as the parking area for the trailhead as well as for fishermen who try their luck in the branches of Trout Brook.

Walking from south to north through the Notch you have less of a climb and also gain an enhanced sense of the transition from a southern Adirondack forest to a northern one. The hemlock at the southern edge of the Notch give way to balsam on the north. It also puts the greatest excitement as well as risk of getting wet near the hike's end, where there are several brook crossings. The streams are certainly more beautiful in high water. I think it is worth risking wet feet toward the trail's end just to make sure there is enough water in the flow that plunges from Washburn Ridge, partway along and not far from the trail. The fall is spectacular.

The lovely high meadow where you park offers another fine view of the Notch. Fire rings show that campers have used the clearing. No signs specifically indicate the trail, but if you head into the woods on the north side of the parking area, beside a "Wilderness" sign, you discover the first of the new yellow DEC trail disks. If you are observant you may also notice here a faint, blue-marked trail heading northwest toward Bailey Pond.

Your route is downhill on an abandoned logging road through a tall and impressive forest with some good-sized white birch. In a hemlock swale the road has been dug out to a depth of several feet. Within fifteen minutes, listen for the West Branch of Trout Brook, which you soon cross on a snowmobile bridge that may not last many more years. In low water the bridge is not needed.

Continue, now uphill, through a lovely forest of pine and birch with a good ground covering of blooming plants. A second bridge and a section of corduroy mark the gentle climb to a very tiny clearing, which has enough clues, apple trees for instance, to indicate that an early settler lived here.

The woods road continues climbing gently through maple and large popple to a fork. Bear right on the fork clearly marked with yellow disks. The road descends a second time and then turns to follow a stream coming in from your left. You are now in a big, deep valley, and only a narrow footpath is worn along the route of the abandoned road. You cross the stream twice within 150 feet.

You are now walking in one of the most stately mixed forests in the Adirondacks, making you wonder if it has ever been logged. Huge yellow birch, tall hemlock and ash, and a few large beech stand out. Continuing through a deep, wet glen to the left of the stream, the roadway is filled with lush ferns and wildflowers. You recross the stream on a very slippery log bridge, pass a section of corduroy, and finally hear a larger stream. Flowing from the Notch, it is the North Branch of Trout Brook.

You can walk to the North Branch in forty minutes. As you turn north along the brook signs point to Big Marsh. Almost no footpath shows on a little-used route that forks right across a bridge over the brook. It is marked for Big Rogers, the local name for Big Pond. Notice the bear scratch high on the balsam beside the bridge. Bear often sharpen their claws by scraping them on the

trunks of trees. The scratches you see on this walk indicate this is bear country, and big bear at that.

Your route is now almost due north beside the North Branch, but you cross many small streams that flow from Washburn Ridge on your left. The valley is almost level, and your route is joyously accompanied by the many small riffles and falls in the brook beside you. Big boulders fill the valley, which is shaded by a magnificent mix of maple and hemlock.

Beside the third intermittent stream crossing, stop to notice a huge yellow birch. Its diameter at chest height exceeds five feet. Next you pass a giant rounded boulder shaped like the back of a sleeping dinosaur and capped with moss and polypody ferns. At one point, a glacial drummond lies between you and the stream, but most of the time you walk close to the water.

For this first hour or so, you have probably been traveling quickly and easily. Now reduce your pace so you can appreciate the details of the deepening valley. There is so much to see. The hillside above the stream on your right, east, rises directly and steeply from the brook. Ledges on the left now crowd the road, and for a time the valley floor is little more than 100 feet across, so there is scarcely room to walk. The trail continues for .5 mile as a narrow footpath through a rich forest floor, threading its way between a jumble of boulders and ledges.

You finally become aware that you are climbing into the Notch. For a time the valley is more open, filled here with giant spruce and pine, through which you can glimpse the top of Texas Ridge on your right.

After an hour and a half—or more if you've kept a leisurely pace—and a distance of just over 3 miles, the trail climbs above an alder meadow. Giant spruce

edge the flow and through them you sense you are seeing the end of the Notch in the distant north. Leave the trail to step out into the sphagnum bog filled with spruce and hemlock stumps and many signs of old beaver work. Again look for bear scratches on the spruce.

The trail, carpeted with violets, continues close to the bog's edge, over which are more views of Texas Ridge. As the valley narrows again, you climb over small ledges beside the marshy stream. You are nearly at the top of the Notch. Look for a giant tree, felled on your left beside the trail. A typical 13½-foot section has been removed from the butt end, but the rest, stretching over 100 feet, has been left to decay, so that a fair-sized birch and several small evergreens grow from its rotted remains.

Erratics and boulders fill the valley, and a balsam thicket crowds a patch of royal fern close to the bog. After a bit more than two hours of walking, a distance of about 4 miles, you see the waters of Big Marsh, which is just over halfway through the Notch. It takes about ten minutes to walk along the marsh to find a picnic rock with a view of the hills to the east.

Cliffs and ledges extend almost to the water's edge, and huge boulders ring the marsh, where an open flow of shallow water reflects the surrounding hills as well as the tall pine and white birch that border the marsh. Texas Ridge rises to the south, and the steep knob to the north is Hornet Cobbles. East, opposite your perch, is the valley cut by a stream flowing from the flanks of the Blue Ridge Range. The peak of Hoffman Mountain rises above that valley.

As you continue the valley broadens. The trail turns away from the marsh to hug the western side, crossing several intermittent streams. The trail is very narrow, with frequent and necessary markers. It takes at least twenty minutes to cross the rest of the Notch and begin the descent, where the old roadway becomes apparent again.

Within thirty minutes you are really descending and can begin to hear Hoffman Notch Brook, which accompanies you most of the remaining distance. You first approach the brook near a wonderful little waterfall. A bridge here across a tributary stream, which flows from the valley between Hoffman Mountain and Texas Ridge, has washed away. So has the bridge farther downstream across Hoffman Notch Brook. You must devise an alternate method of crossing both. In summer, hopping stones to continue on the left bank of Hoffman Notch Brook is no problem. In high water, it is best done upstream from the confluence with the tributary. A short bushwhack along the left bank brings you down to the place the trail used to cross from the east; in fact a new footpath has been worn along most of the left bank here.

You are in the deepest part of the hemlock-shrouded gorge, walking close to the rapids and little falls. The route is rugged, the drop is steep, and the ravine is very deep, but the trek is beautiful. Shortly you pick up the yellow markers again.

Good-sized cliffs and ledges rise on your left, and you occasionally glimpse Hornet Cobbles, which seems to loom incredibly steeply above the trail on the right. When you reach an old logging clearing in a grove of maple saplings, less than an hour's walk from Big Marsh, begin looking carefully to your left. Shortly, you should catch sight of a 100-foot ledge topped with cedars and birch, over which a stream of water shoots, splitting into several cascades, dropping to pools on ledges on the dark black rock face, and then splitting again into a multitude of fine sprays.

If you are tempted to scramble up the talus slope for a better look at the falls, watch out for the horse nettles that cover the hillside and beware of poison ivy. This may be one of the most remote sites reached by that companion of man.

Continuing north beside the stream, you pass a waterfall right beside a giant boulder, an erratic over 30 feet in diameter and more than 15 feet high. Many other boulders fill the valley. Giant cedars grow among the hemlock, which make the stream so dark photographing is impossible. The valley narrows again, so that it is now scarcely 100 yards across. That horse- and oxcarts once traveled this route defies belief . . .

Gradually the brook levels, its route becoming more sinuous but its shores still edged with impressive erratics. Gravel improvements indicate the road's recent use. Trees become smaller, and you pass a small gravel pit, some abandoned and rusted machinery, and many signs of a logging camp. Your route is now high above the stream, which is still lovely in the deep gorge below you. The browns, turquoises, and greens of lichens color its light grey rocks.

After walking an hour and a half from the Notch, you reach a sign that says you have left the Hoffman Notch Wilderness Area. Land ahead is private, but the state has obtained an easement for the trail. Hunting, fishing, and camping are not permitted.

The trail crosses the stream at a spot that could be difficult to ford in high water. In early spring or after a rain, you will surely get wet. In low water, one good-sized jump may be all that is needed. The trail continues level, staying east of the stream on a soft-packed, open roadway, but still within the sound of water. You should arrive at a broad cleared swath below a power line within two hours of leaving Big Marsh.

No sign indicates the trail across the

View of Hoffman Mountain and Notch from Warren Pond

field, and the obvious route straight ahead to the continuing roadway is not the right choice! Walk east in the power line clearing at least 150 yards, then enter the woods on the north below the ledge on which the first of the huge stanchions for the power line is mounted. The spot is poorly marked. It is the beginning of a new route that has been cut and marked with the yellow disks to avoid a beaver flow that flooded the old road and most of the lowlands between you and Blue Ridge Road, your final destination. The trail heads east and almost parallels the power line, staying just below the edge of the trees, and then swings north again to traverse the flooded lands and cross Hoffman Notch Brook on a rickety bridge perched on top of an untended beaver dam. This area has been repeatedly flooded and the trail is in serious need of realignment. Unfortunately, Finch Pruyn & Company, which owns the land through which the lower part of the trail passes, has not permitted further re-alignments. You may get very wet feet.

The trail intersects the roadway again and climbs quickly to the highway. You might want to walk down this short stretch of trail when you spot a car here, before you begin the hike from the south.

If the trail appears to be too flooded for easy passage, you can decide to walk from the south only as far as the marshes in the Notch and return by the same route, eliminating the lovely walk along the gorge until the beaver-flooding-the-trail problem is sorted out.

Boreas Mountain

Distance (round trip): 7.6 miles
Vertical rise: 2,076 feet
Hiking time: 4 hours
Maps: USGS 15' Mount Marcy; USGS 15' Schroon Lake

Facing each other on opposite sides of Elk Lake, both Boreas and Sunrise mountains have spectacular views of the southern sides of the eastern High Peaks. You may still climb Boreas, but because the tower on its summit has been removed, that mountain's magnificent panorama must now be enjoyed in pieces through openings in the trees. A worse fate has befallen Sunrise, which has an unrestricted view toward Mount Marcy from open rock ledges. The trail to its summit, like that of Boreas's, crosses private property. Careless and unthinking hikers have littered the trail and otherwise abused the private land, forcing its owners to limit hikers to guests of the Elk Lake Lodge and groups who have obtained special permission.

Even if you are climbing only Boreas, the Elk Lake Lodge is an elegant place to stay. Guests may canoe around the bays and islands of Elk Lake, surrounded by a sweep of mountains that includes Mount Marcy, Nippletop, and Dix. Hikers find it a delightful base for exploring the area. The regulations governing the use of Elk Lake lands are simple: no camping, hunting, fishing, or building of fires. Only two other trails on the Elk Lake Preserve are open to the public. They lead to Panther Gorge and the Dix Range and are described in *Discover the Adirondack High Peaks.*

The trailhead for Boreas is just outside the gate of the Elk Lake Lodge property, but still on private land. When you hike Boreas, be sure to respect those lands so all may continue to enjoy the mountain.

Now, to the pleasure of the mountain. From many peaks near the periphery of the Adirondacks, the distant horizon has been defined by some aspect of the eastern High Peaks. The hikes in this guide have you approaching the inner mountain range that holds the Adirondacks' highest peaks as you would approach a great sculptural work of art, looking at it from different angles, tracing its lines and curves, examining its shapes and masses, watching the play of light and shadow cast by sun and clouds, pausing to enjoy the brilliance of the white slash of mountain slides or the sparkle reflected from high mountain streams.

When you climb the eastern High Peaks, the views from the summits within this crowded cluster of mountains make you feel on top of the world but few of these vistas rival those from the peaks immediately surrounding the Adirondacks' highest range. Circling this sculptural mass, you find that the most spectacular of all views is from the south, from Boreas and Sunrise, looking to the steepest faces, the deepest mountain passes, and the greatest expanse of bare rock and precipitous slides. This peak, at 3,776 feet, does not even number among the fabled over-4,000 peaks.

From one of the openings between the trees on Boreas you see northeast across Elk Lake to a range that traces the outline of a bracket against the horizon. Hough is the apex, flanked by Dix and McComb mountains, each of which has enormous vertical slides. Farther north, the flanks of Dix and Nippletop form Hunters Pass. From Boreas you see right through the pass to Giant Mountain, marked by the slides surrounding its cirque. North, left, of Nippletop is the row of mountains flanking the east side of the Ausable valley with Blake Mountain and

Mount Colvin clearly identified.

On the north side of the Ausable valley, you see Sawteeth with the sheer face of Gothics right behind. You cannot help but be impressed by its rocky countenance. Continuing left, the tops of Saddleback and Basin lead to the impressive cluster of Skylight, Marcy, and Haystack. (Both Saddleback and Basin have deep slashes of open rock.) The latter group is most easily seen from the top of a rock west of the abandoned tower. From there also you can just barely see the MacIntyre Mountains. Through another small opening west of the tower the North River Mountains are visible over Boreas Ponds. To the right and beyond these mountains is Santanoni, with its distinctive scar. Behind Santanoni and to the north, right, are Seward and Seymour. Next north is Redfield with Allen before it and Ampersand peeping over a cut to Redfield's left.

This is considered the best view of the mountains that border the Ausable valley on the north. Unfortunately, southern landmarks, once visible from the tower, cannot be enjoyed. That view included Pharaoh Mountain on the southeast and Blue Mountain on the southwest.

Unhappily, the trail to these views is not among the Adirondacks' best; over 2 miles of the route are through recently logged lands using a segment of a network of rocky logging roads.

To reach the trailhead, exit from the Adirondack Northway (I-87) at Interchange 29, and turn left, west, on Blue Ridge Road toward Newcomb. In 4 miles, bear north on dirt Elk Lake Road and park at the designated spot in 3.2 miles.

Rerouting of the trail to avoid wet areas, confusion caused by intersecting logging roads, and sparse or concealed markers along parts of the trail make it occasionally difficult to follow.

The first part of the trail is well marked with red DEC disks. It heads west, drops moderately, then more abruptly down to a road where it turns left along the road and at .4 mile crosses The Branch on a good bridge. The only caution here is that on the return trip remember to turn right into the woods after crossing this bridge; the road continues straight ahead and you might be tempted to follow it.

The trail is now circling around a spruce bog. At .6 mile the trail turns to the right up onto a bank for about 100 feet to avoid a wet area, then returns to follow the road again. Watch carefully at a height-of-land at just over 1 mile where the road continues straight ahead down into a wet, marsh area. Here the trail, marked with strips of red plastic as well as the DEC disks, makes a sharp right turn into the woods. If you miss this turn, you will find the old route still has markers and you have to cross a lot of wet ground before the old and new routes meet again.

The trail makes a rock-hop crossing of a stream at 1.4 miles and continues moderately uphill until it emerges in an open area and rejoins the old route. As you leave the open area, avoid the road to the left. On the right is an old road with a stream to the right of it. The trail follows this road along the stream as it continues uphill. At 1.7 miles, the trail takes a sharp left up a steep bank, joins another road and continues uphill to the right.

The trail dips once to cross a stream that has cut across the road, then at 2.2 miles, it turns left and heads down across another stream. As you turn to descend to this crossing, the mountain is straight ahead of you. Across the stream the trail angles right again and continues steadily uphill. There is one more right fork onto a roadway before the trail crosses an eroded area. The trail threads between deep wheel ruts, then continues along the old road and the traditional trail to the cabin site, which you reach at 2.9 miles. The abandoned fire observer's cabin has burned recently and is surrounded by badly scorched trees.

A stream flows behind the cabin site. The trail crosses the stream to the left of the cabin site, plunges into the woods, and immediately begins to climb very steeply. Nearly 1,000 feet remain to climb in the last .9 mile. The forest is cooler and less disturbed but still composed of fairly small trees. The route is a steep, steady climb through balsam and spruce. You cross a small stream on the remains of a washed-out bridge .3 mile from the cabin clearing and recross the stream shortly in a deep draw edged with birch and mountain ash. The third time you cross the stream it has dwindled to barely a trickle.

Within thirty minutes from the cabin site you climb quite steeply through a rocky ravine where the trail is washed out. The grade levels briefly before leading into an incredibly steep pitch, but fifteen minutes

View from Boreas

of hard hiking ("climbing" might be more exact) brings you to a forested spot where blue sky shows through the trees in all directions. After a series of small switchbacks the light breeze alerts you that you are approaching a ridge of the mountain. As you come over the ridge in a meadow of tall ferns, turn left to head up the narrow spine toward the summit.

Within a couple of minutes you will turn left to the summit knoll where the tower once stood.

On the descent you should have no problem with any directions. All the logging roads seem to funnel toward the route you should follow, except at the last fork after you cross The Branch.

Giant Mountain

Distance (one way): 6.6 miles
Vertical rise: 3,000 feet
Hiking time: 6 hours
Maps: USGS 7½' Metric Keene Valley; USGS 7½' Metric
  Elizabethtown
Giant Mountain Wilderness Area

Giant is in every way an appropriate name for the mountain between Pleasant Valley south of Elizabethtown and the East Branch of the Ausable south of Keene Valley. Several trails lead to its summit, and although the route chosen here, from the west, presents the greatest vertical rise of any hike described in this guide, trails from Pleasant Valley on Giant's east side require another thousand feet of climbing. Giant is indeed a giant. It is 4,627 feet tall, the twelfth highest peak in the Adirondacks. The summit commands the best view from the east of the High Peaks, while overlooking almost all of the Champlain Valley and, on south, to the mountains beside Lake George. The climb from Chapel Pond on the west is challenging, and you can descend via the trail along Roaring Brook, also on the west, for a hike as varied as you could wish. If you pause for a picnic lunch on Giant's summit, the day's outing should take at least 7 hours.

If you plan to hike the two trails as described here, two cars are advisable. You can walk along NY 73 between Chapel Pond and Roaring Brook trailheads in less than a half-hour, but the highway is very busy and apt to be dangerous for

pedestrians. If you decide simply to retrace your route, I suggest using the Chapel Pond trail. The unfolding views on that trail far exceed any along the Roaring Brook route. The trip is fairly strenuous, so be sure you carry enough water. The summit is exposed, so also carry extra clothing.

To reach the trailheads, take Exit 30 off the Adirondack Northway (I-87) and head northwest on NY 73, following signs for Keene Valley. Chapel Pond is 3.6 miles beyond the road that forks right toward Elizabethtown. The Roaring Brook trailhead, where your hike ends, is 1.4 miles farther, opposite the southern entrance to the Ausable Club.

After parking at Chapel Pond, and if you can tear yourself away from the views of the cliffs that rise from the pond, as well as those on the shoulder of Giant, walk south 250 yards to the trailhead, which is concealed in a marsh on the east side of the road. An inconspicuous sign denotes the route to Giant via the Ridge Trail.

Orange Adirondack Trail Improvement Society (ATIS) markers indicate the way. You begin to climb immediately after crossing an intermittent stream. Rocks are tumbled everywhere. At .3 mile the trail angles left and a sign points right to a spring that is not dependable in dry weather. New birch railings guide you to a recently rerouted stretch of trail. Follow the prescribed route, which zigzags across the steep slope. A steeper climb is possible but it would hasten erosion. The sparse birch cover tells of raging forest fires, and there is no ground cover to hold the thin soil. The mountainside is amazingly bare, brown, and sterile below the tree cover.

Within fifteen minutes, as you traverse back toward the highway, a glimpse of Round Mountain serves as a gauge on how rapidly you are climbing. In .5 mile you reach a rubble-filled wash and continue under overhanging ledges. The wash was once the outlet of the Giant's Washbowl, a tiny pond on the mountainside. After walking less than a half-hour, you reach an unmarked fork where a footpath leads 50 feet to the left to the edge of a cliff that drops directly to the

highway by Chapel Pond. Notice how the cliffs that overhang the western side of the pond have already shrunk below you. The tops of Armstrong and the Wolfjaws are visible to the west.

Continue on the right fork, almost on the cliff edge, to a second lookout and then turn away from the cliff to drop a few feet to a trail junction .7 mile from the highway. The left fork leads to Saint Huberts, but you continue straight beside the Giant's Washbowl. Pause to enjoy the reflections of the Giant's cliffs. The route heads northeast into a spruce and hemlock grove, which indicates the limits of the fires up the mountain. The trail continues through deep woods with huge cedars for .2 mile to a second marked junction where the fork left also heads towards Saint Huberts, via Roaring Brook.

Bearing right, you start up a steep pitch, and the cover quickly thins. After about an hour of climbing, a slide at 1.2 miles yields views across the valley to Round Mountain and Noonmark. You

View of Chapel Pond

234 *Giant Mountain*

now scramble up bare rock to a second lookout southwest toward Hough and both South and East Dix mountains. The peaks covered by the Range Trail are now visible beyond the Ausable valley.

For the twenty minutes you need to ascend the sheer rock face, cairns guide you along the route. The climb continues between view spots, each providing needed respite. Gothics becomes clearly distinguished between Sawteeth and Wolfjaw. The opening south through the long valley shows Pharaoh Mountain's cone 24 miles away and the Tip of the Tongue and Black Mountain near Lake George 40 miles away.

Cairns direct the trail between the scrubby clumps of spruce, balsam, and blueberries that separate patches of open rock. You come to an overlook east toward Rocky Peak Ridge about the same time you see a false summit on Giant. Chapel Pond seems no bigger than a drop of water. The Ausable Club is visible in the western foreground, and the mountains on the north side of Johns Brook Valley appear above the mountains of the Range Trail.

You continue to scramble through low woods to another sheer slope of open rock. The views of only ten minutes before are even more dramatic, and now you begin to see straight through Hunters Pass, with Dix on the left and Dial on the right. Nippletop is still hidden behind Dial, but Hough, McComb, South Dix, and East Dix now range as separate peaks to the south. Colvin appears on the side of Ausable Lake, and the bare cone of Haystack is apparent between Gothics and Sawteeth.

The trail forks, the way right climbing over and the way left circling a little knob from which the southern end of Giant's summit ridge is visible. The trails rejoin at about 1.8 miles and just under two hours into your hike. You continue across a ridge, looking toward the Giant's cirque, the huge bowl slashed by recent slides, which make this mountain recognizable from such enormous distances.

Beyond a relatively level stretch, the trail rises to another intersection, 2.2 miles from Chapel Pond. The left fork leads down toward Saint Huberts, the way you will return. The right fork leads .7 mile and 700 feet to the summit, a climb you can make in a half hour. You pass a slant rock shelter and then reach a level stretch around the top of the cirque, with a steep rock ledge on your right. The footpath is narrow, winding through trees scarcely taller than hikers' heads. The summit is still .3 mile ahead. One more steep pitch brings you to it. A couple hundred yards before the actual peak, another trail forks right, leading in .7 mile to Rocky Peak Ridge.

Walk along the summit ridge to find overlooks for all directions. Right at your feet extends the new scar of the slide that washed from Giant's summit in a violent series of thunderstorms. Before you, across the deep, scarred valley enclosed by the Giant's arms, spread the Ausable valley with Gothics beyond, a little south of west, and Mount Marcy finally visible above it. Over the wooded slopes north of Gothics lies MacIntyre, with Colden barely visible between it and Marcy.

On the northern side of Johns Brook Valley, Big Slide is to the left of Cascade and Porter, which appear almost as two summits of the same mountain. To the right of MacIntyre on the distant horizon, MacNaughton, Street, and Nye form a ridge ending over Big Slide. To the right of Porter and Cascade, the long ridge with lots of rock is Pitchoff, and beyond it, the Sentinels and Whiteface are visible.

Now, as you look through Hunters Pass, the tower on Boreas is visible. To its right and 43 miles distant are the steep slopes of Puffer and the heart-shaped top of Humphrey to the left. Farther left, Snowy's peak is obvious, and continuing left, Panther and Wakely are visible with good binoculars.

Hurricane is obvious in the northeast, identified by its tower and rock summit. The eastern horizon is filled with the sweep of Lake Champlain; and of the distant Green Mountains, only Camel's Hump and Mount Mansfield are obvious and easily identified. The mountains of Vermont seem to range forever, to both the north and south.

Retrace your route .7 mile to the trail to Saint Huberts. The route is steep enough so that you may need twenty-five minutes to reach the junction. Take the right fork, which heads into deep woods, traversing the steep slopes of Giant, dropping like a rock. The slopes you cross are sometimes pitched at a sixty-degree angle, so even the traverse route is steep. No open places distract you as you keep your eyes on the trail to ensure safe footing.

Thirty minutes from the junction the trail levels out, but you must walk a bit farther before the trees become noticeably taller. As you enter a valley you sense you are near the edge of the glacial cirque, but new growth conceals it from view. The steep descent continues for the better part of an hour on this trail, covering nearly 1.5 miles before reaching a muddy seep within a majestic hemlock grove. From here you can hear the water of Roaring Brook. You cross two streams flowing from your left in .2 mile, and reach a trail junction in another .1 mile. The route left is through the Giant's Nubble. You turn right and shortly cross the brook on the pure white rocks amidst signs of terrifying amounts of water and fallen debris. The rubble from the slide is now uphill above you. A trail to the right heads up the mountain but is quickly obliterated by the slide. You turn left to follow the valley of Roaring Brook, walking through the prettiest wooded section on the hike, a hemlock grove of tall, straight, towering trees.

A path forks left 3.3 miles from the summit, back to the top of Roaring Brook Falls, a place of beauty and danger. The trail continues on a contour around a deep ravine, running first through magnificent hemlock and then past huge birch, and finally dropping to the valley floor. The entire 3.6-mile descent, with time to pause and study the slide and enjoy the falls, takes at least two and a half hours.

Indian Pass

Distance (one way): 10.6 miles
Vertical rise: 674 feet
Hiking time: 7 hours
Maps: USGS 15' Mount Marcy; USGS 15' Santanoni
High Peaks Wilderness Area

In 1836 Professor Ebenezer Emmons was appointed chief geologist in charge of studying the Adirondacks. In the course of this study he visited the "Adirondack Pass" we now know as Indian Pass. Of it he wrote that "in this country there is no object of the kind on a scale so vast and imposing as this. We look upon the Falls of Niagara with awe and a feeling of our insignificance; but much more are we impressed with the great and sublime in the simple and naked rock of the Adirondack Pass." Later nineteenth-century explorers discovered many more dramatic natural features, but Indian Pass remains the most incredibly wild and dramatic spot in the eastern United States.

Indian Pass bisects the Adirondack High Peaks. You can hike through it in one day, if you arrange to leave a car at both the north and south trailheads. I suggest you walk the pass from north to south for both aesthetic and historic reasons. The route is one to anticipate and savor, so set aside ample time to appreciate the marvelous sights and sounds you will encounter.

To heighten the drama read Alfred Billings Street's nineteenth-century classic

The Indian Pass before you go. He used every passionate and romantic adjective to describe the pass's awe-inspiring rocks, cliff, and vistas. For example, a typical summer thunderstorm became a dialogue between the echoing voices of the mountains. For all the excesses of his nineteenth-century prose, you will discover that the pass remains the "magnificent spectacle" he described.

The quirks of sound and echoes that astounded Street will amaze you, for the voices of other hikers seem to reflect from many improbable sources. According to Street, Indians called the pass He-no-do-as-da, the path of the thunder, or Os-ten-wanne, Great Rock, or Otne-yar-heh, the Stonish Giants.

The southern trailhead, where your hike ends, is the Upper Works Trailhead north of Tahawus, the site of National Lead Company's titanium mine. From Exit 29 of the Adirondack Northway (I-87), drive west 13.5 miles on Blue Ridge Road to an intersection marked Tahawus and turn right, or north. From Long Lake on NY 30, take NY 28N east 15.5 miles through Newcomb and turn north at the marked intersection. Just south of the entrance to the mine, a road forks left 3.7

miles to the Upper Works Trailhead.

To reach the northern trailhead, drive to the end of Heart Lake Road which runs south from NY 73 at the hamlet of North Elba, 11.2 miles west of Keene and 3.2 miles east of Lake Placid. Park by the Adirondak Loj, which is owned and managed by the Adirondack Mountain Club. The club charges a nominal parking fee.

The red-marked trail begins west of the parking lot, circles north of the Loj, swings south beside the Natural History Museum, and continues south along the shore of Heart Lake, following a dirt road which gives access to lean-tos and campsites on Loj property.

Within .2 mile you pass a trail that forks right to head up Mount Jo. That trail, which is described excellently in Dr. Edwin Ketchledge's *Guide to the Natural History of Mount Jo,* is short and spectacular. First-time visitors to the High Peaks will find it an excellent introduction. From Mount Jo, the view across Heart Lake to the MacIntyre Mountains is most beautiful.

In less than fifteen minutes, .5 mile from the start, you reach the end of the lake, where a side trail forks left to circle it. Continue straight, passing the sign-in box for the trail, through a birch and cedar second-growth forest over rolling country. Within .1 mile you reach the boundary of state land. For the next 1.5 miles the walking is easy on a good hard-packed trail. Enormous spruce and good-sized balsam dot the hardwood forest of beech, maple, and birch. A rich forest floor supports a wide variety of wildflowers and ferns. In summer the red berries of twisted stalk and the blue berries of clintonia stand out beside the trail. Openings to the right through the trees give hints of the outline of the valley of Indian Pass Brook. While some guidebooks pay scant attention to these first 2 miles you should not, for you are walking in a very fine forest.

In addition to red trail markers, yellow markers with red numbers at .5 mile intervals measure your progress from the Loj. You can easily reach the 2-mile marker within an hour. In another .1 mile, on the far side of a stream crossing, a loop trail heads right, past Rocky Falls and a lean-to. This spur is little more than 200 yards longer than the main trail, so take it and enjoy walking beside Indian Pass Brook with its white stone base and views of the falls that drop into a deep pool from a chute through a deep cleft in the bedrock. Returning to the main trail requires scrambling up a short pitch, but the entire detour, .3 mile long, should take no more than fifteen minutes to walk.

Where you return to the main trail, a benchmark marks the elevation as 2,160 feet. Turn right, south, passing an intermittent stream and then a second stream in a small gorge. Beyond a rocky section you encounter a mud hole, and you pass the 3-mile marker in the midst of a big stretch of mud and corduroy.

There are interesting ledges on your left as the walking continues easy and level. Along this stretch you may encounter a howler, or widowmaker, a treetop leaning on a second tree and rubbing against it to create weird shrieking sounds.

Through openings to the right you should be able to glimpse the shoulders of Street and Nye mountains and the unnamed mountain that conceals Lost Pond near its summit. You cross one and then another creek, where ledges on surrounding hills begin to enclose the pass. As the valley narrows you reach the Scott's Clearing lean-to, 4 miles from the Loj. Ford the creek in front of the lean-to by hopping rocks. The trail then turns right, and within a few minutes you enter

the meadow of Scott's Clearing, which today is filled with raspberries, barrel staves and iron artifacts, and spectacular white birch.

In another .3 mile, a blue-marked trail heads west to Wallface and Scott ponds. Just beyond, a marvelous rock dam creates a flow over which there is a view of Wallface Mountain and Indian Pass. An ancient beaver house stands in the pond, and signs of beaver work abound. A low water-level trail continues toward Indian Pass, but it can be wet even in a dry summer. I suggest you walk an alternate route, which circles a small hill whose cliff face drops directly to the pond. To find it, angle left at the east end of the dam, almost as if to parallel the trail from the lean-to, and walk to the brook. For about 100 yards the trail follows the brook, whose rock base is strangely colored steel gray. It then swings up a draw; and footing is rough among the rocks and roots. Rounding the top of the draw, the trail crosses a height-of-land in a small ravine, turns toward the valley, and starts down through a steep cleft that cuts the cliff wall.

When you return to the level of the flow again, you become aware of how narrow the valley is. A rock wall is now visible on the east. You cross a stream that enters from the left at 4.7 miles. The next section of trail lies too close to Indian Pass Brook, and footing is apt to be wet until you cross a second brook, .2 mile farther. Both streams flow from Algonquin Pass. At 5.1 miles, after about two and a half hours of walking, you intersect a yellow-marked trail that heads east for 3.3 miles to Lake Colden.

Just beyond that trail junction you have a good view of cliffs on an unnamed knob, but then the pass becomes progressively narrower, and vertical cliffs form walls on both sides of the stream. You cross Indian Pass Brook on a grav-

ely wash, and then recross it to follow a smaller flow from the pass. Just beyond you see the outlet of Scott Pond, which flows from the west.

The trail now enters the narrow cleft of Indian Pass and begins to climb rapidly. A faint footpath winds up and over boulders and moss-covered ledges, following the small cold brook that flows from the pass. Steep cliffs face the flanks of MacIntyre to form the pass's eastern wall. Here the pass itself is scarcely 100 feet wide and filled with the rubble of ancient slides. You may often have to use your hands to help yourself along and you will need the one ladder to help you climb the steepest part. The dark, moss-covered canyon with overhanging cliffs ends all too soon. This entrance to the pass is but .4 mile long. It should take twenty minutes to scramble up the 400-foot rise into the pass.

As you reach the end of the ravine, Wallface begins to loom high up on your right, its sheer, vertical cliff cut jaggedly. The pass opens wide, and you climb a few feet on the east side, overlooking a precipitous mass of boulders so rugged the trail could not possibly be routed through the deepest part. As you walk the short distance of the height-of-land, watch for the holes and the mouths of caves among the slabs. On a hot summer day fog and mist rise in cool drafts from these crevices, where ice often persists well into July. The sharply angular tops of the larger boulders support lichens and mosses and even large spruce and birch. Rising above it all, Wallface creates a dramatic backdrop for the wild scene.

The pass developed as a northeast-trending fault at the same time as many other Adirondack fault valleys from pressures created by the Taconic uplift. But while many of these faults are filled with long, thin lakes, rocks and boulders fallen from the cliff of Wallface and the flanks of MacIntyre have filled the pass to its present level.

By the route you have taken it is nearly 5.8 miles to the height-of-land in the pass, a point denoted by a DEC trail marker. As you continue south, the temperature rises noticeably when the trail leads a few feet up a ridge on the east side of the pass. As you make a short descent, the sheer cliffs, columns, and hanging ledges on Wallface seem even higher. You walk through a small meadow, and within ten minutes reach a clearing with a fireplace. This is a good stopping spot for viewing the highest part of the cliffs, which rise nearly 1,000 feet above you.

To continue south, find and cross a small stream. It, like the brook on the north, rises from a spring in the height of the pass. The northern brook makes its way to the West Branch of the Ausable, which empties into Lake Champlain. The one you have just met, confusingly also called Indian Pass Brook, flows south into Lake Henderson, whose outlet joins Calamity Brook to form the Hudson River.

Just beyond the meadow an enormous fallen slab of cliff blocks the trail. You wind around it, climbing slightly before beginning the final descent, which is along a ridge above and on the east side of the gorge. The south side of the pass is drier and more open than the north. Its sides are precipitously steep below you. After a half-hour walk, for it takes that long to enjoy this .4-mile segment, you reach a sign pointing right up a small ladder to a huge boulder, Summit Rock, which marks the southern edge of Indian Pass. It overlooks the broad sweep of the pass as it falls off toward Lake Henderson, with Henderson and Santanoni mountains behind. The sight rivals the majestic grandeur of the vista back toward the cliffs on Wallface. You will stand on the outcrop like the tiny figures of the Hudson River School painters, overlooking an awe-inspiring view, completely overwhelmed by the scale of the rocks and forests around you.

A steep descent of 500 feet over .5 mile to the southern Indian Pass Brook follows. Within a few minutes you reach the first ladder, a necessary convenience because of the cliffs that rim the pass. The jumble of boulders, caves, and overhanging cliffs continues, with side paths leading to some of the larger boulders that emerge above the trees. Then, in a spot not well marked, the trail turns right, east, toward the gorge around a ledge, at the beginning of a very steep sliding descent into the valley. A pair of ladders assist in the descent. Lovely views accompany you on the precipitous route.

By the time you reach these ladders, the valley has become quite broad. The terrain continues to be rugged. A few openings between tree-capped boulders offer dramatic views of Wallface, which seems to loom even higher than it did before. You continue to look down into the depths of the cleft on your right, with everything on a much larger scale than it was along the northern entrance to the pass.

You pass a waterfall just before you actually reach and cross the brook. Here you have your last view back of the cliffs on Wallface. It will probably take you at least a half-hour to cover the .5-mile descent from Summit Rock.

The stream crossing marks a real change in the route, for the trail now enters a deep mature woods. The descent is gentle for a short time, until you reach a boggy section of trail. Cross it, on slippery logs, looking for turtlehead as you go.

You cross the wash of an intermittent stream, which affords views back east to the ridge that makes up the foothills of

Wallface cliffs from the north end of Indian Pass

the MacIntyre Mountains. The trail crosses a larger stream, the outlet of Wallface Ponds, and then continues beneath ledges on the west side of the valley to the Wallface lean-to, 1.2 miles and at least a half-hour from the stream crossing.

A washed-out bridge is all there is for crossing a small stream just below the lean-to. Within twenty minutes the trail angles left up a small rise, where it meets a freshly painted but ambiguous sign, on which is written in elegant script only the word "Bridge." Turn left to follow the trail 100 yards east to the bridge over Indian Pass Brook. A ten-foot-tall crib of boulders supports the bridge's west end, while a single boulder supports the east end. Beyond, the footpath turns south beside the stream and leads to an old clearing with another bridge sign and an incorrect mileage marker where the trail forks. A blue-marked trail heads back east toward Colden. It is .3 mile to the Henderson lean-to, and 2 miles from the clearing to the Upper Works Trailhead. The trail stays near the stream as far as the lean-to, which is less than 100 yards from the boundary of private lands. The red-marked trail continues through private lands. Permission to cross has been granted hikers, but the lands are posted against fishing, hunting, trapping, and camping.

At a major intersection .1 mile south of the boundary, a trail turns right, west, toward Duck Hole and Coreys, west of Ampersand.

Here you pick up a yellow-marked trail heading south along logging roads improved with gravel. Because the surrounding land is private, you never really see Lake Henderson. After a dull, relatively level stretch you cross the Hudson River, just below the outlet of Lake Henderson. In another five minutes you walk downhill to the trailhead and your waiting car.

It takes a full day to enjoy the 10.6-mile walk, but there is still more to see. Immediately south of the Upper Works Trailhead, a row of deserted houses marks the 1833 settlement of Adirondac where the workers of the McIntyre Iron Works were housed.

A mile south of the trailhead stands the stone tower of the mine's blast furnace, erected in 1854. The beauty of the precise angles of the tower's cut stone will remind you of European castles. The tower, nearly 48 feet tall, now bears a crown of cedar and huge birch.

The iron ore was "discovered" in 1826 by a party who made the trip through Indian Pass from North Elba, led by an Indian guide, Lewis Elijah, who knew the site of the ore bed. The group included my great-great-grandfather's brother, Duncan McMartin; David Henderson; a black manservant; and a dog called Wallace. Within a few years, a company formed by Henderson, McMartin, and Archibald McIntyre began mining and shipping out the high-grade iron ore. Unfortunately, high titanium content, which made ore separating difficult, and the problems of shipping the ore from its wilderness location brought an end to the iron mining operation after only a few years.

Driving south toward Newcomb, you cannot help but be aware of the successor company, National Lead, which now mines and ships titanium from pits deep in the earth near Lake Sanford. A short detour to the mine is worthwhile. A parking turnout is provided beside the road for those who wish to stop for samples of the ilmenite from which the titanium is processed, and heavy pieces of magnetite, which contain the iron ore. Above the spot marked as a "Mineral

Collecting Area," you will find one of the Adirondacks' more impressive views. Due east lie the North River Mountains, with Allen to their north, then Redfield leading up to Skylight, with Mount Marcy peeping behind. Just east of north lies Mount Adams, identified by its tower. Northwest, over the mine pit, stands Henderson, with Santanoni beyond.

If you continue on the mine road, you will reach the overlook where you may view the current operation. In a dozen years it has created a hole 3,000 feet long, 1,500 feet wide, and 300 feet deep in the spot where the mining village of Tahawus once existed.

When you return home you will want to relive the pleasures of the hike through Indian Pass by reading Arthur H. Masten's *The Story of Adirondac,* available in reprint. In it you will find a copy of the letter in which David Henderson wrote of his discovery trip through the Pass, as well as the history of the mine. And, you will want to relive the trip, for you will agree it is the most exciting walk in the eastern United States.

Algonquin Peak in the MacIntyre Mountains

Distance (round trip): 8 miles
Vertical rise: 2,936 feet
Hiking time: 6 hours
Map: USGS 15' Mount Marcy
High Peaks Wilderness Area

Algonquin Peak in the MacIntyre Mountains is, at 5,114 feet, the second highest mountain in New York State. But in all other respects, Algonquin is second to none. Standing in the midst of the noblest group of mountains in the Adirondacks, it offers an exciting climb and the best view from within the High Peaks.

The trailhead for Algonquin is an historic site at the end of Heart Lake Road, which heads south from NY 73 in North Elba, 11.2 miles west of Keene and 3.2 miles east of Lake Placid. When you first turn south toward Heart Lake, stop to enjoy the view of the High Peaks; the MacIntyre Mountains completely dominate the skyline.

This northern gateway to the High Peaks is owned and managed by the Adirondack Mountain Club, which maintains a parking lot at the end of Heart Lake Road. The club charges a nominal fee for parking. Public accommodation is available at the club's Loj, and many lean-tos and tent sites near the shores of Heart Lake may also be rented on a daily basis. The Loj was built near the site of an imposing hotel the inventor Henry van Hoevenberg had constructed of massive logs in 1878–1880. Van Hoe-

venberg's fortune financed the lodge he planned to run with his fiancée, Josephine Scofield, for whom he named the mountain behind the lodge, Mount Jo. Disapproving parents and her untimely death brought an end to the marriage plans, and the forest fires of 1903 brought an end to the lodge. Donaldson's *The History of the Adirondacks* contains many fascinating details of the development of this northern gateway to the High Peaks.

The MacIntyre Mountains derived their name from Archibald McIntyre, Comptroller of the State of New York and partner in the McIntyre Iron Mine, south of Indian Pass. Algonquin Peak was named about 1880 by the surveyor Verplank Colvin after the tribe that once controlled most of New England, the Hudson River Valley, and the St. Lawrence River Valley. The tribe, which sided with the French in the French and English wars of the seventeenth century, was gradually overpowered by the Iroquois. Algonquin, according to Russell M.L. Carson in *Peaks and People of the Adirondacks,* "is therefore a monument to the annihilated people, who were the original possessors of the Adirondack Wilderness." (Carson's book is a complete record of the names, early ascents, and trails on the Adirondacks' forty-six peaks over 4,000 feet in elevation.)

The trailhead and registration booth are located at the southeastern edge of the Loj parking lot. For the first mile you follow the newly constructed Van Hoevenberg Trail, which is the principal route to Mount Marcy, denoted with blue markers. The route begins down a small incline and crosses a marsh, an alder swamp, and then the outlet of Heart Lake on a log bridge. After climbing the side of a small hill, you enter state land, and within twenty minutes, or 1 mile, you come to a major trail junction. Here the blue-marked trail to Marcy Dam heads south, or left, and the MacIntyre trails, marked with yellow disks, continue straight ahead.

From the intersection it is 3 miles to the summit of Algonquin, with almost all the ascent yet to come. The Adirondack Mountain Club is proud of the work that has been done to repair sections of the trail and reroute worn areas. Waterbars, stairs, and stone work all help prevent erosion. As a result, the lower sections of the trail are easy to walk.

Within twenty minutes you come to a stretch where large stones have been placed through a muddy swale. A ski-touring trail forks left at 1.4 miles, toward Whales Tail Notch. The Whales Tail is a small knob directly northeast of MacIntyre's northern summit, Wright Peak. Continuing, you walk through a rich hardwood forest whose floor is punctuated by the blooming flowers of understory plants.

Gradually paper birch becomes the predominant tree. This indicates the extent of the fires that burned the mountainside and all the Heart Lake area in the early twentieth century. The spruce and balsam now establishing themselves be-

neath the birch are your clues to the length of time that has passed. You walk through the birch forest for nearly 1 mile, past ledges on the left, climbing moderately. You will hardly be aware of where you cross the old worn trail. At 2.3 miles, an hour and fifteen minutes into your walk, a sign points to the summit 1.6 miles away. The gullied wash leading back to your left is the abandoned trail.

A few minutes later you come to a sign pointing left, east, to a camping area. Just beyond, the trail crosses a brook not shown on the USGS map. In wet seasons a crystal sheet of water falls over a high ledge, creating a charming resting spot.

As you climb again, the balsam become thicker, and ledges on the left are covered with a deep moss carpet. Within fifteen minutes, in a short level, you cross an almost dry stream. Then a jumble of old blowdowns edges a steep section of trail that zigzags through the scrub. In fifteen minutes more, at 2.9 miles, you pass a rock knob on your right, just off the trail. A sign warns you not to proceed farther without proper gear, a caution you should always heed while hiking in the High Peaks.

As you turn left away from the knob to scramble up a very steep section, you have views of a wooded summit, the first of many false summits you glimpse as you climb.

Two hours into your hike, at 3.1 miles, you reach another trail junction. The way left, marked with blue disks, leads in .5 mile to Wright Peak, 385 feet higher than your present location. Continue straight on the yellow-marked trail to begin one of the steepest climbs on a High Peaks trail, an ascent of 912 feet in .9 mile. It may take you a full hour to reach the summit from here.

The route is steep, over ledges, with water usually coursing over the bare rock

Colden from Algonquin

248 *Algonquin Peak in the MacIntyre Mountains*

that constitutes the trail. Scrubby spruce and balsam line the route and cling to the sphagnum that makes up the vertical bogs of the alpine summits. The shallow soil is home to many ground covers, including creeping white winterberry, golden thread, and bunchberry, here blossoming at the end of July, eight weeks later than in the Adirondack lowlands. When you reach a stretch of sheer rock trail, pause to look back, for you can now see the summit of Wright Peak, and you appear to be at about the same elevation. Openings permit views north to Whiteface and McKenzie and east to the precipitous rock face of Gothics. Again you have a view of a summit ahead, but it too is false. The blue leaves of dwarf bilberry and the blue-green and white almost needlelike leaves of bog rosemary show up in the mats of low scrub bushes along the trail. Huge blue crystals of labradorite are imbedded in the anorthosite that makes up the rock base of this and all the eastern High Peaks.

Forty minutes from the junction you reach treeline, with .4 mile left to climb. A sign asks that you please stay on the marked trail so that you do not trample the fragile alpine vegetation. From here on, only arrows painted on bedrock or cairns mark the trail. The route is not hard to follow in good weather, but if clouds should roll in, a not uncommon event on high Adirondack summits, watch carefully for the arrows.

Another false summit looms ahead, but finally you climb over a small ledge and find the true summit. As you climb the open rock slabs, you begin to see the three-leafed cinquefoil of the alpine summits, and in summer you will be surprised to discover bottle gentian blooming at the same time as bunchberry. Adirondack High Peak summers are compressed into a short season.

After you settle in for a picnic, spread out your maps and orient yourself. The most impressive mountain view is southeast to Colden, the stripes of its slides radiating from the summit like the outflow from some gigantic moonscape eruption. Slides from Colden have changed the outlet of Avalanche Lake, which lies hidden between Algonquin and Colden. Colden's famous trap dyke, a narrow gorge carved out in the sheer rock dome, is clearly visible to the left of the major slides. This view of Colden is my favorite scene in the High Peaks, and one of the reasons is that the mountain was for a time called Mount McMartin, after my great-great-grandfather's brother, who was one of the founders of the McIntyre iron mine south of Indian Pass.

On the horizon left, east of Colden, lie Skylight, Gray Peak, and Marcy. Continuing left are Hough, the Dixes, and the mountains of the Range Trail, with Giant almost due east. Hurricane, Porter, and Cascade are visible around to the north, with Van Hoevenburg to the northeast. The Sentinel Range is visible over Van Hoevenburg, and to its left, west, lies Whiteface. You will have no trouble spotting the new Olympic Ski Jump at Lake Placid.

Moving around to the northwest, Street and Nye form a long wooded range that leads to Wallface in the west. The cliffs on Wallface clearly outline Indian Pass.

Starting again with Colden but this time moving right, or west, you should identify first Redfield. Below you lie Lake Colden and Flowed Land. South of Lake Colden and just to the right of Redfield you can see the cliffs on Cliff Mountain. Next comes a small peak, Little Nippletop, and then Calamity Mountain. Flowed Land points to the valley between Cliff and Calamity, through which Opalescent River, the outlet of Flowed Land, exits. Over Calamity Mountain and to the right you should see Henderson, with Santanoni the huge mountain behind. Seward and Seymour mark the western horizon behind Wallface, with the Sawtooth Mountains to its north, followed by Ampersand.

You will need binoculars and exceptionally clear weather to see more distant peaks, but it is possible to pick out Blue Mountain and Vanderwhacker as well as many of the outlying summits described in this guide.

Your return will occupy the better part of two and a half hours, with fifty minutes devoted to the first .9-mile descent. It is that steep! If you are making a midsummer trip, look for Milbert's Tortoise, an uncommon angle-wing butterfly often seen in large numbers on Algonquin.

Algonquin is a fairly strenuous climb, yet it is much easier to reach than the majority of the High Peaks, which require treks from interior backpacking locations. If the introduction to the eastern High Peaks has stimulated your interest in the Adirondacks' higher climbs, sample a few, but do not neglect the outlying mountains, for which there is the *Discover* series of guidebooks. You will find their climbs and views are more than comparable, but you will also discover a sense of wilderness that is becoming rare in the popular High Peaks.

Index

(Only names of places and people important to the trail descriptions are indexed. As in the *Discover* series, the places visible from destinations are not indexed.)

Discover the Adirondacks
A Series of Regional Guides by Barbara McMartin

The 11 guides in the *Discover the Adirondacks* series tell you enough about each area so that you can enjoy it throughout the year, in many different ways. Each guide acquaints you with that region's access roads and trailheads, its trails and unmarked paths, some bushwhack routes and canoe trips, fishing waters, and its best picnic spots, campsites and ski-touring routes.

Some of the destinations are within walking distance of the major highways that ring the areas, while others are miles deep into the wilderness. The sections are grouped in chapters according to their access points. Each chapter contains a brief introduction to that area's history, followed by trail descriptions including accounts of the geological forces that shaped the land and unusual wildflowers and forest stands.

The guiding force behind this series is Barbara McMartin. She and her co-authors and collaborators bring a wealth of experience in local and natural history, geology, and outdoor recreation to the preparation of each guide.

Discover the Adirondack High Peaks by Barbara McMartin, with the assistance of Lee Brenning, Phil Gallos, Don Greene, Ed Ketchledge, Gary Koch, and Willard Reed. Hundreds of excursions, paperback, $14.95

In addition to all marked trails in the High Peaks and in the Dix Mountains Wilderness Area, this guide describes bushwhacks, unmarked paths into hidden valleys and waterfalls, and trips up exhilarating slides. Another major feature of this volume is the information on peak identification, enabling hikers to know what they see from the region's many breathtaking views.

Discover the Central Adirondacks, Four-Season Adventures in the Heart of the North Woods, by Barbara McMartin, with the assistance of Dennis Conroy, James C. Dawson, and Edythe Robbins. 67 excursions, paperback, $8.95.

The guide encompasses the great north woods — Hoffman Notch Wilderness, the little-known Vanderwhacker Wild Forest, and the more familiar Blue Mountain Wild Forest. Discover the beauty of this area's spruce-bordered ponds, cliffs and caves, giant glacial erratics, and cascading rivers and streams.

Discover the Eastern Adirondacks, Four-Season Adventures near Lake George, Pharaoh Lake and Beyond, by Barbara McMartin, with the assistance of Edythe Robbins. 104 excursions, paperback, $9.95.

This guide to one of the most popular and accessible areas in the Adirondacks offers trails to upland ponds, cliffs and open peaks, and unusual geological formations. Includes hiking and horse trails and superb cross-country skiing. A thorough revision of the 1981 Adirondack Mountain Club's *Guide to the Eastern Adirondacks.*

Discover the Northeastern Adirondacks, Four-Season Adventures from Lake Champlain to the Rock-Crowned Eastern Slopes, by Dennis Conroy, James C. Dawson, and Barbara McMartin. 90 excursions, paperback, $9.95.

All of the destinations in this guide are close to the Adirondack Northway. The excursions encompass a great variety of terrain and a 4,400-foot change in elevation from the shores of Lake Champlain to the peak of Giant Mountain.

Discover the Northern Adirondacks, Four-Season Excursions from Lake Placid, Saranac Lake and Points North, by Patricia Collier, James C. Dawson, Phil Gallos, Peter O'Shea, and Barbara McMartin, with the assistance of E.H. Ketchledge. 98 excursions, paperback, $10.95.

From the slopes of Whiteface Mountain to the rolling boreal forest in the park's northern boundary, this guide focuses on hiking, ski-touring, and bushwhacking opportunities. All excursions are easily accessible from Lake Placid and Saranac Lake. More than half a dozen state campgrounds are in this region.

Discover the Northwestern Adirondacks, A Four-Season Guide through the Boreal Forest, by Lee M. Brenning, Barbara McMartin, and Peter O'Shea. $12.95

Explore trails in the Cranberry Lake Wild Forest, the Five Ponds Wilderness Area, and the Pepperbox Wilderness Area. This guide also encompasses all the recent state land aquisitions, including the Wilderness Lakes Tract and the Grass River Area.

Discover the South Central Adirondacks, Including the Siamese Ponds Wilderness Area, by Barbara McMartin, with the assistance of Dennis Conroy. 90 excursions, paperback, $10.95

Explore the part of the Adirondack Park extending from Indian Lake to the Hudson River and from the East Branch of the Sacandaga to Route 28. McMartin presents a wealth of recreational opportunities in this area. This is a thorough revision of the 1979 book *Discover the Adirondacks 1.*

Discover the Southeastern Adirondacks, Four-Season Adventures on Old Roads and Open Peaks, by Barbara McMartin, with the assistance of Willard Reed. 67 excursions, paperback, $8.95.

Enjoy long, level trails through remnants of glacial lakes and make dramatic climbs to a dozen open peaks, some reached by trails, some only by bush-whacks. Covering principally the Wilcox Lake Forest, this guide has an excursion for every taste, and the area is only a short distance from New York's Capital District.

Discover the Southern Adirondacks, Walks, Waterways and Winter Treks, by Barbara McMartin, with the assistance of Stanford Pulrang. 104 excursions, paperback, $10.95.

The Southern Adirondacks contains some of the wildest lands in the state. The area is rich in quiet lakes, streams, quaking bogs, and fields of wildflowers — where hikers and cross-country skiers can explore endlessly, rarely meeting another person. This is the third edition of the 1974 book *Walks and Waterways.*

Discover the Southwestern Adirondacks, Four-Season Adventures in the Wild-Forested Foothills, by Lee M. Brenning, William P. Ehling, and Barbara McMartin, with the assistance of Stanford Pulrang. 117 excursions, paperback, $9.95.

The western foothills' big plateau of rolling hills, deep valleys, and handsome rivers has some of the best level trails in the Adirondacks. Numerous fishing streams and small ponds dot the area.

Discover the West Central Adirondacks, A Guide to the Western Wildernesses and the Moose River Plains, by Barbara McMartin and Lee M. Brenning, with the assistance of Dennis Conroy, Sandy Edwards, and John Edwards. 176 excursions, paperback, $13.95.

Explore four pristine wilderness areas: the West Canada Lakes; Pigeon Lake; Blue Ridge with its easy trails; and tiny Ha-de-ron-dah with its charming ponds. Sandwiched between these wilderness areas are many miles of dirt roads with campsites accessible by car, as well as some of the most remote lakes in the Adirondacks.

Guidebooks from The Countryman Press and Backcountry Publications

Written for people of all ages and experience, these popular and carefully prepared books feature detailed trail and tour directions, notes on points of interest and natural phenomena, maps and photographs.

Walks and Rambles Series

Walks and Rambles on the Delmarva
  Peninsula, $9.95
Walks and Rambles in Dutchess and Putnam
  Counties (NY), $9.95
Walks and Rambles in Rhode Island, $8.95
Walks and Rambles in the Upper Connecticut
  River Valley, $9.95
Walks and Rambles in Westchester (NY) and
  Fairfield (CT) Counties, $7.95

Biking Series

25 Mountain Bike Tours in Vermont, $9.95
25 Bicycle Tours on Delmarva, $8.95
25 Bicycle Tours in Eastern Pennsylvania,
  $8.95
20 Bicycle Tours in the Finger Lakes, $8.95
20 Bicycle Tours in the 5 Boroughs (NYC),
  $8.95
25 Bicycle Tours in the Hudson Valley, $9.95
25 Bicycle Tours in Maine, $9.95
25 Bicycle Tours in New Hampshire, $7.95
25 Bicycle Tours in New Jersey, $8.95
20 Bicycle Tours in and around New York City,
  $7.95
25 Bicycle Tours in Ohio's Western Reserve,
  $9.95
25 Bicycle Tours in Vermont, $8.95

Canoeing Series

Canoe Camping Vermont and New Hampshire
  Rivers, $7.95
Canoeing Central New York, $10.95
Canoeing Massachusetts, Rhode Island and
  Connecticut, $7.95

Hiking Series

50 Hikes in the Adirondacks, $11.95
50 Hikes in Central New York, $9.95
50 Hikes in Central Pennsylvania, $9.95
50 Hikes in Eastern Pennsylvania, $10.95
50 Hikes in the Hudson Valley, $9.95
50 Hikes in Massachusetts, $11.95
50 More Hikes in New Hampshire, $9.95
50 Hikes in New Jersey, $10.95
50 Hikes in Northern Maine, $10.95
50 Hikes in Ohio, $12.95
50 Hikes in Southern Maine, $10.95
50 Hikes in Vermont, $11.95
50 Hikes in West Virginia, $9.95
50 Hikes in Western New York, $11.95
50 Hikes in Western Pennsylvania, $11.95
50 Hikes in the White Mountains, $12.95

Adirondack Series

Discover the Adirondack High Peaks, $14.95
Discover the Central Adirondacks, $8.95
Discover the Eastern Adirondacks, $9.95
Discover the Northeastern Adirondacks, $9.95
Discover the Northern Adirondacks, $10.95
Discover the Northwestern Adirondacks, $12.95
Discover the South Central Adirondacks, $10.95
Discover the Southeastern Adirondacks, $8.95
Discover the Southern Adirondacks, $10.95
Discover the Southwestern Adirondacks, $9.95
Discover the West Central Adirondacks, $13.95

Ski-Touring Series

25 Ski Tours in Central New York, $7.95
25 Ski Tours in New Hampshire, $8.95

Other Guides

Maine: An Explorer's Guide, $14.95
New England's Special Places, $12.95
New Jersey's Special Places, $12.95
New York State's Special Places, $12.95
Pennsylvania Trout Streams and their Hatches,
  $14.95
State Parks and Campgrounds in Northern New
  York, $9.95
Vermont: An Explorer's Guide, $14.95
Waterfalls of the White Mountains, $14.95

The above titles are available at bookstores and at certain sporting goods stores or may be ordered directly from the publisher. For complete descriptions of these and other guides, write: The Countryman Press, P.O. Box 175, Woodstock, VT 05091.